About the Author
Michael J. Tougias (Pronounced TOH-gis)

Michael Tougias is a lecturer and *New York Times* bestselling author and co-author of thirty-one books for adults and six for young adults and children.

Fatal Forecast: An Incredible True Tale of Disaster and Survival at Sea was praised by the *Los Angeles Times* as "a breathtaking book- Tougias spins a marvelous and terrifying story." *The Finest Hours*, which Tougias co-authored, tells the true story of the Coast Guard's most daring rescue. A finalist for the Massachusetts Book Award, the book was made into a movie by Disney. *Ten Hours Until Dawn: The True Story of Heroism and Tragedy Aboard the Can Do in the Blizzard of 78*, was selected by the American Library Association as one of the "Top Books of the Year" and described as a "white-knuckle read, the best book of its kind." His latest books are *A Storm Too Soon, Rescue of the Bounty in Superstorm Sandy*, and *Above & Beyond*.

Several of Tougias's books were adapted for middle readers (ages 8-13) and for chapter books with MacMillan Publishers. His series is "The True Rescue Series" and it includes *Into the Blizzard, Attacked At Sea, A Storm Too Soon*, and *The Finest Hours*.

Tougias's most popular books include:

- *Rescue of the Bounty: A True Story of Disaster and Survival in Superstorm Sandy*, Simon & Schuster, co-author Douglas Campbell

- *A Storm Too Soon: A True Story of Disaster, Survival, and an Incredible Rescue*, Simon & Schuster

- *Overboard! A True Blue-Water Odyssey of Disaster and Survival*, Simon & Schuster

- *Fatal Forecast: An Incredible True Story of Disaster and Survival at Sea*, Simon & Schuster

- *Ten Hours Until Dawn: The True Story of Heroism and Tragedy Aboard the Can Do*, St. Martin's Press, American Library Association Best Book of the Year Selection

- *The Finest Hours: The True Story of the US Coast Guard's Most Daring Sea Rescue*, Simon & Schuster, co-author Casey Sherman, finalist for the Massachusetts Book Award

- *The Waters Between Us: A Boy, A Father, Outdoor Misadventures, and the Healing Power of Nature*

- *Until I Have No Country: A Novel of King Philip's Indian War*, Lemur Press

- *King Philip's War: The History and Legacy of America's Forgotten Conflict*, WW Norton, co-author Eric Schultz

- *Above & Beyond: John F. Kennedy and America's Most Dangerous Spy Mission*, Public Affairs, co-author Casey Sherman

- *There's a Porcupine in My Outhouse: Misadventures of a Mountain Man Wannabe*, On Cape Publications, winner of the Independent Publishers Association Best Nature Book of the Year Award

- *So Close to Home: A True Story of an American Family's Fight for Survival During WWII*, Pegasus Books, co-author Alison O'Leary

- *River Days: Exploring the Connecticut River from Source to Sea*, Lemur Press

- *AMC's Best Day Hikes Near Boston*, Appalachian Mountain Club

- *Nature Walks in Central and Western MA,* Lemur Press

- *Exploring the Hidden Charles,* Lemur Press

- *Country Roads of Massachusetts,* Lemur Press

- *Quiet Places of Massachusetts,* Lemur Press

- *New England Wild Places,* Lemur Press

- *The Cringe Chronicles* (with Kristin Tougias), Lemur Press

- Middle reader adaptations: *The Finest Hours, A Storm Too Soon, Attacked At Sea and Into the Blizzard*

- *Quabbin: A History and Explorers Guide*, Lemur Press

- *The Blizzard of '78*, Lemur Press

Michael Tougias has been featured on ABC's *20/20*, the Weather Channel, National NPR among other appearances. He offers slide lectures for each of his books and speaks at libraries, lecture series, schools and colleges across the country. He also speaks to business groups and associations on leadership and decision-making including such programs as Leadership Lessons from the Finest Hours; Survival Lessons: Decision Making Under Pressure; and Fourteen Steps to Strategic Decision Making: JFK and the Cuban Missile Crisis. He lives in Florida and Massachusetts. For more information, videos of some of the rescues Tougias writes about, or to contact the author, visit www.michaeltougias.com.

Nature Walks in Central and Western Massachusetts

2d edition

Michael Tougias
René Laubach

LEMUR PRESS

LEMUR PRESS

Contents

Acknowledgments vii
Locator Map x
Walks and Highlights Chart xii
Introduction xviii
    A Few Suggestions xix
    Trail Courtesy xx
    Wildlife Watching xx
    Nature Walking with Children xxiii
    Recommended Walks with Younger Children xxiv
How to Use this Book xxvi

Middlesex and Worcester Counties

1.   Groton Place and Sabine Woods 1
     Groton

2.   Flat Rock Wildlife Sanctuary 6
     Fitchburg

3.   Lincoln Woods 11
     Leominster

4.   Wachusett Mountain State Reservation 15
     Princeton

5.   Broad Meadow Brook Wildlife Sanctuary 20
     Worcester

6.   Purgatory Chasm State Reservation 25
     Sutton

7.   Blackstone River and Canal Heritage State Park 29
     Northbridge/Uxbridge

8.   Douglas State Forest 34
     Douglas

9.   Royalston Falls 38
     Royalston

10. Jacobs Hill Reservation 42
Royalston

11. Doane's Falls 46
Royalston

12. Elliot Laurel Reservation 50
Phillipston

13. North Common Meadow 54
Petersham

14. Swift River Reservation 58
Petersham

15. Quabbin Reservoir—Gate 45 63
Hardwick

16. Rock House Reservation 69
West Brookfield

17. Tantiusques Reservation 74
Sturbridge

18. Cook's Canyon 78
Barre

19. Harvard Forest 82
Petersham

20. Crow Hill at Leominster State Forest 88
Leominster

Franklin County

21. Bear's Den 93
New Salem

22. Mt. Grace State Forest 97
Warwick

23. Northfield Mountain Recreation
and Environmental Center 102
Northfield

24. Erving State Forest 108
    Erving/Warwick/Orange

25. Wendell State Forest 113
    Wendell

26. Mt. Sugarloaf State Reservation 119
    South Deerfield

27. High Ledges Wildlife Sanctuary 123
    Shelburne

28. Bear Swamp Reservation 128
    Ashfield

29. Chapelbrook Reservation 134
    South Ashfield

30. D.A.R. State Forest 138
    Goshen/Ashfield

31. Kenneth Dubuque Memorial State Forest 143
    Hawley/Plainfield/Savoy

32. Mohawk Trail State Forest 148
    Charlemont/Savoy/Hawley

33. Mt. Toby Forest 154
    Sunderland

34. Sachem Head 161
    Greenfield

35. Dunbar Brook 167
    Monroe/Florida

Hampshire and Hampden Counties

36. Buffam Falls Conservation Area 175
    Pelham

37. William Cullen Bryant Homestead 179
    Cummington

38. Chesterfield Gorge 183
    Chesterfield

39. Glendale Falls Reservation 188
Middlefield

40. Arcadia Wildlife Sanctuary 193
Easthampton/Northampton

41. Joseph Allen Skinner State Park 197
Hadley/South Hadley

42. Holyoke Range State Park 203
Amherst/Granby

43. Mt. Tom State Reservation 209
Holyoke/Easthampton

44. Sanderson Brook Falls 215
Chester/Blandford

45. Tolland State Forest
Tolland/Blandford/Otis/Sandisfield .219

46. Granville State Forest
Granville/Tolland 225

47. The Meadows
Longmeadow 230

48. Laughing Brook Education
Center and Wildlife Sanctuary 234
Hampden

49. Norcross Wildlife Sanctuary 241
Monson/Wales

50. Mt. Orient and Amethyst Brook Conservation Area 248
Amherst/Pelham

Recommended References and Reading
About the Authors
About the AMC
Index

Acknowledgments

Many people helped with the first edition and this revision, and we sincerely thank them for sharing their time and knowledge. In particular we would like to thank Dick O'Brien and Paul Grzgbowski, who supervise the central region for The Trustees of Reservations, and Steve McMahon, who supervises the western region; Don Reid and James Caffrey of The Trustees of Reservations; Jeanne Andersen, Doug Kimball, Tom Tyning, and Ron Wolannin of Massachusetts Audubon Society; Shawn Cameron, Doug Clark, Dennis G. Moore, James McNair, Michael M. Smyth, and others at the Massachusetts Department of Environmental Management who reviewed manuscripts; Matthew Kelty of the University of Massachusetts's Department of Forestry and Wildlife Management; Karl Meyer of Northeast Utilities' Northfield Mountain Recreation and Environmental Center; Joseph A. Catalano and the staff of the Norcross Foundation; and Dan Laroche of the town of Greenfield's Office of Planning and Community Development. Thanks also to Ellsworth (Dutch) Barnard, Simon Geary, and Bob and Jani Leverett for their knowledge, advice, and assistance. A note of appreciation to the editor of the first edition, Gordon Hardy, and his ability to bring a manuscript to a higher level while allowing the individual writer's style to flourish. Thanks also to Mark Russell, the editor of this revised and expanded edition, for his initiative and guidance.

Lastly, we would like to thank our families for joining us on walks and for giving us the time to work on the manuscript. René wishes to thank especially his wife, Christyna, for being a wonderful companion and a great help in the field.

*To my son, Brian, who brings me so much joy.
We always find little adventures when walking
in the woods. And to my brother, Bob, a long-
time hiking companion in the forests of Quabbin.*
—Michael Tougias

*For my sister, Doris, whose courage, determina-
tion, and sense of humor inspired all who were
fortunate enough to have known her.*
—René Laubach

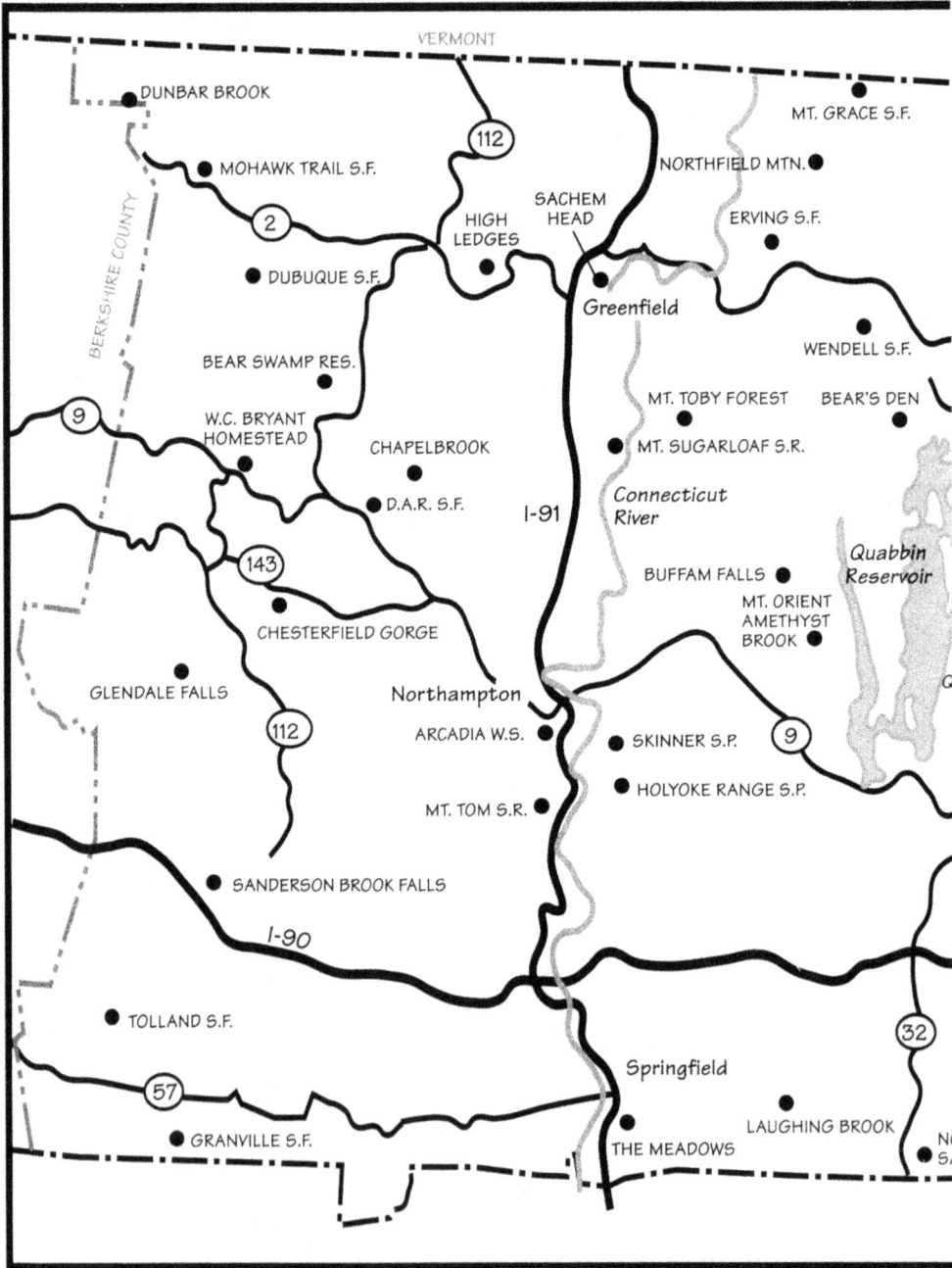

Locator Map

VERMONT

DUNBAR BROOK

MT. GRACE S.F.

112

MOHAWK TRAIL S.F.

NORTHFIELD MTN.

SACHEM HEAD

ERVING S.F.

2

HIGH LEDGES

BERKSHIRE COUNTY

DUBUQUE S.F.

Greenfield

WENDELL S.F.

BEAR SWAMP RES.

MT. TOBY FOREST

BEAR'S DEN

9

W.C. BRYANT HOMESTEAD

CHAPELBROOK

MT. SUGARLOAF S.R.

Connecticut River

D.A.R. S.F.

I-91

Quabbin Reservoir

143

BUFFAM FALLS

MT. ORIENT AMETHYST BROOK

CHESTERFIELD GORGE

GLENDALE FALLS

Northampton

112

ARCADIA W.S.

SKINNER S.P.

9

HOLYOKE RANGE S.P.

MT. TOM S.R.

SANDERSON BROOK FALLS

I-90

TOLLAND S.F.

32

Springfield

57

LAUGHING BROOK

GRANVILLE S.F.

THE MEADOWS

N SA

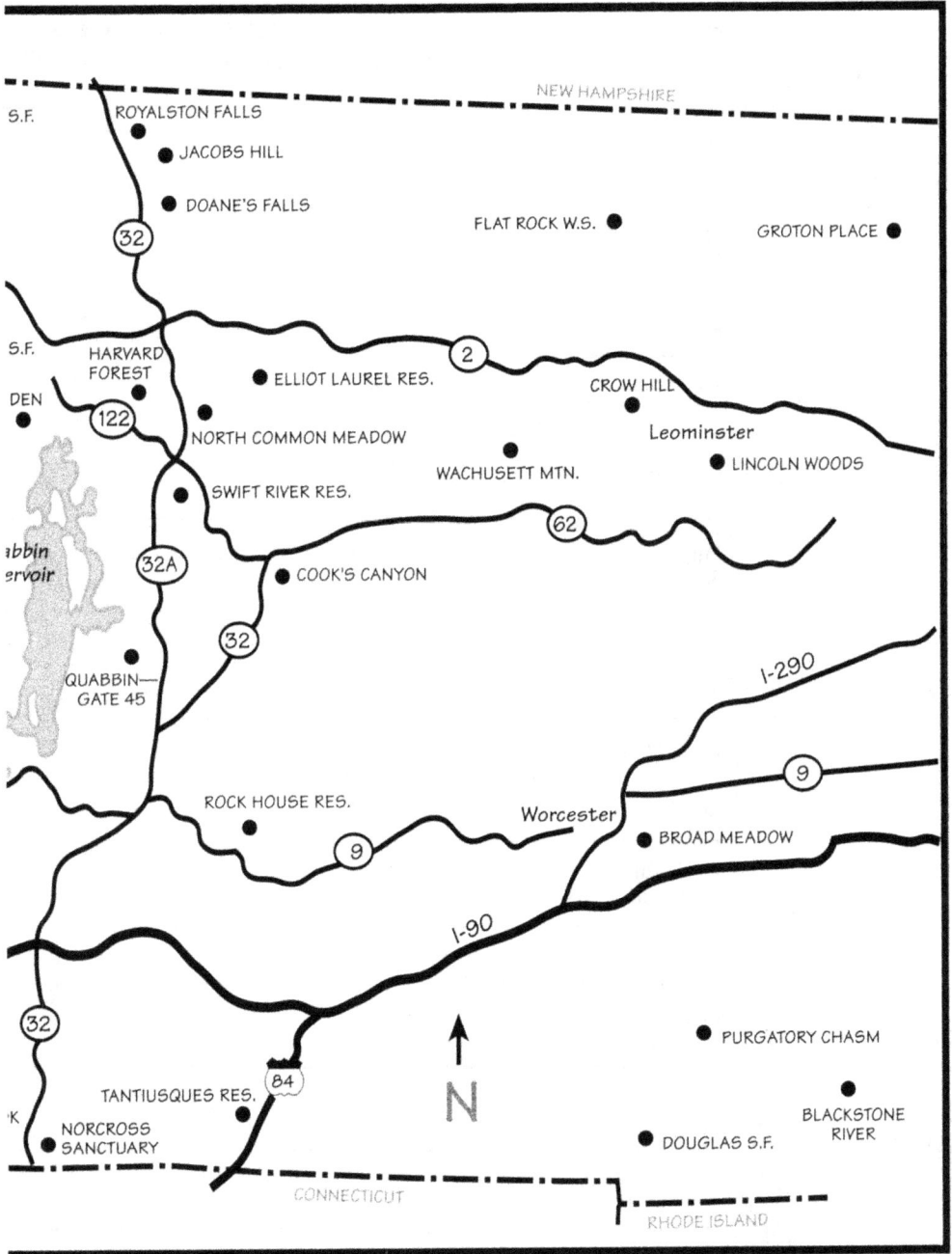

Walks and Highlights

Region	Hike	Page Number	Difficulty Level (for children)	Distance (miles RT)
Middlesex and Worcester counties	Groton Place and Sabine Woods	1	easy	2.5
	Flat Rock Wildlife Sanctuary	6	moderate	1.5
	Lincoln Woods	11	easy	1.0
	Wachusett Mtn. State Reservation	15	challenging	1.5
	Broad Meadow Brook Wildlife Sanctuary	20	easy	2.5
	Purgatory Chasm State Reservation	25	moderate	.5
	Blackstone River and Canal Heritage State Park	29	moderate	3.0
	Douglas State Forest	34	easy	1.0
	Royalston Falls	38	easy/mod.	3.0
	Jacobs Hill Reservation	42	moderate	2.5
	Doane's Falls	46	easy	1.0
	Elliot Laurel Reservation	50	easy	1.0
	North Common Meadow	54	easy	1.25
	Swift River Reservation	58	moderate	1.75
	Quabbin Reservoir Gate 45	63	moderate	5.0

*Area Manager: A=Audubon; T=Trustees; SP=State Park; O=Other

River or Brook	Falls or Gorge	Lake or Pond	Scenic Vista	Rocky Ledges	Wooden Bridges	Special Geology	Area*
✔							O
			✔				A
					✔		A
			✔				SP
✔							A
				✔		✔	SP
✔	✔	✔	✔	✔			SP
		✔				✔	SP
✔	✔						T
✔	✔	✔	✔	✔			T
✔	✔	✔					T
				✔			T
		✔					T
✔			✔	✔			T
✔		✔					O

Region	Hike	Page Number	Difficulty Level (for children)	Distance (miles RT)
Middlesex and Worcester counties	Rock House Reservation	69	easy	1.5
	Tantiusques Reservation	74	easy	1.75
	Cook's Canyon	78	easy	1.5
	Harvard Forest	86	easy	1.5
	Crow Hill	88	moderate	1.5
Franklin County	Bear's Den	93	easy	.375
	Mt. Grace State Forest	97	difficult	2.8
	Northfield Mountain	102	moderate	4.5
	Erving State Forest	108	easy	0.9
	Wendell State Forest	113	easy	1.4
	Mt. Sugarloaf	119	difficult	2.2
	High Ledges Wildlife Sanctuary	123	moderate	1.7
	Bear Swamp Reservation	128	moderate	2.5
	Chapelbrook Reservation	134	moderate	1.75
	D.A.R. State Forest	138	moderate	2.5
	Kenneth Dubuque Memorial State Forest	143	moderate	4.5
	Mohawk Trail State Forest	148	difficult	4.0
	Mt. Toby	154	moderate	4.2

*Area Manager: A=Audubon; T=Trustees; SP=State Park; O=Other

River or Brook	Falls or Gorge	Lake or Pond	Scenic Vista	Rocky Ledges	Wooden Bridges	Special Geology	Area*
		✔	✔	✔		✔	T
				✔			T
✔	✔	✔	✔	✔			A
							O
			✔	✔			S
✔	✔			✔			T
✔			✔				SP
		✔	✔	✔		✔	O
✔		✔	✔	✔			SP
✔		✔		✔			SP
			✔	✔		✔	SP
✔		✔	✔	✔			A
✔		✔	✔	✔			T
✔	✔		✔	✔			T
		✔	✔				SP
✔		✔					SP
✔			✔	✔			SP
✔			✔			✔	O

Region	Hike	Page Number	Difficulty Level (for children)	Distance (miles RT)
Franklin County	Sachem Head	161	easy	1.8
	Dunbar Brook	167	moderate	5.5
Hampshire and Hampden counties	Buffam Falls Conservation Area	175	easy	1.0
	William Cullen Bryant Homestead	179	easy	0.9
	Chesterfield Gorge	183	easy	3.0
	Glendale Falls Reservation	188	moderate	1.2
	Arcadia Wildlife Sanctuary	193	easy	1.75
	Joseph Allen Skinner State Park	197	difficult	1.75
	Holyoke Range State Park	203	moderate	2.75
	Mt. Tom State Reservation	209	difficult	4.5
	Sanderson Brook Falls	215	easy	2.0
	Tolland State Forest	219	moderate	3.3
	Granville State Forest	225	moderate	2.0
	The Meadows	230	moderate	3.0
	Laughing Brook Educ. Ctr. and W.S.	234	easy	2.2
	Norcross Sanctuary	241	easy	1.5
	Mr. Orient/Amethyst Brook	248	moderate	3.0

*Area Manager: A=Audubon; T=Trustees; SP=State Park; O=Other

River Brook	Falls or Gorge	Lake or Pond	Scenic Vista	Rocky Ledges	Wooden Bridges	Special Geology	Area*
			✔	✔		✔	O
✔							SP
✔	✔			✔			O
✔			✔				T
✔	✔		✔			✔	T
✔	✔		✔	✔			T
✔		✔	✔			✔	A
			✔	✔		✔	SP
			✔	✔		✔	SP
			✔	✔		✔	SP
✔	✔			✔			SP
✔		✔	✔				SP
✔	✔	✔					SP
✔		✔					O
✔		✔		✔	✔	✔	A
✔							O
✔			✔	✔			O

Introduction

A weekend is just not a weekend without a walk in the woods. The physical joy of walking combined with the potential of seeing wildlife make for a winning combination. A special day outdoors can make your spirits soar. Maybe it's a walk on a crisp, colorful autumn day, or a winter's trek just after a heavy snow, or perhaps the first warm day of spring when all the earth seems to be awakening.

Central and western Massachusetts affords a number of diverse pockets of wilderness where you can walk in solitude. Properties range in size from the few acres around the waterfall at Bear's Den to the sprawling forests protecting Quabbin Reservoir. One of our toughest challenges was deciding which of the 100 or so properties we researched to include in the 50 reviewed in the book. Ultimately the selection was narrowed down to include properties that had the most diversity. There are hilltop overlooks, quaking cedar bogs, riverfront trails, glacial eskers and erratics, and walks that will take you by lesser-known historic sites.

Each location review includes directions, suggested trails, a map, wildlife and plants to be seen, estimated hiking time, trail conditions, and scenic views. If there is a nearby point of interest we give a brief description and directions. The initials at the end of each section indicate whether it was written by Michael Tougias (M.T.) or René Laubach (R.L.).

We have also included a level of difficulty for each walk. In general we have rated walks under three miles on fairly level terrain as *easy* and walks of three miles or more as *medium*. Walks that are over five miles or go up steep hills are rated as *difficult*.

Thoreau viewed walking as a way to lose oneself: "What business have I in the woods, if I am thinking of something out of the woods?" He walked often and far afield: "I think that I cannot preserve my health and spirits, unless I spend four hours a day at least—and it is commonly more than that—sauntering through the woods and over the hills and fields, absolutely free from all worldly engagements." And if Thoreau saw wildlife, all the better. It was not unusual for him to sit and wait patiently for some creature to appear or to stop his walk to watch wildlife for the rest of the day. Your walks can be more enjoyable if you follow Thoreau's examples.

We wrote this book to share some of our special places with you and hope that by raising appreciation for nature we can protect more wild places before they are forever lost to development.

A Few Suggestions

- To make your hikes more enjoyable bring binoculars, a camera, water, and a snack (food tastes better in the outdoors).

- Bring extra film—we always seem to run out when the best picture presents itself.

- Unfortunately, it's not advisable for women to hike alone. Ask a friend who shares your love of the outdoors, or better yet, pick a friend who spends more time in the malls than the woods, and introduce him or her to the joys of walking in the great outdoors.

- Getting lost in the woods is no fun. If you are unfamiliar with an area be sure to allow plenty of time before dark when you set out. Even at the smaller properties it's possible to get lost. Always tell someone what properties you plan to explore.

- The tiny ticks that can carry Lyme disease are spread nearly throughout New England. Always wear long pants, preferably with the pants tucked beneath your socks. Use bug repellent on your skin, socks, and pants. Avoid fields of tall grass during the warm-weather months. And to be on the safe side, give yourself a "tick check" after every hike by examining yourself all over, especially the scalp, neck, armpits, groin, and ankles. The most common initial symptoms of Lyme disease include swollen lymph nodes near the site of the bite, flulike symptoms, and a rash around site of the bite. The rash expands from the center out, and it may look like a bull's-eye.

- Be on the lookout for poison ivy—identified by its three shiny leaves. Again, long pants are recommended.

- During warm-weather months carry a small backpack or fanny pack with water and bug spray. (It's a good idea to have a pack permanently loaded for nature walks, so that all you need do is fill the water bottle.)

- During cold-weather months layer your clothes, so that you can peel off or add items easily. The best layering is a moisture-wicking inner layer, a warm insulating middle layer, and a waterproof/windproof outer layer. Be sure to wear warm, waterproof boots. Always bring a hat.

- Deer hunting season is in the fall; wear a blaze orange hat to be on the safe side—even when in a no-hunting area.

- Learn how to use a map and compass—there are several good introductory books and workshops available through the AMC and other organizations. Bring them along on your hikes.

Trail Courtesy

Respect for nature involves a few basic rules.

- Be sure to follow the "carry-in, carry-out" principle when it comes to trash. If you want to be an extra-good citizen, carry along a small trash bag and collect litter left by less thoughtful individuals.

- Do not remove any plants or animals from the woods. Return logs and rocks that you move to their original positions.

- Keep to the established trails.

- Give wildlife a wide berth. Binoculars (7 – 10 × 40) and a telephoto lens on your camera will allow you to view the wildlife without forcing it to flee.

By becoming involved in local conservation efforts, we can all help to keep our woods and waters in a clean, natural state, where wildlife has a chance to flourish. Besides local conservation commissions and watershed associations, there are also regional and statewide organizations such as the Appalachian Mountain Club, The Trustees of Reservations, and Massachusetts Audubon Society that have active conservation programs.

Wildlife Watching

The reservations, sanctuaries, and conservation lands reviewed in this book are all rich in wildlife. Seeing that wildlife, however, depends on both luck and one's knowledge of the creatures themselves. We can't do much about luck, but there are a number of steps that can be taken to increase your odds of spotting the many birds, mammals, reptiles, amphibians, and insects that live in central and western Massachusetts.

Thoreau was an expert "wildlife watcher," patient and full of curiosity. He would think nothing of sitting for an hour to watch a bird or animal gather food. "True men of science," he wrote, "will know nature better by his finer organizations; he will smell, taste, see, hear, feel, better than other men. His will be a deeper and finer experience." Nature reveals more of her subtleties when we focus all our senses into the natural surroundings. Try following Thoreau's example and let yourself become absorbed by the forests, fields, and water—even if you don't see wildlife, the walks themselves are more rewarding and refreshing.

Two of the key components of wildlife watching are knowing where and when to look. The best time to see most wildlife is at dawn and dusk. Many creatures are nocturnal, and there is also some overlap at dawn and dusk with the daytime birds and animals. Spring and fall are the two best seasons, especially for migratory birds. Animals that hibernate will be active during the spring after a long winter, and in the fall they will eat as much as possible in preparation for the cold months to come. Winter has the least activity but it does offer some advantages, such as easier long-range viewing (no foliage), easily visible tracks in fresh snow, the potential to see some animals crossing the ice (such as coyotes); also animals are often easier to spot against a background of white snow.

Experienced wildlife watchers look everywhere: in the fields, on the forest floor, under logs and stones, on the water or ice, along shorelines, in trees, and in the sky. Perhaps the single most productive spot for seeing wildlife is the edge of a field. Hawks and owls often perch here, and many animals make their dens and burrows where the woods meet the meadows. Creatures feel safer around the edges—deer often stay close to these fringe areas before entering a field at nightfall. Red fox and coyotes hunt the edges, and they can sometimes be seen trotting through tall grass on their rounds.

Other productive areas are along riverbanks and shorelines. Mink, weasels, muskrat, and raccoons, just to mention a few, are commonly observed foraging next to water. And of course shorebirds, wading birds, and ducks are found here. Scanning a shoreline with a pair of binoculars can be extremely rewarding—you may see a number of different wildlife species. Many of the wild areas in this book offer excellent canoeing, and this, too, affords opportunities for nature study at close range.

Obviously, when walking through the woods you must do so quietly if you hope to get near wildlife, but being quiet is not enough. Most creatures would prefer to hide than run, and they will sit tight and let you walk right by. You should give the surrounding areas more than a casual glance. For example, when trying to spot deer, look for parts of the animal between the trees rather than for the entire body. Look for the horizontal lines of the deer's back contrasting with the vertical trees. Knowing the size of the animal also helps; when scanning for deer most people would do so at eye level, yet deer are only about three feet high at the shoulder.

Many animals blend in with their surroundings so well it's almost impossible to see them. The American bittern, for example, sometimes hides by freezing with its head and long neck in an upright position to match tall reeds and vegetation around it. A snapping turtle in shallow water looks just like a rock, and ruffed grouse can be indistinguishable from the fallen leaves on the forest floor. Even great blue herons will stop feeding and wait, silent and unmoving, until perceived danger passes.

Another key factor to consider is wind direction, which can carry your scent to wildlife. As you walk down a trail try looking upwind—animals will detect your scent on your downwind side. If you have a choice when beginning a hike, travel into the wind. The same holds true when approaching a known feeding area. Serious wildlife photographers even go as far as wearing rubber boots to stop the scent from their feet from escaping into the air!

It is important, by the way, that we humans do not approach creatures too closely. Birds will take wing and animals will run away, thus expending valuable energy to avoid us. If you keep your distance many creatures will allow you to observe them, so long as you do not walk directly at them or linger too long.

Some animals are almost never seen because they are nocturnal and secretive. But you don't have to see them to know that they are present. They leave clues. You will find the tracks of otter, heron, raccoon, and deer along the soft margin of a river or lake. Looking for fresh tracks after a snowfall can be especially rewarding. Some astute trackers can also identify creatures by the droppings they leave behind. The burrows and dens of animals reveal where animals such as the fox and groundhog live. Owls disgorge pellets, which can identify their presence and what they have been feeding on. Look for them underneath large pine trees. Deer leave a number of signs: the trails they use between feeding and resting grounds and the scrapes and scars on saplings caused by a buck rubbing its antlers. Peeled bark can mean deer, mice, rabbit, or others, depending on the teeth marks, shape, and height of the marking.

The time and patience required to find and identify clues can be significant, but so too are the rewards. It is satisfying to solve the wildlife "puzzle," not only in learning of a species' presence but to also deduce what its activities were. Children especially enjoy this detective work.

Besides using your eyes, you should use your ears to help in wildlife identification. Learning the songs and calls of birds will greatly enhance your enjoyment of the outdoors. Many of us have heard the hooting of an owl at night or the daytime drumming of the male ruffed grouse. It appears that more and more folks in the outer suburbs will soon be hearing the wild and eerie yapping and howling of coyotes. Some animal sounds are quite surprising. Creatures you wouldn't expect to make a peep can be quite vocal at times. We've heard deer snort, porcupines scream, and woodchucks grunt and click their teeth.

Knowing the behavior of birds and animals can often explain their actions. For example, if a ruffed grouse pulls the "wounded wing act," you can be sure its chicks are near and it is trying to draw you away. The mother grouse makes a commotion, dragging its wing in a way sure to get your attention. After watching the mother's act, take a moment to scan the forest floor and you just might see the chicks (look, but don't touch, and be careful where you step). Some other creatures give warnings if you get too close. A goshawk guarding its nest will give a warning of "kak, kak, kak"; don't go any closer, it may attack you. (Never get too close to nesting birds or chase or corner an animal. Oftentimes the best way to get a second look at an animal is to remain perfectly still. They may return out of curiosity.)

Nature study is all the more fascinating when you learn the habits of each wild animal; what it eats, where and when it feeds and rests, whether it is active in the winter or hibernates. Birds can be studied in a similar way, and of course migration patterns are crucial to understanding when and for how long certain birds are in our region. Amphibians and reptiles are generally only active in the warm-weather months, relying on their behavior and surroundings to control their internal temperatures. The relatively few amphibians and reptiles that live in Massachusetts must overwinter in holes or burrows below the frost line. Some (e.g., wood frog) can survive freezing! The best time to see some of them is in the late spring or early summer (usually June); for example, that's when the snapping turtle comes out of the water to lay its eggs on land.

For wildlife photography, you need a zoom lens and a tripod. High-quality shots are extremely difficult to achieve. It's hard enough just locating an animal or uncommon bird, but finding a clear shot for a picture can be quite frustrating. Patience is the key—that's why professional wildlife photographers often spend days in the woods working from a blind.

Consider searching for "small game." Colorful butterflies nectaring on wildflowers, dragonflies hawking for insects along a pond shore, and red-spotted newts courting at the edge of a beaver pond can be just as fascinating as an encounter with a larger creature. The key is to look closely.

Finally, don't discount dumb luck. Much of wildlife we have seen has been by accident, but we greatly increased our odds by repeat visits to favorite properties.

Nature Walking with Children

A walk in the woods with a child can be a wonderful experience or a potential nightmare! The most important step you can take is simply to be flexible. High expectations can ruin any trip. Be ready to turn back anytime, and don't force your goals on a child. When a child shows signs of fatigue take a rest, then turn back—or you might find yourself carrying the child back to the car. And remember that walking in the snow, sand, or mud can use up twice as much energy as a walk of the same length on hard ground.

We have found that a little preparation goes a long way in ensuring that both adult and child have a good time. Bring a **snack**; oftentimes the child will be more interested in the snack than in the natural world. (There's nothing wrong with that; the idea here is to have fun and make the trip a pleasant one.) Bring a **field guide** to birds, animals, reptiles, amphibians, insects, and plants (see the recommended list on p. 253).

A guide enables the child to work with you in identifying the natural world around them. **Binoculars** are always a big hit, and if you do spot wildlife, binoculars might allow the child to see much more than a fleeting glimpse. A hand lens can open up a whole new world. Let the child hold the **map**, and have them help decide which way to go while you teach them how to interpret the map. You might also want to purchase the child a **small backpack**; from the child's viewpoint this seems to somehow make the trip more of an adventure, as if you are going to explore some far-off place. Pack a whistle in the child's backpack, and explain that it is to be used (blown at regular intervals) only if the child becomes separated from the parent.

Spending a day outdoors with a child is a great way to become closer and at the same time teach them a respect for nature. You can show them responsibility through your own actions, such as picking up trash—even if it's not yours. Try to see the world through their eyes and enjoy the simple things that feed their enthusiasm. (If the location has water, it's a good bet the child will want to spend some time throwing twigs or stones.) When you take a rest, that's a good time to tell stories about nature or browse through the field guide together. Remember to praise and encourage the child each time he or she learns something new or completes a walk.

Recommended Walks with Younger Children

All the walks rated easy or medium are good for children. Generally, the walks listed here have fairly level terrain and well-maintained routes. On a few of the longer walks you should not attempt to do the whole route described in the book but rather a small portion, depending on the age and interest of the child.

Children love to explore rocky ledges, boulders, the edges of ponds and streams, lookouts, wooden footbridges, and observation towers. The following places are personal favorites for introducing youngsters to the natural world:

Middlesex and Worcester Counties

Lincoln Woods
Wachusett Mountain State Reservation
Broad Meadow Brook Wildlife Sanctuary
Purgatory Chasm State Reservation
Douglas State Park
Jacobs Hill Reservation
Bear's Den Reservation
Swift River Reservation
Rock House Reservation
Tantiusques Reservation

Franklin County

Northfield Mountain Recreation and Environmental Center
Erving State Forest
Wendell State Forest
High Ledges Wildlife Sanctuary

Hampshire and Hampden Counties

Buffam Falls Conservation Area
William Cullen Bryant Homestead
Chesterfield Gorge
Glendale Falls Reservation
Norcross Wildlife Sanctuary
Arcadia Wildlife Sanctuary
Sanderson Brook Falls
Granville State Forest
Laughing Brook Education Center and Wildlife Sanctuary

How to Use this Book

The walks are grouped into three sections according to the counties they are in. (See the locator map before the introduction.) Once you have selected the location you want to explore, and have read the property description, look up directions to the site under "Getting There," found at the end of each walk.

The approximate time it takes to make the recommended walk is given at the beginning of each entry, as well as the level of difficulty. The time-to-mileage ratio used is about 30 minutes for each mile, but if you're like us you will want to allow more time to enjoy the environment. This ratio was used in some cases to figure approximate trail mileage.

You will want to take the book with you so that you can use the map if you are unfamiliar with the property. A P designates the parking area found at the entrance to each site. Each map shows north to orient you, and we have included an approximate scale in either feet or miles. A heavy dashed line indicates the route described in the text, and the lighter dashed line indicates other trails in the area.

If you are walking with children, see the recommended walks found earlier in this introduction.

Conditions of trails do change from time to time, and we would appreciate hearing about any changes you find. Address them to Appalachian Mountain Club Books, 5 Joy Street, Boston, MA 02108.

Middlesex and Worcester Counties

1 Groton Place and Sabine Woods

Groton

200 acres

❖ 2.5 miles

❖ 1.5 hours

❖ easy

Groton Place and Sabine Woods are two little-known properties situated along the eastern side of the **Nashua River** in Groton. They cover a total of 200 acres of forest and fields and are managed by the New England Forestry Foundation. Some **massive white pines** grow here, as well as rhododendron, azaleas, oaks, maples, and birch. Adjacent to the properties is a strip of land owned by the Groton Conservation Trust, and together the three tracts protect more than 1,800 feet of river frontage.

The walk through the properties is a relatively easy two-and-a-half-mile outing forming a large circular route. The highlight of the walk is the path along the Nashua River, which is lined by old-growth pines.

From the parking area near the river, enter the property through the large metal gate. (When leaving your car unattended, always lock any valuables out of sight in the trunk.) You will cross a narrow cove and enter a field where an old stone horse trough rests directly ahead. Bear left on the trail leading into the woods. The trail forks again in about 100 feet at a large stand of **rhododendron** bushes. Bear to the left again. White pines are the dominant tree here along with a scattering of oaks. The trail is fairly level and makes a great path for cross-country skiing. Horseback riders also enjoy the flat terrain, and it's quite likely you will see riders on the weekend. Soon an old stone wall parallels the trail on the left. About 15 minutes into the walk (stay on the main trail) you will pass a sign for Sabine Woods, erected for people coming down the trail the other way.

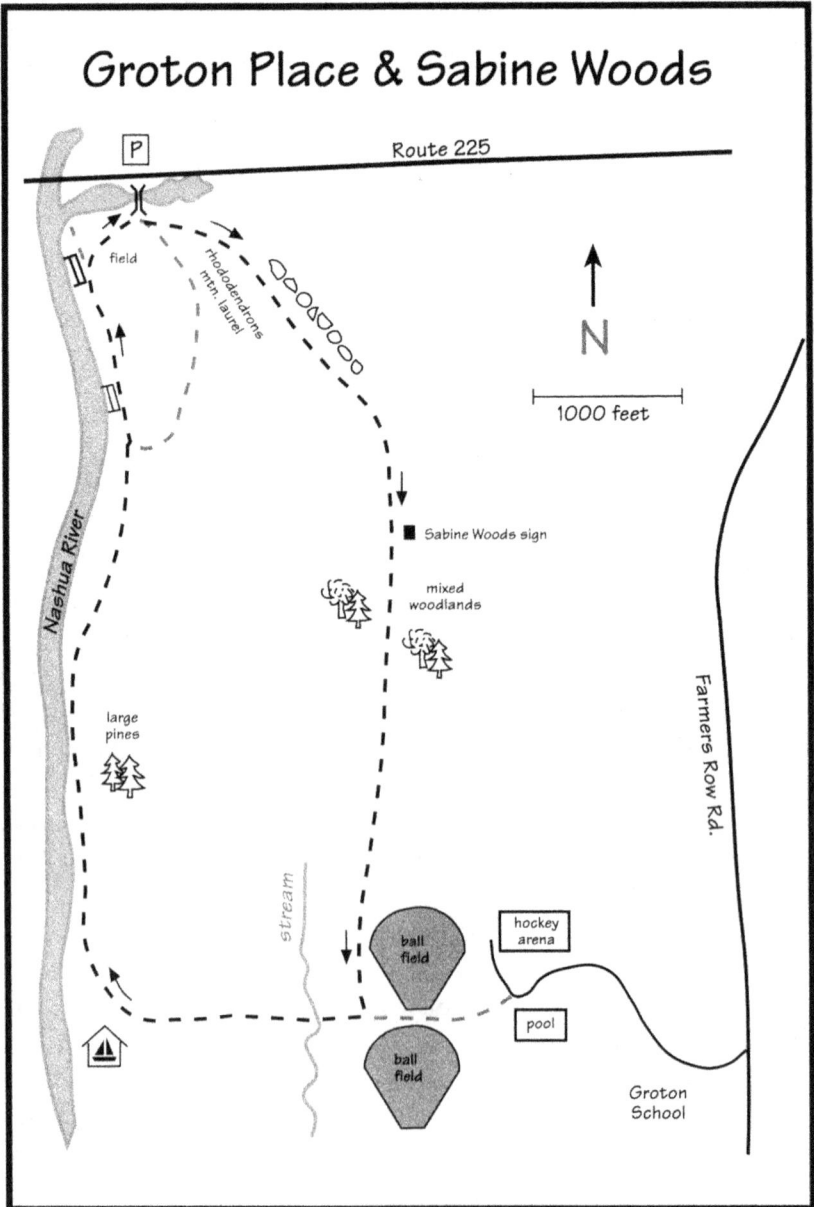

Groton Place & Sabine Woods

P

Route 225

field

rhododendrons
mtn. laurel

N

1000 feet

Nashua River

Sabine Woods sign

mixed
woodlands

large
pines

stream

Farmers Row Rd.

hockey
arena

ball
field

pool

ball
field

Groton
School

After walking another 10 minutes you will pass a ball field on your left. This is part of the sprawling campus of the Groton School. At the next intersection in a grassy area, turn right to continue your loop. You will soon reenter the woods. There is a greater variety of trees here, with oak, maple, pine, and a scattering of white birch. Look for cottontails, which are active year-round, particularly at night and early morning when they emerge from their concealed resting places to feed. They will eat all kinds of green vegetation including bark, twigs, buds, and grass. The trail passes over a small stream that flows north.

From the ball field, proceed down this trail for about 20 minutes until you reach a boathouse on the banks of the Nashua River. The river is quite a success story. In the 1960s it was considered one of the most polluted rivers in the country. Since that time, cleanup efforts have restored much of the river to a Class B rating (fishable/swimmable), and a large portion of its banks are now protected. It is one of the few north-flowing rivers in Massachusetts and drains more than 530 square miles. The watershed includes three main tributaries: the Squannacook, the Stillwater, and the Nissitissit. Groton Place and Sabine Woods are part of a larger greenway connecting open space along the Nashua River.

At the boathouse, take the trail that follows the river's flow northward. The enormous white pines that line the trail were once sought after as timber for ships' masts. In fact, the British Admiralty, through a king's decree in 1688, reserved all pines with trunk diameters of 24 inches or greater for the British navy. A broad arrow was stamped on the tree, signifying that these were crown property—a long-standing source of irritation to the colonists who worked the land.

Pines are sun-loving trees and when New England agriculture began to decline in the late nineteenth century, pines reclaimed the abandoned fields. In just a few years a thick stand of pines would dominate a field. In the understory, shade-tolerant hardwood saplings eventually appeared, and when the pines were logged or died of old age, the hardwoods took over.

The riverside trail you are walking has good views of the water, and it's possible to see wading birds such as great blue heron standing in the river or flying just above the water's surface. **Great blue heron** have wingspans of 70 inches and fly with necks folded. They are often seen standing motionless at the edge of the river watching for fish or frogs. **Green heron** are also seen here. They can be identified by the green-gray coloring of their back and wings, with chestnut-colored head and neck. They are considerably smaller than the great blue heron, and they have a comparatively shorter neck. Mammals such as raccoons, deer, fox, and weasels are active along the banks of the river. You probably have your best chance of spotting wildlife by walking the trail at dawn.

After walking along the path for 15 minutes you will reach an area where **hemlock** and **spruce** are mixed with the pines. Stay straight and do not turn on the small path entering on the right. A cement circular bench overlooking the water makes a good resting spot. (Notice the interesting statue of a resting dog next to the bench. The owner of this former estate, Mr. Frederick Dumaine, was a fox hunter and dog lover. The ashes of Mr. Dumaine are under the millstone next to the bench, and his favorite horse is buried nearby. The statue of the dog is said to be guarding this final resting place.) Just a hundred feet beyond this point is another bench—this one is situated in a field by the river so it usually receives full sunlight. It's also a good place to stop for a snack and watch for birds, such as bluebirds, that prefer the open areas rather than the forest.

A great blue heron pauses from fishing.

To return to your car, simply walk away from the river, opposite the second set of benches, and follow the trail right through the grass. In five minutes you will be at the horse trough and bridge over the cove near the metal entrance gate where you parked. (If it's springtime, be sure to take a few moments to walk back up the trail to its first split where rhododendrons grow, as marked on the map. By staying to the right at the fork instead of going left as directed earlier, you make a short loop back toward the benches by the river.)

Getting There

From Route 495, take Exit 31 (Route 119/Groton) and follow Route 119 west 7.1 miles into Groton center. Bear left onto Route 225 west and follow for 0.7 mile. Route 225 will turn to the right. Follow it for another 0.7 mile. The turnoff for parking is just before the bridge over the river on the left. A brick and iron gate marks the entrance to the property.

Open year-round, seven days a week, no admission fee, no rest rooms.

—M.T.

Flat Rock
Wildlife Sanctuary

2

Fitchburg
340 acres

❖ 1.5 miles

❖ 1 hour

❖ medium

❖ great for children

Walking the trails of Flat Rock Wildlife Sanctuary, it seems as though you are miles from civilization, instead of a few minutes from downtown Fitchburg. Beech, hemlock, and birch form a canopy above mountain laurel. Below these is a rich diversity of ferns, moss, and ground cover such as winterberry and partridgeberry. The trail system is quite extensive with multiple entry points to this 340-acre sanctuary managed by the Massachusetts Audubon Society (MAS). This walk covers the westernmost portion of the property near the main entrance on Ashburnham Hill Road.

On my first trip to Flat Rock, I had the pleasure of walking the property with Gail Howe, a Massachusetts Audubon Society naturalist. Gail's keen eye for nature's subtleties gave me a perspective of the sanctuary I would have missed had I gone alone. We also had the good fortune of walking in mid-October under a crystal blue sky that highlighted the brilliant foliage.

We started our trip by following the trail that begins adjacent to the little barn by the parking area (two large posts mark the beginning of the trail). It's an uphill climb, passing old stone walls and **witch hazel**, which has small yellow flowers blooming in the fall. The flowers appear in clusters of two or three in the axils of the leaves. A furry woody seed capsule of the previous season appears with the flowers, and when this capsule splits it ejects the seed, propelling it for many yards. Witch hazel is a tall shrub (usually about 10 feet) with dull, deep olive green leaves from two to six inches long. In the autumn when the flowers begin to open, the leaves turn a spotted, dull gold. A little higher up on the trail, the smooth gray trunks of beech trees dominate the woodlands. In autumn their yellow-bronze leaves flutter in the breeze. Gail pointed out a multitude of chipmunk holes (about one and a half inches in diameter) along the side of the trail, and we saw quite a few busily gathering acorns.

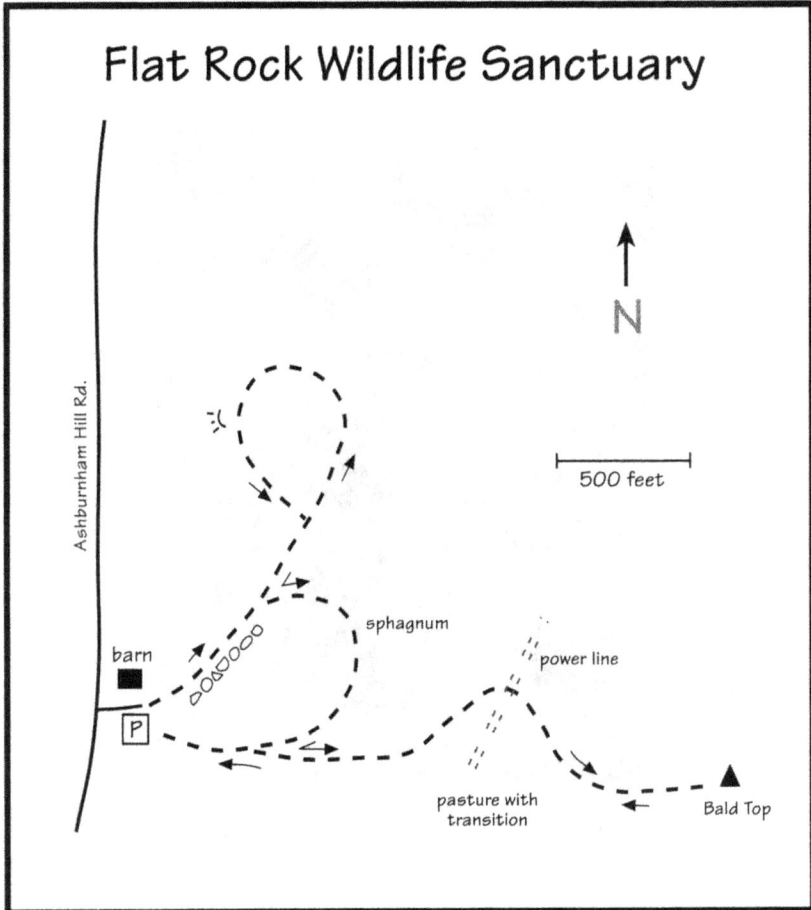

Flat Rock Wildlife Sanctuary

Gail also identified a sign of the **pileated woodpecker**—a pile of chips at the base of a dead tree where it had chiseled into the soft wood in search of wood-boring insects such as carpenter ants. Nearby, we saw the tracks of white-tailed deer that had also used this trail, probably to feed on the popple trees near the summit. (Popple and poplar are names given to the American aspen.) Deer tracks can be identified by a heart-shaped footprint with a ridge in the center. The animal is traveling in the direction at which the narrow end is pointed. Deer are quite abundant in Massachusetts now, but it was not always so: in Thoreau's essay *The Natural History of Massachusetts,* written in 1842, I was surprised by his lament that "the bear, wolf, lynx, wildcat, deer, beaver and marten have disappeared...."

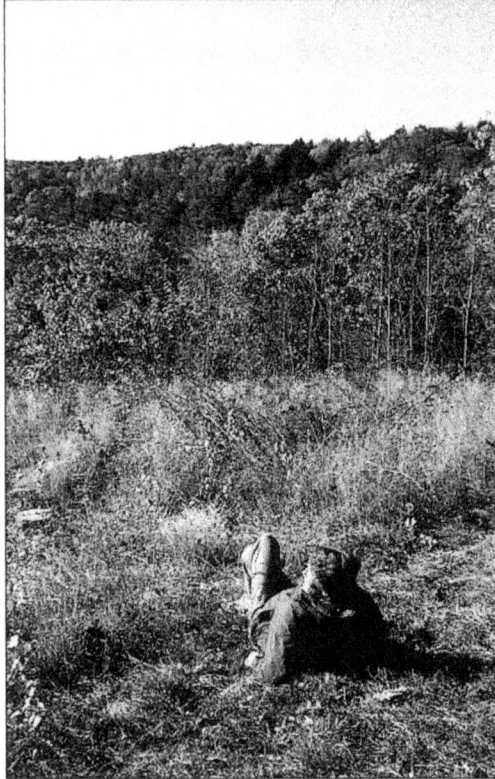

Enjoying the sun and vista at Flat Rock.

If you look closely at the surrounding woods, it's possible to see the signs of a fire that burned much of the underbrush in 1992. You will also see staghorn sumac, so named because the stems feel like the velvet antlers on a deer during the summer months while the antlers are still growing. In late summer, the sumac's red fruit brightens the margins of the deeper woods, and in the fall the leaves turn a rich crimson. The sumac usually grows only to 10 or 12 feet but occasionally reaches heights up to 45 feet.

It grows in large clumps in old pastures and open areas but never in deep, shaded woods. Sumac leaves are large (12 to 24 inches) and are made up of 11 to 31 toothed leaflets.

By staying on the main trail, you will first pass a trail branching off to the right after 10 minutes; continue straight and in 5 minutes you'll reach a vista that overlooks a meadow and the hills to the southwest. This is a nice spot to rest in the sun, before completing a small loop that takes you back to the main trail. Head back down the hill a short distance (past the start of the loop), and turn onto the first path to the left. On this trail, Gail pointed out club moss, growing like miniature pine trees, and the sprouts of American chestnut coming out of an old stump. Unfortunately, chestnut blight, a disease introduced to this country from Asia early in this century, kills the chestnut before the sprouts have a chance to mature. Gail observed that the tree "perseveres, keeps trying to come back." Scientists are working hard to conquer chestnut blight; perhaps someday the stately chestnuts will once again fill the New England woods.

This side trail is rather narrow and rocky, with glacial erratics scattered about and mountain laurel growing in the shallow soil beneath the woods of beech. About 10 minutes down this path, be on the lookout for a tiny patch of **sphagnum** in a moist area to the left of the trail. (Feel how spongy the sphagnum is—because of its ability to absorb water, Native Americans used it for diapers.) Bogs form in wet places, such as old glacial lakes created when blocks of ice deposited by the glaciers melted. Peat often accumulates to considerable depths. Because peat is deficient in many minerals needed for plant growth, only a few specialized species such as sphagnum mosses can grow in the extremely acidic, nutrient-poor soil.

After walking a few more minutes, you will see a trail on the left with blue paint dots on trees, indicating this trail leads away from the parking area (yellow dots signify that you are going toward the parking area). Take this trail to the left to extend your walk. It is referred to as the Link Trail and heads to the east. Within 10 minutes you will pass beneath power lines and then through land that is in transition from pasture to forest. Small white pines, oaks, and blueberry are scattered about. The small birch trees you see here are gray birch, which rarely grow beyond 30 feet tall and often occur in clumps. Gray birch typically grows in poor soil of old fields or burned-out areas. Although it is of little value as lumber, the seeds and buds are eaten by ruffed grouse and songbirds.

Ahead is a bald area of granite rock ledge that makes a nice sunny spot to picnic. To return to the parking area simply retrace your steps back on the Link Trail, and then bear left at its end for a short walk to your car.

(Intrepid explorers may want to continue toward the east from the bald area, but the trails can be a bit confusing. Gail told me she once found a huge pellet from an owl at the base of a large pine just east of the bald. The pellet had the entire skull of a squirrel in it!)

Getting There (main entrance)

From Fitchburg center at the intersection of Routes 2A, 13, and 31, follow Route 2A west to West Street, and take the second right onto Ashburnham Hill Road. Sanctuary entrance is 1.0 mile on the right.

Open year-round, Tuesday–Sunday (closed on Monday except on major holidays), admission fee (MAS members free), no rest rooms.

—M.T.

3 Lincoln Woods

Leominster
68 acres

❖ 1 mile

❖ 30 minutes

❖ easy

❖ great for children

Just one mile beyond the center of Leominster, Lincoln Woods features an esker (a glacial ridge) and vernal pools that attract wildlife. The walk in this Massachusetts Audubon property is an easy one and is recommended for young children.

Begin by following the trail behind the signboard at the parking area. The woods are comprised of white pine, oak, and maple, with Canada mayflower growing in abundance among the pine needles on the forest floor. At the first split in the trail, about 150 feet from the signboard and near an activities building on the right, take the path to the right that leads into a meadow.

A stone wall runs along the edge of the meadow where garter snakes, black racers, and other snakes sometimes sun themselves. Garter snakes can be identified by the stripes running down either side of their body and a pale yellow or orange stripe running down the center of their backs. Black racers are somewhat larger and are usually a black or slate gray color.

Other wildlife here includes deer, opossum, fox, raccoon, and a wide assortment of birds, including the pileated woodpecker. Pileated woodpeckers, uncommon in Massachusetts, are large birds, 15 inches from head to tail. They use sharply pointed bills to dig into trees to get at wood-boring insects. While "drumming" into the tree the woodpecker steadies itself with its stiff tail. It can be identified by its black back and brilliant red pointed crest on the head.

Lincoln Woods

P

226

building

pine
forest

meadow

N

200 feet

vernal
pool

ball
field

vernal
pool

vernal
pools

esker

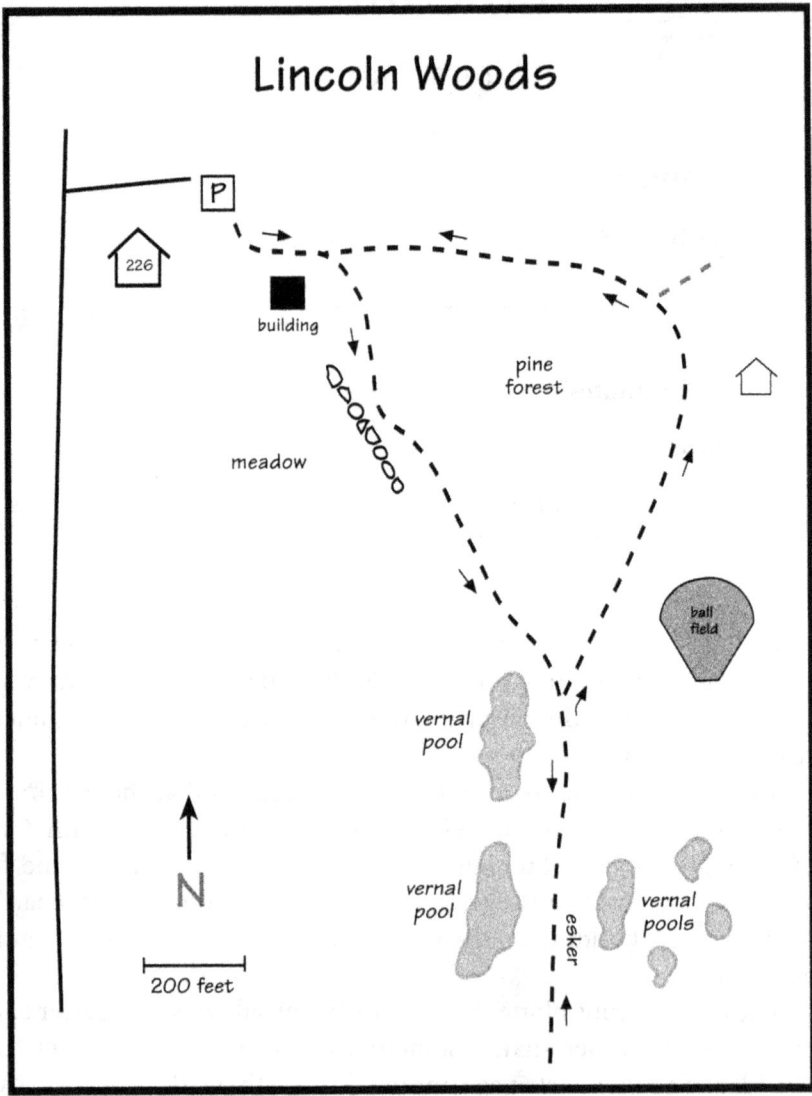

After the trail crosses the meadow, it reenters the pine forest and soon passes by the first vernal pool on the right. A vernal pool is temporary, filling with water in the spring and fall but usually drying in the summer. Because fish are absent from such pools, amphibians can breed here with less threat of being eaten. These unique pools are used by wood frogs and various salamanders as breeding sites; invertebrates such as fairy shrimp spend their entire lives here. Bring along a magnifying glass so children can explore the vernal pools with you.

Blue-spotted salamanders, an endangered species classified as of "special concern," live in forests that have vernal pools. During the breeding season in spring, they lay their eggs at the bottom of vernal pools. During the rest of the year this amphibian lives entirely underground, burrowing beneath the leaf litter of the woods. They can be identified by the sky blue spots on their sides and should not be disturbed if seen.

As you walk the trail, note that you are climbing a ridge of land separating the hollows on either side. This ridge, running north-south, is an esker formed by the glaciers. Eskers are comprised of gravel deposited by a meltwater stream as it flowed through a tunnel under the ice that covered New England from 20,000 to 10,000 years ago. In some places here at Lincoln Woods, the esker is quite high and narrow.

Follow the trail to the south as it climbs the esker. More vernal pools lie to the right and left. An old stone wall parallels the trail on the left, indicating that the land here was once cleared for pasture.

Trails pass old stone walls leading into Lincoln Woods.

The trail ends at the southern section of the property. Retrace your steps back past the vernal pools, then bear right at the fork in the trail to make a loop of the woods. You will pass a ball field and private home on right. The total walk is only about a mile and is on fairly level terrain.

Getting There

Take the Leominster-Route 12 exit (Exit 31) off Route 2. Follow Route 12 south 1.9 miles to Union Street on the right. (You will have passed Leominster center.) Go right on Union Street for 0.6 mile and look for the Audubon sign on the left. There is a small entrance road just to the left of the caretaker's house (226 Union Street). Follow this road to a small parking lot.

Open year-round, closed Mondays except for major holidays, admission fee (free for MAS members), no rest rooms.

—M.T.

4 Wachusett Mountain State Reservation

Princeton
2,050 acres

- ❖ 1.5 miles

- ❖ 1 hour, 15 minutes if you descend via the Pine Hill Trail

- ❖ moderate/difficult

- ❖ great for older children

Thoreau called it "the blue wall," and the Native Americans called it Wachusett, meaning "by the great hill." Both are apt descriptions. Seen from a distance, Wachusett does look like a blue wall standing alone in the lowlands, and it is a large and great hill for this area of Massachusetts, rising to 2,006 feet. The sprawling reservation that covers the mountain and the surrounding forest is one of our better state parks, with a great number of well-marked trails, excellent wildlife habitat, and some super views. The walk to the top is not especially difficult, and, with a couple of rests, most people should have little trouble.

The relatively short walk to the summit described here is just one of several ways to reach the top, and the reservation is worthy of many visits. At the visitor center you can obtain a free map that shows all the trails, including those on the Westminster side of the mountain. The Westminster area includes "Balance Rock," left behind by retreating glaciers; streams; and an old-growth red oak forest. In fact, it's worth taking a circular drive around the mountain to see the beautiful countryside. And for anyone who is mobility impaired, the access road to the summit is open for driving during warm-weather months.

Begin your walk at the reservation's main parking lot and follow the Bicentennial Trail. (Blue triangular blazes mark all the trails.) It's only a few minutes to a sign for the Loop Trail, where you should turn right and begin the ascent of the mountain. This trail has plenty of rocks, so keep an eye on the ground to see where to plant your next step. Be sure to stop and admire the oak woods and scan the hills ahead for wildlife such as grouse, fox, or deer.

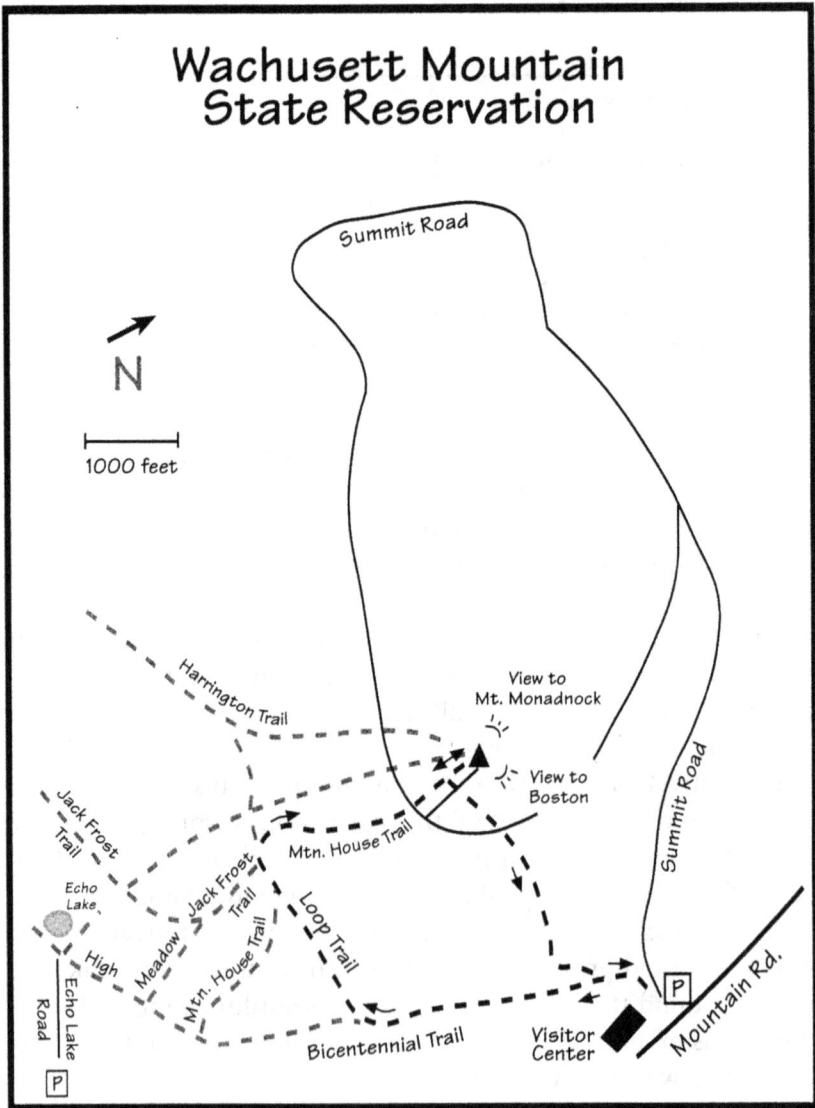

Wachusett Mountain State Reservation

Soon a view opens up on the left. This is a good place to pause and catch your breath. The scene is to the east, and on a clear day you can see the Boston skyline in the distance. Notice that the land stretching toward Boston is relatively flat. Wachusett Mountain is a **monadnock**, a mountain that rises high and virtually alone above the flat plateau. Formed more than 100 million years ago, the mountain is composed of once molten granite. Over the course of millions of years the mountain has been worn down by wind, water, and glacial erosion. It is estimated that at one time Wachusett was thousands of feet taller, perhaps as high as 23,000 feet above sea level. Other mountains made of softer rock than granite once surrounded Wachusett, but they were completely leveled by erosion.

A hawk surveys surrounding terrain from its perch.

The surrounding woods are primarily comprised of oaks, and I've observed many woodpecker holes in the dead wood, possibly from pileated woodpeckers. The pileated woodpecker is an elusive bird, but because of its large size (about as big as a crow) you might get lucky and spot one. Listen for its drumming, which begins loud, then slows, and finally is softer before ending. The birds are best identified by the distinctive red crest and solid black back.

As you climb the trail, try to find your rhythm as you pick your way over the rocks. Mountain hikes can be incredibly relaxing when you focus solely on the hike and forget the outside world. In about 20 minutes you will arrive at the junction with the Mountain House Trail. Turn right and head north toward the summit.

Once I hiked up Wachusett in November, and this area of the mountain was especially beautiful. The bare trees stood out boldly against the granite rocks and the crystal blue southwestern sky. A scattering of beech trees showed off their smooth gray trunks, and a few yellow leaves clung tenaciously to lower branches. Another advantage of hiking here in November is that the access road to the summit is closed, so you may have the summit to yourself. As with any fall hike, be sure to wear something red or orange during hunting season.

The open mountaintop appears in another 20-minute walk, and you are rewarded with views in all directions. To the northwest you can see the outline of Mt. Monadnock and in the distance the smooth rolling shape of Vermont's Green Mountains. On clear days, Mt. Tom can be seen far to the west along the Connecticut River valley.

Thoreau camped on Wachusett's summit, writing, "It was thrilling to hear the wind roar over the rocks." When he awakened he wrote of the vista as dawn reached its prime: "We enjoyed the view of a distinct horizon line, and could fancy ourselves at sea, and the distant hills the waves in the horizon, as seen from the deck of a vessel." Later in the 1800s a summit house was built on the mountain, signaling the beginning of recreation on Wachusett. The hotel was three stories tall and attracted visitors from Boston and New York. Princeton had 12 hotels and was a thriving tourist town for visitors to escape the heat and hustle of the city and enjoy the clean mountain air.

The view of the surrounding lowlands from the summit in those days would have been far different than it is today. Instead of the green canopy of trees, the landscape was one of fields and pasture. Agriculture was king in Massachusetts until the late 1800s, when farmers were drawn west, away from its stony fields. First white pine, gray birch, sumac, and aspen reclaimed a field, followed by oak, beech, and hemlock. The forest, still changing today, will reach the climax stage when hickory, hemlock, sugar maple, oak, and beech dominate.

September is a wonderful time to visit Wachusett because that is when the hawk migration is in full force. Thousands of broad-winged and lesser numbers of sharp-shinned hawks ride the thermals above the ridges. Sometimes other species such as eagles and turkey vultures pass through. The migration is a thrilling sight if you hit it right. However, be warned that in mid-September you won't have the mountaintop to yourself, as many others will be there to enjoy the annual event.

There are many different routes you can take to descend the mountain. You might try the Jack Frost Trail, which has stands of hemlock and mountain laurel in its lower reaches. The Jack Frost Trail connects to the High Meadow Trail, and you can walk southwest to see Echo Lake before heading back to the parking area via the Bicentennial Trail. Echo Lake is a small, shallow lake with a picnic table and stone fireplace at its eastern end. High Meadow is an area of transition where the once open field is being reclaimed by the forest, now covered with birch, sumac, and blackberry bushes. It affords a partial view to the southeast.

The quickest way off the summit is to descend via the Pine Hill Trail, but this route should be taken only in dry weather because it is very steep and much of the trail is exposed bedrock. The trail has some great views to the east. Hemlocks and white birch line the trail and, in the springtime, mayflowers bloom. Descending on this trail only takes about 15 minutes.

Be sure to stop in at the visitor center—the displays are excellent.

Getting There

From Route 2 take Exit 25, Route 140 south, and go south on Route 140 for 2.6 miles. Turn right at the State Park sign and follow Mile Hill Road, which soon turns into Mountain Road. Parking is 1.8 miles from Route 140.

No admission fee; rest rooms in visitor center; open seven days a week, year-round.

—M.T.

5 Broad Meadow Brook Wildlife Sanctuary

Worcester
272 acres

❖ 2.5 miles

❖ 1.5 hours

❖ easy

❖ great for children

Broad Meadow Brook Wildlife Sanctuary is like an oasis of green in the urbanized area around Worcester. It acts as a resting place for many migratory birds and is home to a surprising amount of wildlife such as mink, deer, raccoon, red fox, rabbit, opossum, and woodchuck. The 272-acre property, with marsh, brooks, and woods, is the largest urban wildlife sanctuary in New England.

The walk begins by following the Holdridge Trail around to the left of the visitor center and into a woods of maple, quaking aspen, ash, and oak. About five minutes into the walk, you come to a boardwalk at marker number 1 and turn left. (Markers are placed at all trail intersections.) This is the Cutover Trail, which leads past a tiny frog pond on your left. On my last visit, with my family in late September, we spotted two frogs and a large **snake** beneath the cattails. We waited for the snake to show more of itself so we could try to identify it, but it was content to lie motionless, with just its head sticking out of the water.

The trail soon passes by some private homes on the left, and in five minutes you will have reached the end of the Cutover Trail. On your right will be the Sprague Trail, a wide, flat path that borders an old stone wall. It is an excellent place for birding because of its openness. The sanctuary is home to some 60 species of **birds** that breed on the property, such as ruffed grouse, red-tailed hawk, northern flicker, and hairy woodpecker. Smaller birds such as eastern wood-pewee, common yellowthroats, bluebirds, and warblers are often present. Wood ducks, great horned owls, eastern screech owls, and wild turkeys also have been observed.

About an eighth of a mile down the Sprague Trail, Broad Meadow Brook passes under the trail, flowing south toward the Blackstone River. The granite slab that serves as a bridge over the brook is a perfect place to sit and rest. Look down into the pool below the small waterfall for crayfish and minnows. Some lucky explorers have seen muskrat and raccoon at this spot. **Mink** are also known to frequent this pool. Adult males can grow as long as 35 inches including their tail, yet the weight of a mink that size would be only about two and a half pounds. They are crafty hunters that prey primarily on small rodents but will also take birds, snakes, frogs, crayfish, and even muskrat.

Broad Meadow Brook Wildlife Sanctuary

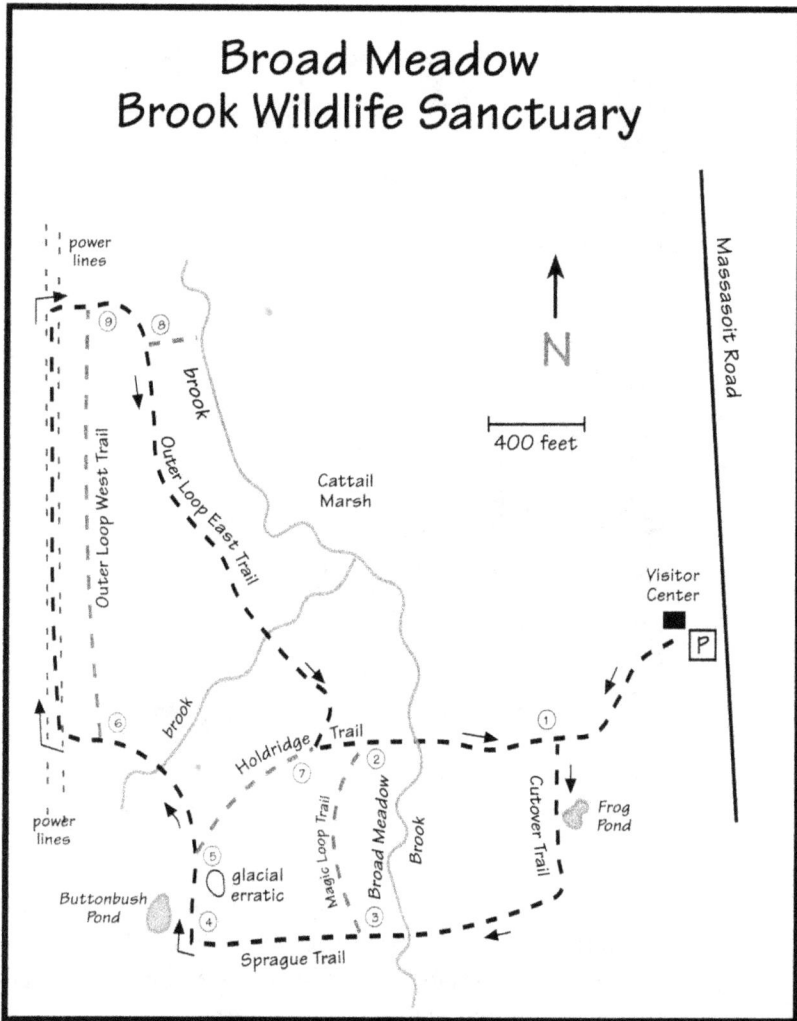

On the edge of the brook you might notice a slender plant two to four feet tall with bright red flowers blooming during late summer. This is the **cardinal flower**, which grows in wet places throughout New England. You may also notice skunk cabbage and other plants that prefer swampy areas. While identifying plant life, be sure to look closely at the muddy banks along the stream—chances are you will find the tracks of raccoons that make nocturnal visits to pools such as this and use their sensitive forefeet, with humanlike fingers, to feel for frogs, mussels, and crayfish. The tracks are relatively easy to distinguish from other animals because the developed "toes" and "fingers" make the tracks look similar to a child's handprint.

Hikers at Broad Meadow pause for a streamside rest.

The Sprague Trail narrows after crossing the stream and rises through a woodland where ferns grow alongside the path, and oaks become the dominant tree. Pass marker number 3 and the Magic Loop Trail branching to the right. Continue on for about five more minutes of walking to marker number 4. Bear right here, and you will pass tiny **Buttonbush Pond** on the left, home to spotted turtles and spotted salamanders. The buttonbush has distinctive ball-like white-colored flowers on stems that range from 3 to 10 feet tall. Because the vegetation is thick here, the best time to see the turtles is in the early spring, before the vegetation obscures your view. Look for turtles basking in the sun on a log.

Just beyond Buttonbush Pond, there is a **glacial erratic** on the right that kids will enjoy climbing. Large boulders such as this are called erratics because during the Ice Age glaciers carried them many miles and deposited them in areas of different bedrock. The glacier that advanced on New England carved valleys where none had previously existed, scoured existing river valleys, and plucked stones off ledges and ground them before depositing when the ice began to melt 10,000 to 15,000 years ago. Many erratics appear in unusual locations, often balanced high on a hilltop.

Not far from the boulder is marker number 5, where you should bear left. This is the Outer Loop West Trail, which leads toward the western perimeter of the property. About five minutes down this trail, after crossing a brook, reach marker number 6. Here either bear right and stay on the Outer Loop West Trail, which goes northward through the woods, or walk beneath the adjacent power lines and follow them to the right.

I prefer the power line trail, because it is a good place to spot **butterflies** such as monarchs and black swallowtails. Beneath the sunny opening of the power lines grow many wildflowers, such as Queen Anne's lace, asters, and goldenrod. After walking about 10 or 15 minutes under the power lines, look for a footpath on the right that leads back into the woods of the sanctuary. (Look for this path just before the power line service road swings to the left side of the power lines.) The Outer Loop West Trail will also enter from the right.

Walk through a birch and poplar grove, pass marker number 9, and within a couple minutes reach marker number 8 where you should bear slightly to the right. The Outer Loop East Trail hugs a ridge, and to the left is a low-lying area where water collects. It is a good 15-minute walk on this trail, which allows your mind to roam while your legs carry you on automatic pilot.

When you reach marker number 7, bear left onto the Holdridge Trail, which leads back toward the parking area. There are some wonderful old oak trees that spread their canopies above this trail. Just stay straight and you will return to the visitor center. Plan on spending about an hour and a half for this walk, a bit longer if you are with children. Chances are, kids will want to revisit the frog pond to look for more snakes, frogs, and tadpoles.

Getting There

From the Massachusetts Turnpike, take the Millbury exit (Exit 11) and turn left off the ramp onto Route 122 heading north. Follow Route 122 for 0.7 mile and then go left on Route 20 west. Proceed 0.9 mile and then turn right on Massasoit Road at the first traffic light. The sanctuary is 0.5 mile ahead on the left.

From Route 290 west, take Exit 13/Vernon Street and turn left (if on Route 290 east take Exit 13 and turn right). Proceed up Vernon Street and take the left fork onto Winthrop Street. Follow Winthrop Street past Providence Street and St. Vincent's Hospital, where it becomes Heywood Street. Go straight on Heywood to the bottom of the hill, and turn right onto Massasoit Road. The sanctuary is 1.4 miles ahead on the right.

Open Tuesday through Sunday, dawn to dusk. Admission fee for nonmembers of Massachusetts Audubon; free to the residents of Worcester Tuesday–Friday. Visitor center and rest room open 9:00 A.M. to 4:00 P.M.

—M.T.

Purgatory Chasm
State Reservation

6

Sutton
960 acres

❖ 0.5 mile

❖ 30 minutes

❖ medium

❖ great for children

A good name always piques my curiosity and Purgatory Chasm certainly has one. Sometimes the name builds you up for a big letdown when you actually visit the place, but that's not the case here. The chasm, with its sheer rock walls towering 70 feet above the trail, is a dramatic place to explore.

From the parking area, follow the sign to the chasm and begin your descent into the base of the crevice. You must pick your way around **massive boulders**, and children should be accompanied by an adult. Be sure to wear rubber-soled shoes or hiking boots. (Because the footing can be treacherous during periods of snow and ice, the chasm is usually closed December through March.) The jumble of rocks forms a series of small dark caves, crevices, and jagged outcrops, adding to the mysterious, otherworldly feeling.

One can't help but wonder how the chasm was formed. Did the earth open during an earthquake? Did the glaciers split the bedrock? Park Ranger Dave Podles told me the most likely theory: the chasm was formed when a giant glacial lake released its water and ice, which tore through the rock and opened the crevice. Later, freezing and thawing made the sides split and rocks tumbled to the bottom.

It takes about 10 minutes to reach the base of the chasm, where a few trees somehow manage to grow. A couple of **old-growth hemlock** trees are truly spectacular. Towering overhead, their crowns extend beyond the edge of the cliff above. They are perhaps 300 years old. It was impractical for eighteenth- and nineteenth-century loggers to haul them out of here, and thus they were spared the fate of so many other large ancient New England trees. Take a moment to examine the roots of the trees, which snake around the boulders, searching for a bit of dirt to sink into. A scattering of ferns and lichens is about the only other vegetation that can grow in the shadows of the chasm.

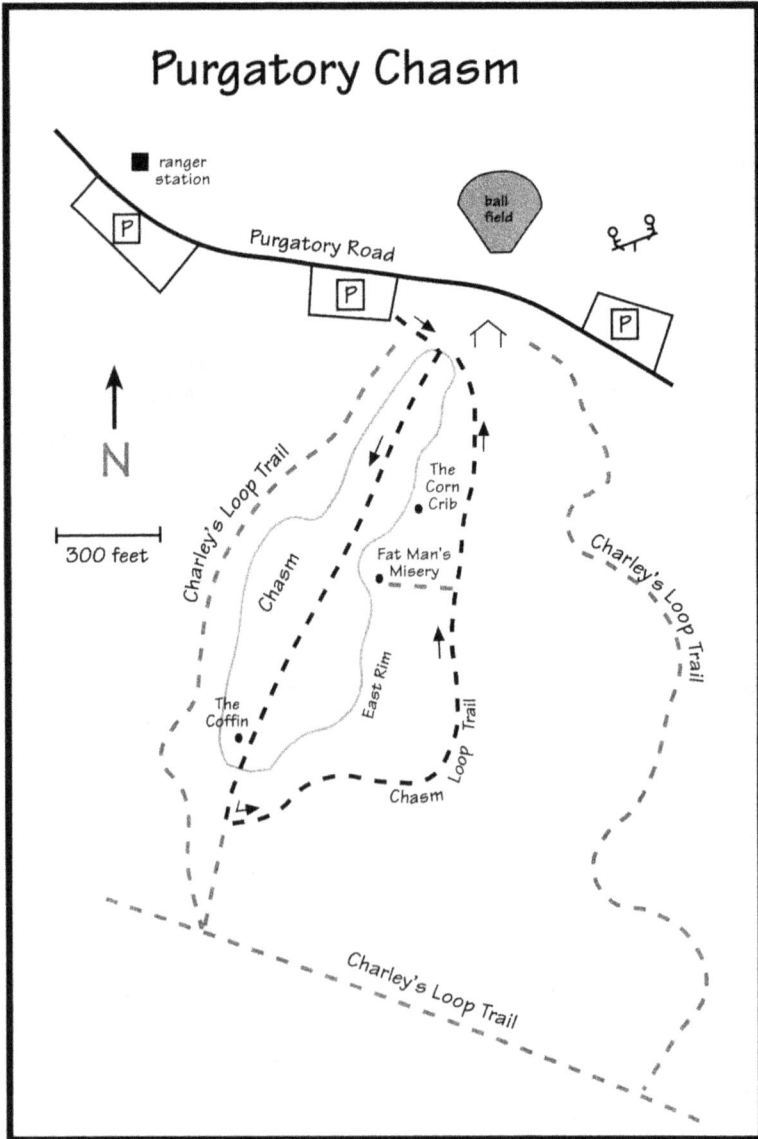

Purgatory Chasm

It seems remarkable to me that the floor of the chasm stays dry because it looks like a river gorge without the water. Perhaps that's why it's been called New England's Grand Canyon. This canyon is just one-fourth-mile long, though, and soon you leave the granite cliffs behind. Mixed with the granite are small sections of quartz, mica, and gneiss.

When you reach the end of the chasm, turn left and walk back toward the parking area via the eastern rim on the Chasm Loop Trail. There are a few overlooks that allow a view down into the chasm, but be sure to exercise caution. Some of the **unique geological formations** in the rim have been named. Fat Man's Misery is a narrow crack in the rock—big enough for a thin person to walk through but trouble for someone with a few extra pounds. On my visits, I opt not to test the dark alley.

Fat Man's Misery.

"The Coffin" and "The Corn Crib" were originally called the devil's coffin and devil's corncrib by the Puritans, who likened the chasm to a descent toward Hades. The coffin has a rock in the shape of a coffin, and the corncrib looks like an early settler's corncrib.

The walk along the rim is relatively easy compared to the climb down into the chasm. The whole loop only takes about half an hour, and you may want to explore some of the less frequented nearby trails through woods of oak, white pine, and hemlock. Charley's Loop Trail begins at the pavilion near the parking area and heads in a southerly direction for half a mile until a T junction, where you should turn right. Follow the trail for about a quarter of a mile and then take the next right, which will bring you to the far end of the chasm. From here you can return to the parking lot by going through the chasm or walking either rim trail.

(Photography in the chasm can be a real challenge. One thing I've learned from repeat visits is that to better capture the scale of the boulders, trees, and cliffs, it's best to have people in the shot. Besides adding a sense of dimension, a person hiking through the chasm gives the photo needed contrast against the dark gray, shadowy rocks.)

Climbing the chasm walls is strictly prohibited without a permit. Serious injuries have occurred here. Wear rubber-soled shoes or hiking books as the trails are slippery, and stay away from the edges of the chasm.

Getting There

Purgatory Chasm is located just off Route 146 in Sutton. (Route 146 runs from the Worcester area southward to Uxbridge on the Rhode Island border.) Exit Route 146 at the Purgatory Road Sutton exit. (If coming from the south, you will see Purgatory Chasm on the sign.) Signs will direct you to the reservation, about a half mile west on Purgatory Road.

Closed during periods of snow and ice, otherwise open seven days a week, no admission fee, rest rooms.

—M.T.

Blackstone River and Canal Heritage State Park

Northbridge/Uxbridge
1,005 acres

- ❖ 3 miles
- ❖ 1.5 hours
- ❖ medium

When William Blackstone, the first European settler of Shawmut Peninsula (now Boston), decided he needed a little more elbow room, he went westward, settling along the river that now bears his name. His solitude was short-lived as other settlers followed him, cutting the virgin timber to farm the rolling hills and erecting mills along the river.

Today, one can get a sense of how this landscape must have looked when Blackstone first arrived by taking a walk to the top of King Philip's Rock. A **panoramic** view to the south encompasses the river, the wooded hills, and almost no signs of mankind.

To reach this hilltop, begin your walk by following the King Philip Trail adjacent to the office of the Department of Environmental Management on East Hartford Avenue. The gravel trail leads northward through a field where bluebird boxes have been erected. About a hundred yards from the start, the trail turns to the right (follow the blue markers) and enters a forest of white pines and oaks. Picnic tables are scattered in the shade.

On your left is **Rice City Pond**, an impoundment on the Blackstone River. The pond, wetlands, and woods around it are home to raccoon, white-tailed deer, red fox, partridge, quail, turtles, and snakes. Herons, ospreys, and hawks visit the pond, and once, a rare Eurasian widgeon was seen. (Canoeists enjoy exploring the quiet, placid waters. You may want to make a day trip to the park, canoeing half the day and taking this walk the other half.)

Follow the trail for about 10 minutes, then pass through an old gravel pit and bear left at the fork on the opposite side. A couple of minutes farther on you come to an opening that overlooks the pond. If you look to the right you can see King Philip's Rock along the hillside.

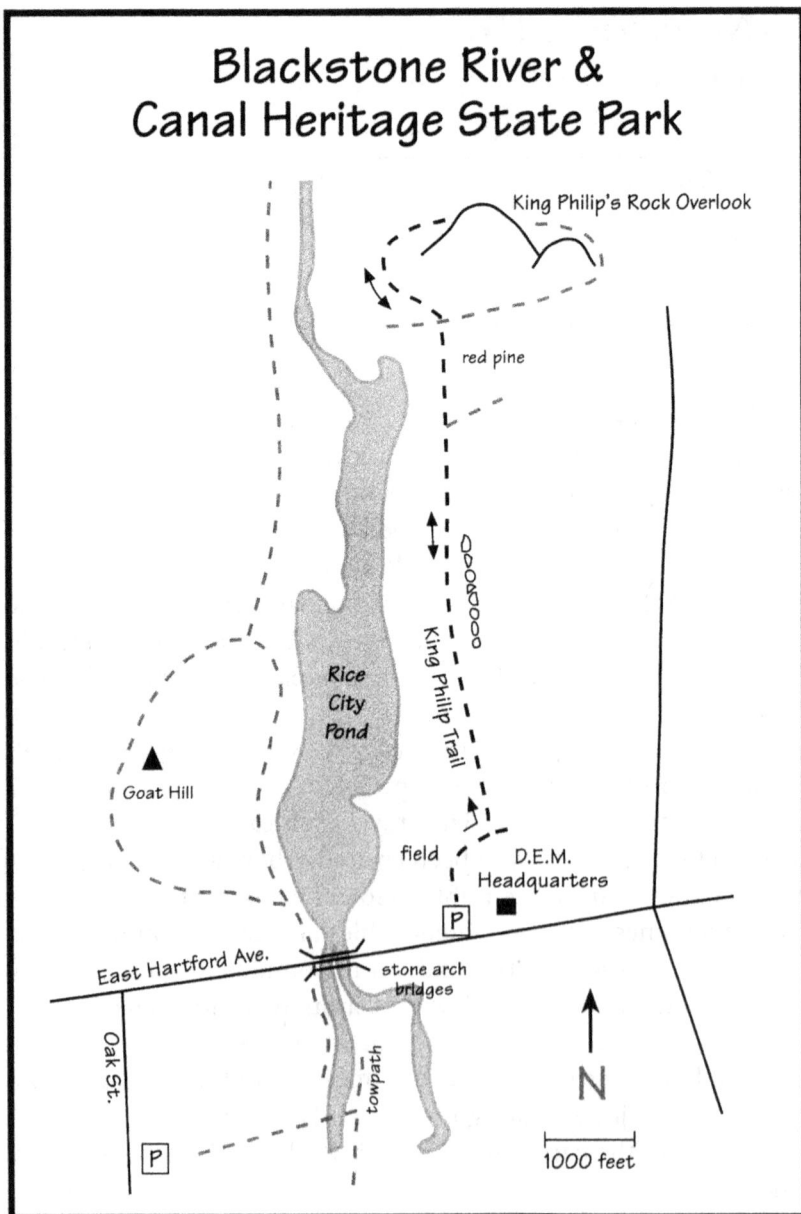

Blackstone River & Canal Heritage State Park

King Philip's Rock Overlook

red pine

Rice City Pond

King Philip Trail

▲ Goat Hill

field

D.E.M. Headquarters

P

East Hartford Ave.

stone arch bridges

Oak St.

towpath

P

N

1000 feet

Next, the trail hugs a boulder-strewn slope, where you must pick your way among the rocks and exposed roots. Notice the smooth gray trunks of small beech trees that begin to appear. Also seen are sections of stone walls, indicating that this land was once cleared for pasture or crops.

About 30 minutes from the start of your hike the trail forks; follow the blue markers to the left, passing over a small stream and through a plantation of **red pine**. A few minutes later you are near the base of King Philip's Rock (also called Look-out Rock), at a four-way intersection. Take the second trail to your left that leads around the sheer rock ledges toward the direction of Rice City Pond. (You can also reach the summit by following the blue markers to the right. This trail makes a more graded climb to the top but takes a little longer.)

Walking trail on the original towpath adjacent to the Blackstone Canal.

The trail swings around to the left and then makes a steep climb to the top of the hill. The summit makes a great place to picnic or simply relax and enjoy the view of the meandering river and pond below. In the spring, I enjoy seeing the pattern of dark green pines mix with the lighter colored new growth of deciduous trees. Autumn brings the orange-brown of oaks and the reds of swamp maples. Often, cool breezes sweep over the hill, refreshing after the 40-minute walk through the lowlands.

King Philip's Rock was named for the Wampanoag leader Metacom, whom the English called Philip. It was Metacom who led the 1675–76 uprising of a number of regional tribes against the settlers pushing westward from coastal areas. Like so many rocky bluffs in Massachusetts, local legend has it that this spot was one of the places where Philip and his followers camped during King Philip's War. While we may never know where Philip actually set foot, the hilltop offers the best view of the Blackstone River, whose historic tale is as interesting as its natural one.

Originating in Worcester, the Blackstone drains an area of 640 square miles during its south-southeastward course to Rhode Island's Narragansett Bay. Along the way there are a number of historic points of interest, most involving the mills and the **canal** that connected Worcester to Providence.

The Slater Mill (1793), located by the river in Pawtucket, Rhode Island, was America's first mechanized textile mill. More mills quickly followed, and the explosion of manufacturing along the banks of the river led to the area being labeled as the "Birthplace of the American Industrial Revolution." Mill villages with holding ponds, dams, old brick factories, and simple mill housing are found all along the river.

In 1824, construction of the canal began. Using shovels, axes, picks, wheelbarrows, and ox carts, laborers (mostly immigrants from Ireland who were paid $12 a month) dug the 45-mile canal. Canal owners installed expensive granite locks rather than the more economical wooden locks and planted trees along both sides of the canal for erosion control. But their investment did not reap long-term profits. In 1848, the completion of the Providence and Worcester Railroad marked the beginning of the end for the canal.

After you follow the original trail back off the hill and retrace your path to the parking area, take the time to walk the old towpath along the canal. My favorite spot is near the new River Bend Farm Visitor Center on Oak Street. The visitor center features exhibits depicting the history of the Blackstone River valley. From the parking lot at River Bend Farm, walk down to the canal and cross the handsome bridge to the towpath. If you walk to the right (south), the trail passes through an open area with the river on one side and the canal on the other (this trail goes all the way to Stanley Woolen Mill, about one and a half miles away). The path also follows the canal to the north, where a 10-minute walk will bring you to the beautiful falls at the stone arch bridges, and extends another two miles north to Plummers Landing.

Getting There

From the intersection of Routes 16 and 122 in Uxbridge take Route 122 north 1.3 miles to Hartford Avenue. Go right on Hartford Avenue 1.0 mile to the river. For the trail to King Philip's Rock cross the river and park at the lot at the Department of Environmental Management headquarters on the left. To walk along the canal turn south on Oak Street (on the west side of the Hartford Avenue bridge over the river). After a thousand feet, a sign will welcome you to the state park.

Open year-round, seven days a week, no admission fee, rest rooms located in the River Bend Farm visitor center.

—M.T.

8 Douglas State Forest

Douglas
4,555 acres

❖ 1 mile

❖ 30 minutes

❖ easy

❖ great for children

Douglas State Park has something for almost everyone: a lake for swimming, boating, and fishing; miles of forest roads for mountain biking and hiking; and an **Atlantic white cedar swamp** for nature study. You will see unique plants that grow in the cedar swamp that are not found in common marshes.

The Cedar Swamp Trail begins near the lake. From the main parking area, follow the path to the beach, then bear right past the rest rooms and small nature center to a sign that points to the trail. (In the off-season, you can park at the boat ramp adjacent to the beach.)

The trail begins as a narrow path winding through a forest of oak and maple with mountain laurel beneath. You will pass the intersection with the returning trail on your right, and you should bear left. Soon a sign points to a bird blind, located just a few feet off the Cedar Swamp Trail. The blind looks out over a slope where birdhouses and bird feeders have been erected. Look for titmice, chickadees, and blue jays at the feeders, and look for ruffed grouse on the forest floor.

Back on the Cedar Swamp Trail, the path climbs exposed granite ledges where small hemlocks grow. An interpretive sign directs your attention to **American chestnut tree sprouts**. The sprouts you see rarely grow beyond 20 feet tall before the blight, which began killing American chestnuts in 1904, enters the trees through cracks in the bark and kills them.

Once common throughout the New England forest, the grand chestnut trees are no more.

Just 10 minutes into our walk, the Cedar Swamp Trail crosses the Coffee Loop Trail and descends down a hill, onto a boardwalk. Pass skunk cabbage (which Native Americans rubbed on themselves when hunting to cover their scent), cinnamon ferns, and sweet pepperbush, known for its late-summer fragrance. Skunk cabbage can be identified not only by its odor but also by its large green leaves that resemble rhubarb. It likes to have moist feet.

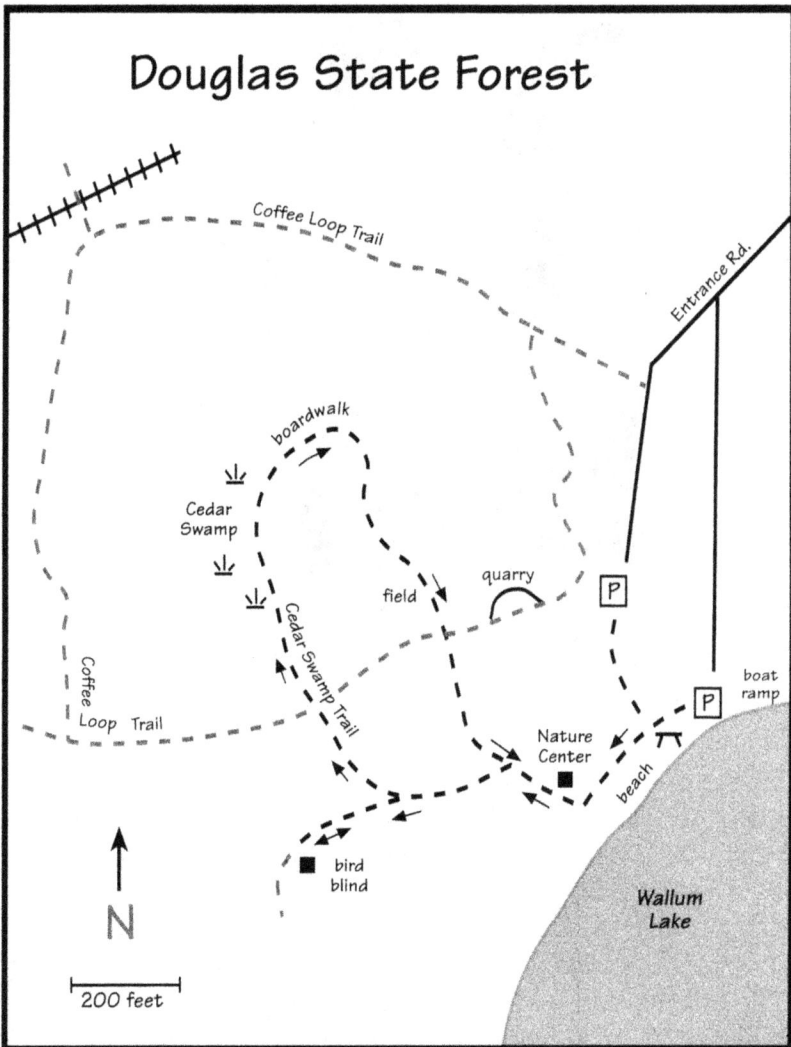

Douglas State Forest

Coffee Loop Trail

Entrance Rd.

boardwalk

Cedar
Swamp

Cedar Swamp Trail

field

quarry

P

Coffee
Loop Trail

P

boat
ramp

Nature
Center

beach

bird
blind

N

Wallum
Lake

200 feet

You are now entering the Atlantic white cedar swamp. The woods begin to feel entirely different: cooler, moister, quieter. A stand of Atlantic white cedar such as this is relatively uncommon because so many of the trees have been cut for lumber. The stand is also unusual because this is about the northernmost location for the species, with most of the New England stands being near the warmer coast. The trees grow from 40 to 50 feet in height and have scalelike, flattened green leaves.

The shores of Wallum Lake offer great picnic spots.

Atlantic white cedar was popular because of its decay-resistant quality and light weight, making it perfect for fence posts, floorboards, joists, and shingles. The trees you see around you are about 70 years old and six to eight inches in diameter.

A thick expanse of sphagnum, or peat moss, covers the ground like a spongy carpet. The moss is capable of holding 20 times its weight in water, and Native Americans lined their babies' pants with it because of its absorbent nature. Also growing in the swamp is an insect-eating plant called the sundew. It is a small plant with rounded leaves and white or pink flowers growing just inches off the ground. Insects get trapped in the sticky fluid on its leaves and are digested by the plant.

The boardwalk ends at a rocky area where a **glacial erratic**, so named because the boulder was deposited here from far away by the retreating glacier, can be seen. Farther along the path, you come to another section of boardwalk leading through more cedars to the lower end of a field.

Approach the field quietly and be on the lookout for white-tailed deer feeding along the edge of the meadow. Red fox, ruffed grouse, and cotton-tail rabbits have also been seen here. Dawn and dusk are the best times to view wildlife.

Go straight through the field and follow the middle trail (which inter-sects the Coffee Loop Trail) to return to the **beach**. The beach is well main-tained, and Wallum Lake looks like a perfect place for a dip after a walk. It is also a great area for picnicking—my favorite spot is a secluded portion of shoreline to the right (as you face the water) where three picnic tables are located by the water's edge.

For a longer walk try the Coffee Loop Trail, which makes a 2.2-mile circle of the cedar swamp.

Getting There

From the east: at the intersection of Routes 146 and 16 go west on Route 16 (passing through East Douglas and Douglas) for about 7.0 miles. At Cedar Street (1.6 miles past the Douglas town common) turn left. Signs direct you to the park entrance, 1.7 miles from your turn onto Cedar Street.

From the west: take Route 395 to the Route 16 exit (Douglas/Web-ster) and follow Route 16 east for 5.0 miles. Follow the signs for the park by turning right on Cedar Street.

Open year-round, seven days a week, fee during summer months, rest rooms.

—M.T.

9 Royalston Falls

Royalston
205 acres

❖ 3 miles

❖ 1.5–2 hours

❖ easy to medium, depending on
  where you park

One of the reasons I like Royalston Falls so much is the walk down the secluded country road to reach the property where the waterfall is located. Four-wheel-drive vehicles can drive this latter part of Falls Road to the trailhead, but the walk down the road is half the fun. Old stone walls, large hemlocks, birch, and maples line the road and are best enjoyed on foot. This way you can relish the scents, sounds, and tranquillity of the woods.

The first part of Falls Road is maintained by the town and you should drive down the road about two and a half miles to where it becomes rough and a sign says Seasonal Use. Park near the sign or at a turnoff about 100 feet past the sign. Be sure you do not block the road.

The walk down the road from the Seasonal Use sign to the Trustees' sign welcoming you to Royalston Falls takes about 25 minutes. The Royalston Falls sign is on the left just after a sharp bend in the road as it climbs a hill. A narrow trail to the falls begins here. This half-mile foot trail goes over small hills of pines, hemlocks, and oaks.

These woods are home to just about every type of animal found in Massachusetts including the **fisher**, a member of the weasel family. It is a skillful predator, tracking down mice, squirrels, snowshoe hares, chipmunks, birds, and frogs. It is one of the few animals that can kill a porcupine and does so by circling the porcupine, biting its head, and wearing the creature down before moving in for the kill.

Soon you will hear the **falls** ahead. Descend a steep slope to the edge of a cliff above the falls where a railing has been erected for your safety.

Falls Brook plunges about 70 feet below into a spray of mist and foam, truly a beautiful sight. The falls are inaccessible, but if you want to do a bit of bushwhacking you can follow the Falls Brook upstream along a faint path that is actually part of the Metacomet-Monadnock Trail. You can also go to the left as you face the falls and descend a slope that leads downstream into an open area about a hundred yards from the falls. It's a beautiful spot where the stream fans out into a pool framed by ferns and rocky outcrops.

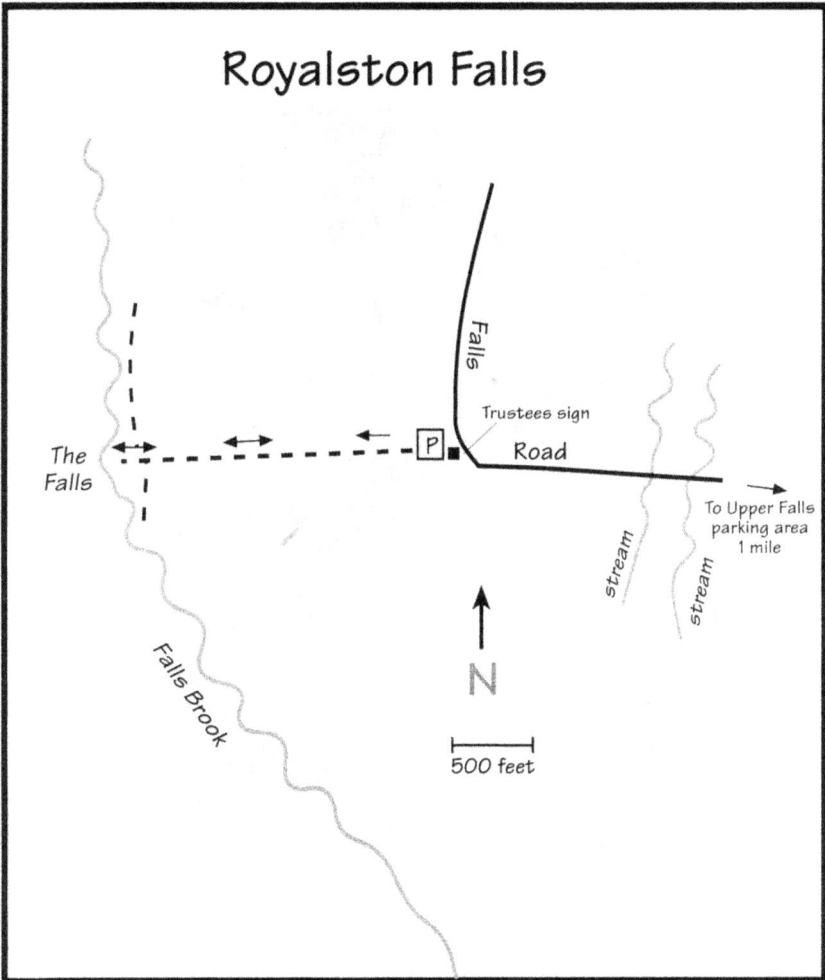

Royalston Falls

The Falls

Falls

Trustees sign

P Road

To Upper Falls parking area 1 mile

stream

stream

Falls Brook

N

500 feet

Streamside vegetation includes cinnamon fern, a tall (three- to five-foot) plant whose fronds are covered by tufts of cinnamon brown wool in spring as well as separate brown-colored spore-producing fronds. These brown stalks wither as the season progresses, while green vegetative fronds persist. In the early spring look for skunk cabbage identified by its large purple-green shell-like spathe, which emerges from damp earth, later to be encircled by dark green cabbagelike leaves. It has a fetid odor that is especially strong if the leaves are bruised. The odor lures insects that pollinate the skunk cabbage. Its growth is so fast in the spring that the heat from its cellular respiration can actually melt snow or ice around it! Other plants you may notice are cardinal flowers, which have many brilliant red tubular flowers that bloom from July into September.

Royalston Falls tumbles over ancient rock formations.

Retrace your steps on the trail to return to Falls Road. From this point, it's about a 25-minute walk back to the parking area. Because Royalston Falls is so far off the beaten path, it **receives few visitors**. The trail to the falls makes a great walk in the autumn when the mosquitoes and black-flies are gone and the hardwoods put on their annual show of color. The yellow leaves of the birches are especially beautiful, made more so by the contrast of the dark green needles of pines and hemlocks. The white birch is also known as paper birch and canoe birch because the Native Americans in northern New England used birch bark canoes.

Spring snowmelt is a spectacular time to see the falls, when the water thunders into the pool below. Blackflies are usually in full force by late April and early May, so pack bug spray. Because Royalston is at the northern border of Massachusetts, these shaded woods may still have snow cover when areas to the south and east have none. Wear hiking boots for protection and proper footing.

Getting There

From the center of Royalston take Route 68 north 1.4 miles (passing Jacobs Hill Reservation). Turn right on Falls Road and travel 3.2 miles. (Note: last 0.8 mile is not maintained by the town. If you don't have four-wheel drive, walk down this last section of roadway.)

(One of the easiest ways to get to Royalston center is to exit Route 2 onto Route 202 north. Follow for 2.4 miles and turn left onto Route 68 north and travel 8.6 miles to the center of Royalston.)

Open year-round, seven days a week, no admission fee, no rest rooms.

—M.T.

10 Jacobs Hill Reservation

Royalston
135 acres

❖ 2.5 miles

❖ 2 hours

❖ medium

❖ great for children

For such a beautiful property, Jacobs Hill sure is a well-kept secret! **Spectacular views**, forested hills, a **beaver pond**, and a **waterfall** await your discovery. Best of all, the top of Jacobs Hill can be reached in an easy 15-minute walk, while more challenging terrain awaits those who want to extend their trip and explore Spirit Falls to the south. Richard O'Brien, Central Region supervisor for The Trustees of Reservations, has seen a wide array of animals here including **coyote, bobcat, porcupine, fisher, deer,** and **beaver.**

From the parking area follow the trail through woods of hemlock and beech with an understory of mountain laurel. About 200 yards down the path you will cross under a power line, and the trail resumes on the other side. (Look for highbush and lowbush blueberries in the sunny opening beneath the power line.)

Follow the yellow markers as the trail begins to climb the ridge known as Jacobs Hill. About 10 minutes from the start of your walk the trail forks—bear right. About 3 minutes later you arrive at an intersection where you should bear left. Within a couple of minutes you will be at the edge of the ridge. Turn right to reach the scenic view lookout.

On your way to the exposed ridge top look for large woodpecker holes in a hemlock, perhaps the work of a **pileated woodpecker.** A rather uncommon bird, the pileated woodpecker is sometimes seen in this forest, its pecking noise reverberating through the woods. It is a large bird with a distinctive red head.

Jacobs Hill

Route 68

Little Pond

P

East Branch Tully River

power lines

Long Pond

N

500 feet

beaver
pond

stream

Spirit Falls

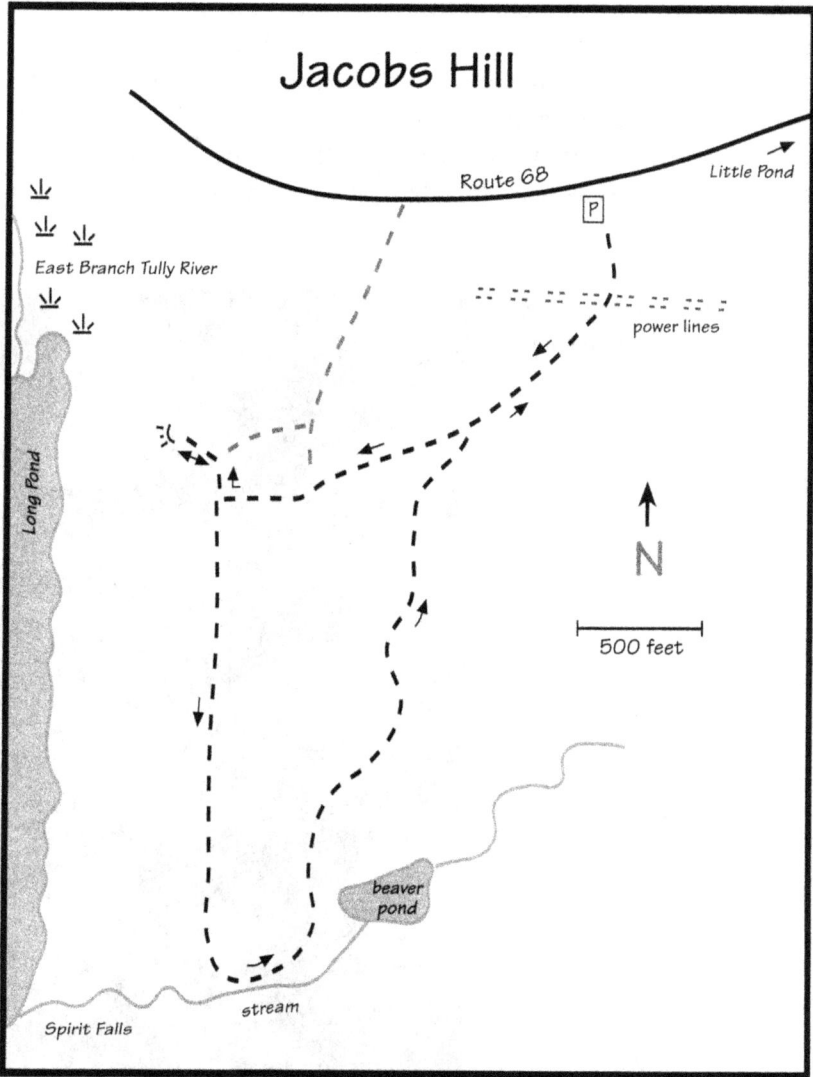

Within five minutes you will have reached the open area that looks out over Long Pond and the rolling hills to the west. This ridge rises 300 feet above the pond, and you can look out over the water and see the forested slopes of Tully Mountain, Mt. Grace, and other rolling hills. I love this spot, often sitting here for extended periods of time with a pair of binoculars. I've seen turkey vultures and hawks ride the thermals above the pond below and sometimes they pass within 20 or 30 feet of my perch. I also like to scan the marshy area to the north, where the East Branch of the Tully River winds its way into the valley and pond. It looks like moose country, and although I've yet to see one, I think it's just a matter of time. Every year more and more moose sightings are recorded in Massachusetts.

Westerly breezes wash over Jacobs Hill, making this the perfect place to relax and enjoy quiet contemplation. When I visit I'm reminded of a quote by English writer Aldous Huxley: "My father considered a walk among the mountains as the equivalent of churchgoing." Amen.

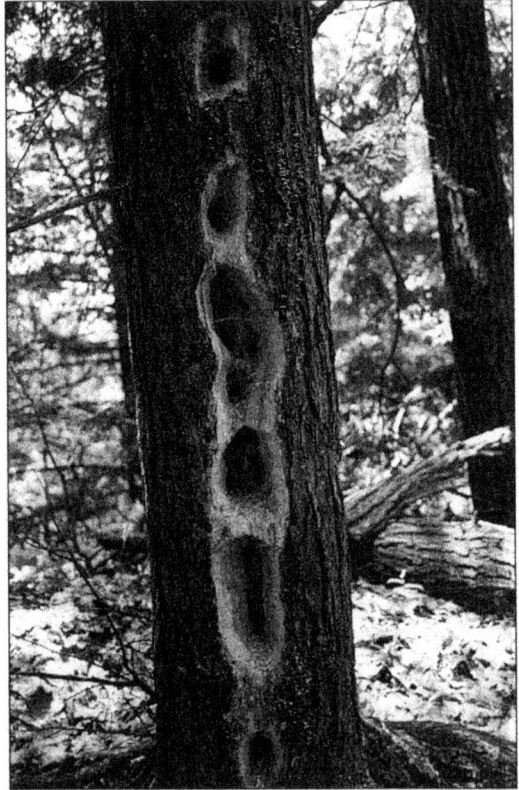

Pileated woodpecker holes open the heart of a hemlock tree on the ridge at Jacobs Hill.

To continue toward Spirit Falls, retrace your steps along the ridge (passing the path that heads toward the parking area) and continue straight in a southerly direction. The trail you are on is quite rocky but relatively straight, hugging the ridge top. If it's wintertime, look for the pigeon-toed tracks of the **porcupine** and its quill marks caused by the dragging tail. One of the surest ways to identify a porcupine trail is to look for signs of its browse: branches cut at 45-degree angles often litter the forest floor beneath a tree where a porcupine has been feeding. I once hiked near

Jacobs Hill with expert tracker and author Paul Rezendes. He pointed out hemlock trees thoroughly stunted by browsing porcupines. A well-worn trail through the snow led from the hemlocks to an exposed rock ledge where we found numerous porcupine dens. While hiking the forest of Jacobs Hill, look up into the trees; you just might spot the dark shape of porcupines quietly feeding.

You will reach the stream that feeds Spirit Falls after about a 10- or 15-minute walk from the lookout area atop Jacobs Hill. A series of cascades lies downstream and it's a difficult climb, with no real trail to follow. For that reason I don't advise families with children to make the climb, nor would I recommend it during winter when the footing is treacherous. During the other seasons you might want to test your "mountain goat legs" and follow the stream down the hillside to watch the stream cascade over moss-covered ledges of granite. Enormous hemlocks and pines grow among the boulders here, and I enjoy photographing this special place.

To complete your loop and head back to the parking area, go back to the main trail and follow it upstream. Within a couple minutes you reach a marshy area. On my last visit there was a large beaver dam blocking the stream's progress, forming a shallow pond for the beavers. Approach this section quietly and you may spot one of nature's engineers paddling about. If you do, get ready for the loud "thwack" of its tail. This warning has caught me off guard more than once.

The trail turns back to the north here. It's about a 25-minute walk to the intersection with the trail you used to climb Jacobs Hill earlier. If you turn right here, the trail will lead you back under the power lines and to the parking lot.

About 2,000 feet east on Route 68 is a short road on the south side of the road that leads into Little Pond. The pond is becoming a bog, surrounded by black spruce, sheep laurel, leatherleaf, and tamarack. A sphagnum moss mat can be seen growing around the edge of the open water.

Getting There

From the center of Royalston, take Route 68 north 0.5 mile. Entrance and parking are on the left.

(One of the easiest ways to get to the center of Royalston is to exit Route 2 onto Route 202 north. Follow for 2.4 miles and turn left onto Route 68 north and travel 8.6 miles to the town's center.)

Open year-round, seven days a week, no admission fee, no rest rooms.

—M.T.

1.1 Doane's Falls

Royalston
31.5 acres

❖ 1 mile

❖ 30–40 minutes

❖ easy

The surging water at Doane's Falls is a thing of beauty but also one of danger. A visitor can't help but notice the large warning sign that lists the four teenagers who drowned here between 1960 and 1991. Cold water, dangerous currents, and no life guards mean these falls are for visual enjoyment, not swimming. Parents should also keep children away from the slippery ledges.

Now that the warnings are out of the way, enjoy a hike along one of the most impressive **waterfalls** in central Massachusetts. Begin your outing by taking the path that follows the water downstream adjacent to the falls. The falls are part of Lawrence Brook, which flows southwestward toward Tully Lake. In the spring, the brook gushes and swirls through the steep granite walls, and you walk with the roar of falling water in your ears.

There are plenty of spots to stop and take pictures of the falls; I like the shot looking back upstream of the water pouring from beneath the stone bridge. On the trail you will see an old **millstone** and stone blocks indicating this was once a mill site. According to The Trustees of Reservations (the nonprofit organization that owns this property), the first mill was built in 1753. At one time or another the falls powered a gristmill, a sawmill, a scouring and fulling mill, and a mill that produced wooden pails and tubs. The falls are named for the Doane family, who built the last mill here in the early 1800s. (On my walks through the state, I've found evidence of mills on almost every good-sized stream and river, even in places you would think had never been settled.)

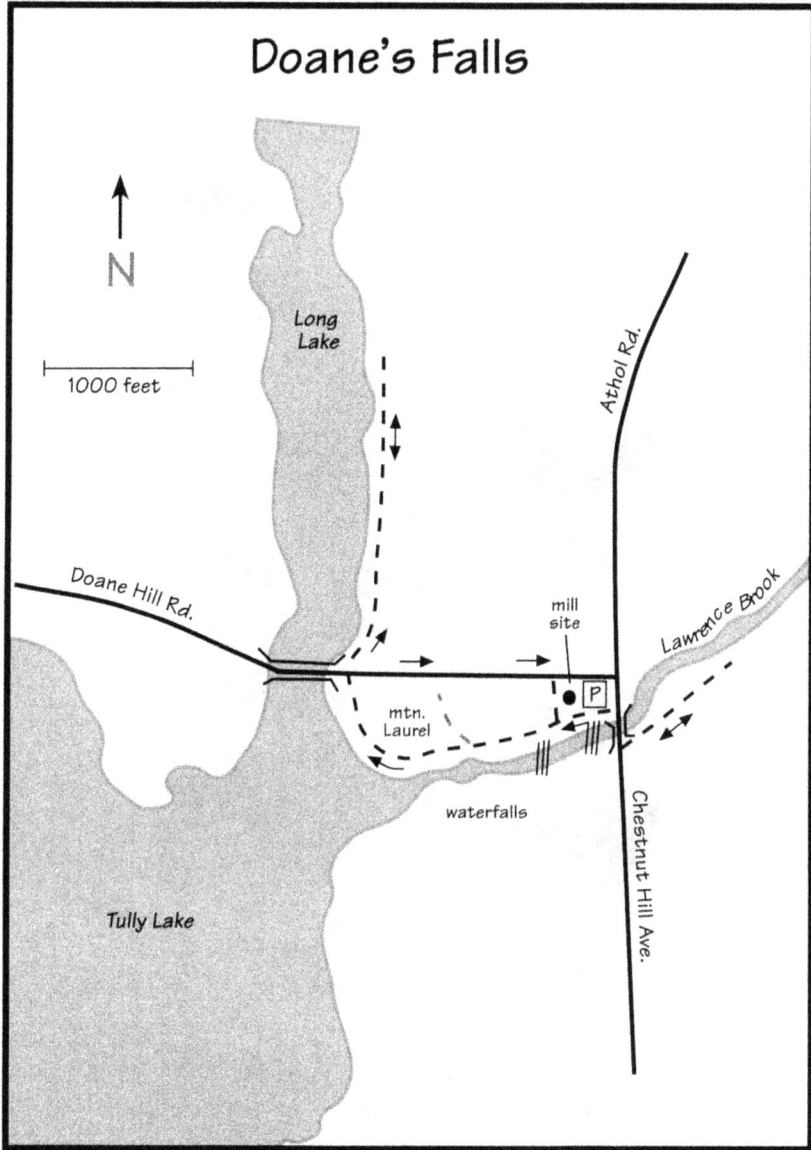

Doane's Falls

N

1000 feet

Long Lake

Athol Rd.

Doane Hill Rd.

mill site

Lawrence Brook

P

mtn. Laurel

Chestnut Hill Ave.

waterfalls

Tully Lake

At some places on the trail, you must pick your way through granite boulders of various sizes as you descend the gorge and the footing is a bit tricky. More waterfalls appear as you follow the trail downstream. (Looking at a topographical map, one can see how the brook is constricted by the steep terrain at the southern end of Jacobs Hill.)

The falls are shaded by pine and hemlock, and some of the trees are quite large, apparently saved from the logger's ax because of the difficulty of the terrain. The rest of the forest is comprised of white pine, maple, oak, and white birch.

Spring snowmelt swells the brook near Doane's Falls.

Soon you will pass a branch of the trail on the right, and by continuing straight (close to the river), you arrive at a quiet pool where mountain laurel thickets surround the stream. In the late summer, look for the brilliant red petals of the cardinal flower. This slender, two- to four-foot plant grows along stream banks and other moist places.

The trail is rather faint here, but a 10-minute walk will lead you to where the stream enters Tully Lake. There is a nice southwest-facing slope here to sit on and soak up the sun. The waters of the lake are shallow, and you may see waterfowl bobbing on the surface. Early morning hikers may see **beavers** in this area. The beaver is one of the recent environmental success stories in Massachusetts, after having been trapped out of existence in the 1800s. The Massachusetts Division of Fisheries and Wildlife started reintroducing beavers in the 1940s, and today they have spread to most areas of the state.

My most powerful memory of a beaver occurred during an evening fishing outing when I was in college. A group of us were bass fishing and having good luck as the last remnant of daylight sank behind the western horizon. Crickets were chirping, and the woods seemed a peaceful place until the water literally exploded in front of us. I'm sorry to say I dropped my fishing rod and ran for cover; it seemed like a boulder had landed in the water. At the time I had never heard the "thwack!" of a beaver's tail, a sound you don't forget in the dark. The beaver was telling us this was its pond, and we were intruders.

Tully Lake, which stretches out before you, covers approximately 300 acres and was built by the U.S. Army Corps of Engineers in 1947. The lake is surrounded by 1,250 acres of public land, supervised by the Commonwealth of Massachusetts Department of Environmental Management. Fishing for warm-water species is very productive on the lake, and there is a boat launch off Route 32 (10 horsepower limit).

By following the trail to the right (north) you will reach Doane Hill Road in 5 or 10 minutes. From there you can walk up the road to the east to reach your car, or retrace your steps back on the wooded trail along Lawrence Brook.

If you wish for more exploration, you can cross Doane Hill Road and follow the trail behind the yellow gate. This trail leads northward along the narrow part of Tully Lake for about a mile and half toward Long Lake and Spirit Falls. Another option is to return to your car and follow a trail that parallels Lawrence Brook in an upstream direction. More remains of mills can be seen, and the water moves quickly beneath hemlocks, pines, and maples.

Getting There

These directions first take you past Tully Lake and dam. From the intersection of Routes 2A and 32 in Athol, take Route 32 north 4.5 miles, and just beyond the dam at Tully Lake turn right on Doane Hill Road. Go to the end of the road and turn right. Parking is immediately on the right.

The Trustees of Reservations guidebooks offer an alternative way to reach the property: "From intersection of Route 2A and 32 in Athol, cross the Millers River bridge and bear right on Royalston-Athol Road. Proceed 4 miles. Entrance is on left after the stone bridge over Lawrence Brook, at intersection with Doane Hill Road."

Open year-round, seven days a week, no admission fee, no rest rooms.

—M.T.

Elliot Laurel Reservation

Phillipston
33 acres

- ❖ 1 mile
- ❖ 35 minutes
- ❖ easy

Elliot Laurel Reservation lives up to its name; the **mountain laurel** that blankets the southern end of the property is truly impressive. If possible, time your trip to coincide with the blooming period in June. The reservation also has mature stands of hemlock, a red maple swamp, and a meadow.

Begin your walk on the main trail that passes through an opening in a stone wall adjacent to the parking area. Before entering the woods take a moment to scan the adjacent **field** for signs of wildlife. This is a good spot to observe deer, fox, rabbit, and maybe even a coyote. Not too long ago I had the thrill of seeing a **coyote** on the property. I was surprised at the size of the canine—larger than a fox—and I realized why they are sometimes called "little wolves." Coyote have expanded their range throughout Massachusetts and have even been sighted on Cape Cod. (In the winter, with the aid of a telescope, it sometimes is possible to spot a pack of coyote at nearby Quabbin Reservoir when they cross the ice or look for carrion. The Enfield Lookout is a good viewing spot.)

As soon as you enter the woods of Elliot Laurel you will notice the dark green leaves of the mountain laurel beneath the white pines and hemlocks. I love the enclosed feeling of walking through thick stands of laurel—it seems to add a bit of enchantment to the woods. Its flowers are saucer shaped, grow in dense clusters, and usually remain on the stems into mid-July. Colors range from white to pink to rose. Mountain laurel is sometimes confused with rhododendron, but the easiest way to tell them apart is by the leaves: laurel leaves are only 3 to 4 inches long, while rhododendron leaves are as long as 10 inches with a greater width.

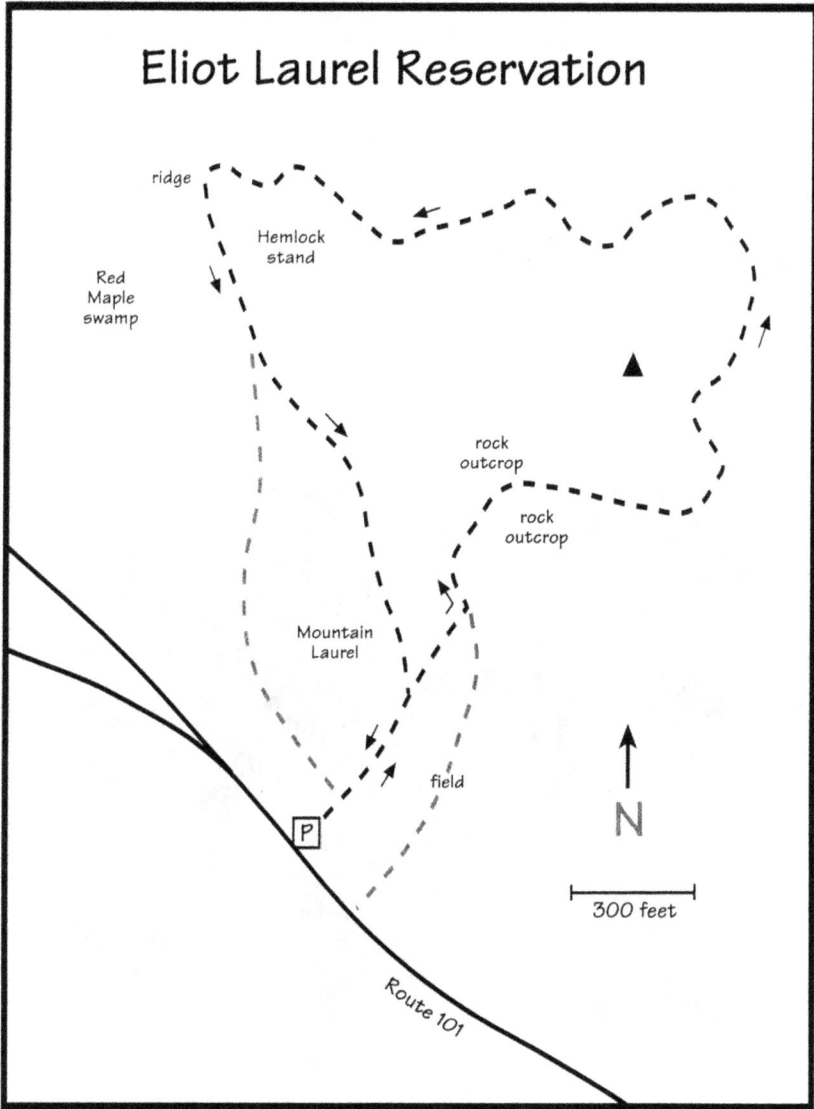

Eliot Laurel Reservation

ridge

Hemlock stand

Red Maple swamp

rock outcrop

rock outcrop

Mountain Laurel

field

P

N

300 feet

Route 101

The path forks a few feet down the trail; stay to the right, following an old stone wall that separates the woods from the field to your right. Soon there will be another fork and again you should stay right. Chipmunks and red squirrels are often seen in this evergreen forest. The feisty red squirrel is especially at home here, eating the buds of evergreens and the pine nuts. They usually den in old tree stumps, crevices, or underground dens, and sometimes make nests in trees using twigs and leaves. It's likely there are **flying squirrels** living in the area, but because they are nocturnal, they are difficult to see. I once was fortunate to view a flying squirrel up close and personal—it had hitched a ride inside by sleeping in our Christmas tree! Flying squirrels glide through the air by spreading skin flaps that stretch from the wrists to the ankles.

When the trail reaches the back of the field, it turns left (a faint trail from the field also enters on the right here) and soon begins to climb a bit, passing exposed ledges of granite covered with moss, ferns, and lichen. Yellow paint dots on a few trees help guide you along. This can be a beautiful area in the fall because the few maple trees scattered about really stand out against the dark evergreens. Winter also has its charm as the laurels' evergreen foliage sparkles against a backdrop of white snow.

The field near the entrance to Elliot Laurel is a good spot to watch for deer, fox, rabbit, and even coyote.

About 20 minutes (three-quarters of a mile) into your walk, the trail begins to descend the hill you have been climbing and heads in a westerly direction. It was on this section of the property that I once got a glimpse of a goshawk, the largest member of the accipiter family. They are rapid-flying hawks at home winging through thick forest understory hunting for birds, squirrels, and other small mammals. Look for a gray belly and broad white eye stripe on this 19-inch-long accipiter. In my opinion they are the most magnificent of all the hawks. Should you see one and it gives a high-pitched "auk, auk, auk," back away so as not to disturb its nest or territory. Goshawks will swoop down and attack intruders that threaten nesting areas.

After another 10 minutes of walking, the trail will bear south. On your right is a **red maple swamp**. Medium-sized trees, growing 50 to 75 feet tall, they are typically found in poorly drained places but can also grow in drier habitats. The bark of young red maples (also called swamp maples) is smooth and light gray, while older trees have dark gray bark that is ridged and broken into scales. Although there is no trail toward the swamp, I sometimes bushwack 50 yards along the ridge and rest against a rock on the hillside. Blue jays, chickadees, and titmice will usually keep you company, even in the winter. You never know what other forms of wildlife may happen past.

Back on the trail, walk through a stately stand of **hemlocks**, where little vegetation grows beneath the sweeping branches. Between an absence of sun and the acidity caused by the hemlock leaves, few plants can tolerate those conditions. The mountain laurel, however, does well in acidic, sandy soil in semishaded areas. Hemlock can be identified by its needles, which have blunt tips and are shorter than fir and most spruce. The branches are pendulous and will sway away from prevailing winds. Cones are light brown and about three-quarters of an inch long, hanging from the tips of tiny branchlets.

Bear left where a faint trail comes in on the right, and then in a short distance, the trail you are following intersects with the trail you started on. Simply bear right and you will be back at the car in five minutes. Elliot Laurel Reservation was given to The Trustees of Reservations in 1941 by Fredrick W. Elliot in memory of his mother. It is open to all for nature study, walking, and cross-country skiing.

Getting There

From Route 2 west, take Exit 21. Bear right at intersection, and follow Route 2A west 1.1 miles. Bear left at intersection, and follow Route 101 south 3.9 miles. Entrance is on the right.

From intersection of Routes 32 and 101 in Petersham, take Route 101 north 3.7 miles. Entrance is on left.

Open year-round, seven days a week, no admission fee, no rest rooms.

—M.T.

North Common Meadow

Petersham
24.5 acres

❖ 1.25 miles

❖ 40 minutes

❖ easy

North Common Meadow may be small in size but it has big rewards for those who walk its fields. The meadow is filled with **wildflowers** and a trail leads down to a quiet pond by the edge of woods. This combination of open fields, freshwater, and woods provides excellent habitat for birds such as meadowlarks, bobolinks, red-winged blackbirds, and passing hawks and owls. Adjacent to the property is the Brooks Woodland Preserve, where forested trails follow the clear-flowing waters of the East Branch of the Swift River.

Your walk begins at the trail next to the Brooks Law Office (built in 1835), which has a few beautiful old maples scattered around it. This spot offers a fine vista of the entire meadow and the pond below. I love the view in the spring, when many wildflowers are blooming, and again in autumn, when maples flame red and goldenrod blankets the slope near the pond.

The upper part of the meadow is a hay field that is mowed, and the lower section, closer to the pond, is a wildflower meadow. In the eighteenth and nineteenth centuries, this is how most of Massachusetts looked; much of the state had been cleared for farming or pastureland, and very few trees escaped the ax. The forests that now cover most of the region are second and third growth, with only a few isolated acres still in virgin condition.

The meadow gently slopes down toward the pond, and a trail has been cut through the field. In just a few feet the trail forks; head to the left. Pass bluebird houses erected on poles. **Eastern bluebirds** prefer an open field like this, and it's important that the entrance hole is only one and a half inches across, enabling bluebirds to enter but keeping out larger birds, such as starlings. The male bluebird is the more colorful of the sexes with dark blue on the head, back, wings, and tail. Its throat is reddish brown and its belly is white. The female has light reddish coloring extending from chin over breast and back along flanks. Its head is light gray tinged with blue, and its back is dull brownish gray. Blue on the tail and wings is not always seen when the bird is perched.

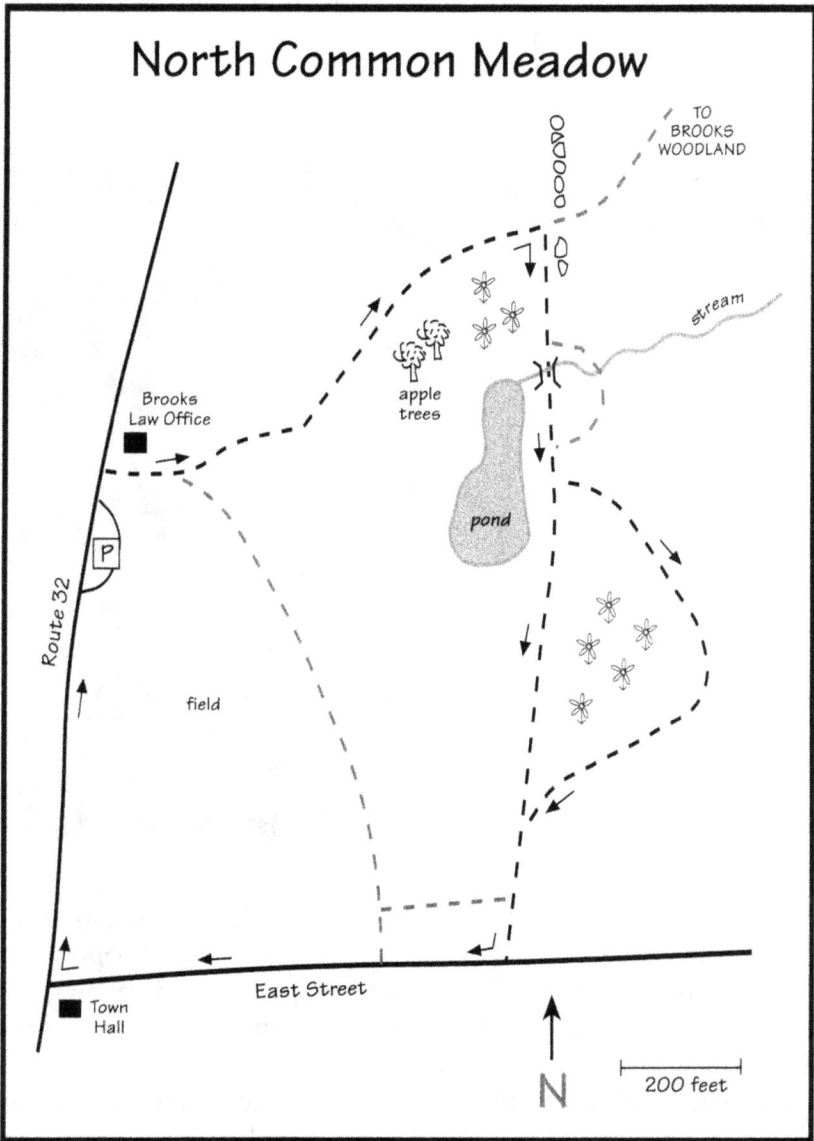

North Common Meadow

Meadowlarks and **bobolinks** also prefer fields such as these. In the fall you might see a concentration of bobolinks near the marsh area as they gather for the fall migration. They resemble house sparrows but have crown stripes and narrow tail feathers. In the spring the male's underside is almost black, but as summer approaches it turns tan. The eastern meadowlark is identified by a black V on a bright yellow breast with white outer tail feathers. Meadowlarks are a joy to watch in flight, flapping and sailing above the meadow. Thoreau makes mention of meadowlarks and bluebirds in his essay *The Natural History of Massachusetts,* writing that "the plaintive note of the lark comes clear and sweet from the meadow: and the bluebird, like an azure ray, glances past us in our walk."

A cottontail rabbit nibbles on grass at North Common Meadow.

The trail passes some old apple trees, then leaves the hay field and enters the meadow of wildflowers. On my last visit, in mid-September, the asters and goldenrod made a kaleidoscope of purples and yellows, mixing with the browns and various shades of green from grasses and clover. Butterflies rose from the flowers by the side of the trail.

Where the path meets the woods at the stone wall, bear right toward the pond. If you were to go straight, you would be entering the Brooks Woodland Preserve (more about the preserve at the end of this chapter).

Follow the trail to the edge of the small **pond** by a tiny stream and stop to scan the cattails and lily pads that grow from its water. Some shadbush, dogwood, and iris grow near the pond's edge. Be on the lookout for frogs, turtles, wood ducks, and swallows.

The path forks near the southern end of the pond; the trail to the left makes a small loop and rejoins the trail. From the pond it is a 10-minute walk to East Street. Here you can either head back to your car by following East Street, or follow a path paralleling East Street that eventually leads to another path heading north through the hay field back toward your car. Wildflowers most easily identified will be the showy clusters of the tiny yellow-rayed flowers of goldenrod and blue or violet flowers of aster that grow singly rather than in tight clusters.

I prefer to walk on East Street, a quiet country lane, because it leads into the center of Petersham, one of the loveliest towns in the commonwealth. Most of the buildings that ring the town common are on the National Register of Historic Places, and many are in the Greek Revival style with white pillars. You can stop in at the Country Store for a cold beverage in the summer, or during the winter try a piece of pie with a hot drink.

The Brooks Woodland Preserve is a wonderful place to explore and is comprised of two tracts. The Roaring Brook Tract can be accessed from the previously mentioned spot at North Common Meadow or by going down East Street 0.8 mile from Petersham center. To reach the Swift River Tract, follow Route 32 south from Petersham center to the intersection of Routes 32 and 122. Go south on Routes 32/122 for 1.5 miles, then turn left on Quaker Drive. There are two entrances on both sides of the bridge over the East Branch of the Swift. This is a large property, more than 500 acres, and the wildlife is quite diverse. It is hilly country forested with hemlock, ash, maple, beech, birch, and white pine. There are scattered boulders and several outcroppings of rock. It will take you multiple trips to explore all the trails, but once you make your first visit, chances are you will be back soon.)

Getting There

From Route 2, take Exit 16 to Route 202 south. Go 2.0 miles to the intersection of Routes 202 and 122. Take Route 122 south about 8.0 miles to its intersection with Route 32. Turn onto Route 32 heading north and reach Petersham center in about a quarter of a mile. Just beyond the town green on Route 32 you will see the Brooks Law Office and North Common Meadow on your right. Pull off the road and park here.

Open year-round, seven days a week, no rest rooms.

—M.T.

14 Swift River Reservation

Petersham
439 acres
(The reservation is comprised of three separate tracts of land)

Slab City Tract—

- ❖ 1.75 miles
- ❖ 1 hour, 15 minutes
- ❖ medium
- ❖ great for children

The Slab City Tract at the Swift River Reservation (managed by The Trustees of Reservations) features a combination that's hard to beat: a clear-flowing river, old-growth timber, and a hilltop offering a far-reaching vista. The East Branch of the Swift River passes through the reservation and is a good spot to see wood ducks, heron, and beaver. If you arrive early you might see a deer, fox, or coyote cross the field near the parking area. Porcupine and ruffed grouse have also been seen here, although they tend to stay in the woods.

To begin your outing, follow the woods road from the parking area about 500 yards to where another old woods road enters on the left. Take this left, which leads up through a field and past an **old cellar hole** on the left. The cellar hole once supported the home of Avery Williams, who operated a sawmill on the river in the mid-1800s. Nearby is a rectangular stone enclosure where the farm animals were kept. Soon after these signs of the old Avery mill and farm, the road forks. Bear left, toward the river, which has spilled into a broad marsh. There are a couple of spots where you can view the marsh, perhaps observing the head of a swimming muskrat or beaver. The trail parallels the marsh to where the river exits the wetlands, passing beneath **enormous hemlocks and white pines**, only about 15 minutes from the start of the walk.

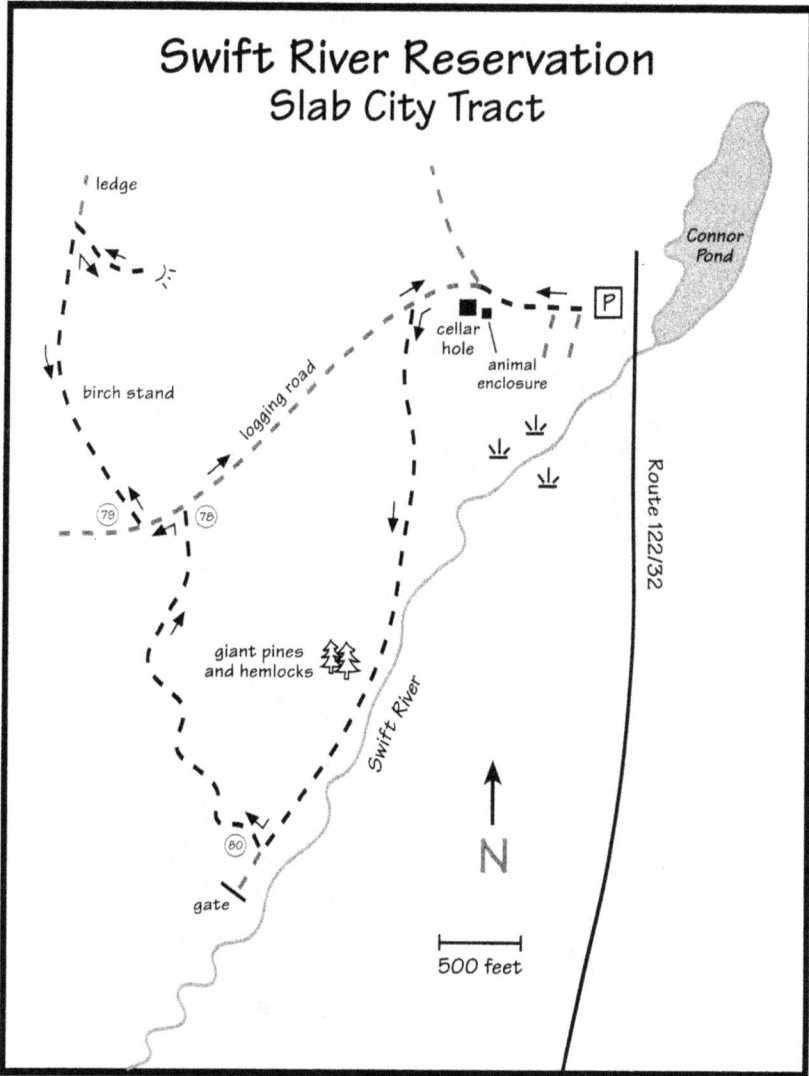

**Swift River Reservation
Slab City Tract**

ledge

birch stand

logging road

Connor Pond

cellar hole

animal enclosure

P

Route 122/32

79 78

giant pines and hemlocks

Swift River

80

gate

N

500 feet

I've always thought this was one of the most beautiful **river walks** in all the Bay State. The Swift courses over rocks and around boulders, seeming to sing on its way to fill the Quabbin. Take a moment to sit by the river and feel the peace of this enchanting spot. Look for the ring of rising trout as they feed on insects that have either fallen in the water or hatched from the streambed.

The hemlocks and pines here are home to red squirrel, raccoon, fisher, and owl. Though their population was reduced by the rabies epidemic of the 1990s, you will still find **raccoons**. They are most active at sundown when they prowl about in search of food. Their food is quite varied—toads, frogs, crayfish, grubs, turtle and birds' eggs, and plants (anyone growing corn knows the 'coon's perfect timing for raiding a garden). In the wintertime, raccoons may sleep for many days in protected places, such as hollow trees, to withstand the coldest temperatures. While they do not actually hibernate and sometimes venture out of their nests, raccoons may lose up to 50 percent of their fall body weight during the course of the winter.

A young hiker rests on a granite ledge at Swift River Reservation.

The river trail extends for about a quarter of a mile and then ends at a green gate, marking the reservation's boundary. About 20 feet before the gate is a narrow trail on the right that zigzags uphill, away from the river.

(There will be a marker #80 nailed to a tree.) Take this trail, and follow the yellow paint dots on the trees marking its path. This seems to be an area favored by **grouse**, and more than once I've been surprised by one suddenly exploding skyward. There are only a few evergreens mixed with small maples, and in the fall you can see through the understory. You might catch a glimpse of a deer's white tail as it bounds off.

Continue on this narrow path until it intersects with a logging road at marker #78 where a power line crosses the trail (about a 15-minute walk from the river). To reach the **scenic overlook**, turn left here and then bear right where the road forks at marker #79. To the south and east, the woods are owned by The Trustees of Reservations, while ahead, to the north, the property is part of the Harvard Forest. It's only a 10-minute gradual climb (passing a private field on the left and a nice stand of birch on the right) until you should turn right on a small path that leads to the outcrop of rock at the overlook. (This can be a difficult trail to spot—look for it just before a large section of exposed rock ledge on the right.)

This is one of my favorite hilltops. Few people seem to know about the place and you usually have the summit all to yourself. Roughly half the summit is open ledge, allowing for an unobstructed view to the east. The body of water seen below is Connor Pond. Beyond that, the wooded hills are part of Massachusetts Audubon's Rutland Brook Sanctuary, a property designated for wildlife only. Along the ridge where you are standing, I've seen lots of porcupine signs. In the winter you may see tracks and nipped hemlock boughs. Porcupines den in the nooks and crannies of the rock ledge, and in this general area it's possible to see porcupine scat near the entrance to these little caves.

After enjoying the view, retrace your steps to marker #78 near the power line. Instead of turning right on the trail you came up, you can go straight down this woods road for a shortcut to the parking area. Maples and hemlocks line the power line path. (During one of my hikes I had the rare treat of seeing a goshawk perched in a tree where the woods meet the field at the end of this road.) It's only a 15- to 20-minute downhill walk to your car, covering about half a mile.

More ambitious walkers may want to explore another tract of the Swift River Reservation. The Davis Tract is located off Glen Valley Road, and it, too, has a scenic overlook and river trail. Cellar holes and stone walls remind walkers of the days when these woods were cleared for pasture. The Nichewaug Tract is on the north side of Swift River, and its entrance is found on Nichewaug Road. Miles of trails lead through woods and old pastures. Like the others, Nichewaug Tract has a ledge outcrop offering a scenic view. Together, the three sections total 439 acres of wild lands—secluded enough for larger animals such as black bear, bobcat, and coyote. And if you are really lucky, you just might spot a moose. An increasing number of sightings have occurred in this area, and tracks have been seen at the Swift River Reservation. Bring your camera!

Getting There

All areas are between Nichewaug Road and Routes 122/32.

Slab City Tract: from intersection of Routes 122 and 32, south of Petersham center, go south on Routes 122/32, 2.0 miles to Connor Pond. Entrance is on the right, across from the dam.

Nichewaug Tract: from intersection of Routes 122 and 32, south of Petersham center, take South Street 0.9 mile. Turn right on Nichewaug Road and travel 0.6 mile. Entrance is on left.

Davis Tract: from intersection of Routes 122 and 32, south of Petersham center, go south on Routes 122/32, 3.3 miles. Turn right on Glen Valley Road and proceed 0.9 mile to intersection of Carter Pond Road. Entrance is on the right.

Open year-round, seven days a week, no admission fee, no rest rooms.

—M.T.

15 Quabbin Reservoir Gate 45

Hardwick
(119 miles of shoreline surround entire reservoir)

❖ 2.5–3 hours

❖ 5 miles

❖ moderate

For the outdoors lover, the forests of Quabbin Reservoir are nothing short of paradise. The 39-square-mile reservoir, one of the largest reservoirs in the world built for domestic supply, has 119 miles of shoreline, not including the many islands rising from its depths. Quabbin means "meeting of the waters" in the Nipmuck language, and before the creation of the reservoir this valley was exactly that. The three branches of the Swift River converged here, making the valley the ideal spot for a reservoir. The fact that people lived in the valley did not stop the city of Boston from getting the water it needed. The towns of Enfield, Prescott, Dana, and Greenwich were "drowned" when dams were constructed at the valley's southern end.

There is a silver lining to the flooding of the Swift River valley—the watershed needs protection and thousands of surrounding acres have been left in their natural state, open only for passive recreation such as walking. The wildlife here is diverse and abundant, and for that reason I've been a regular visitor to the reservoir during the past 20 years. With so many entry gates to choose from, each trip finds me at a different gate, discovering a new trail, new stream, or new meadow. Gate 45 is a fascinating area. It's one of the less frequented entrances into the forest, and the walk described here leads to the **reservoir** itself, with a return stop at a **beaver pond** where great blue herons nest.

After parking your car on the shoulder of Lyman Road at Gate 45, go around the gate and start your walk down this old roadway. The fieldstone walls that line the road might cause you to reflect on how this land looked prior to the reservoir's creation. Farms and small mills dotted the valley. The acres around you were probably pastures before the start of construction of the reservoir in 1928. Some of the original **maples** that shaded the road are still standing along the stone wall, while the woods beyond are filled with younger pines and oaks.

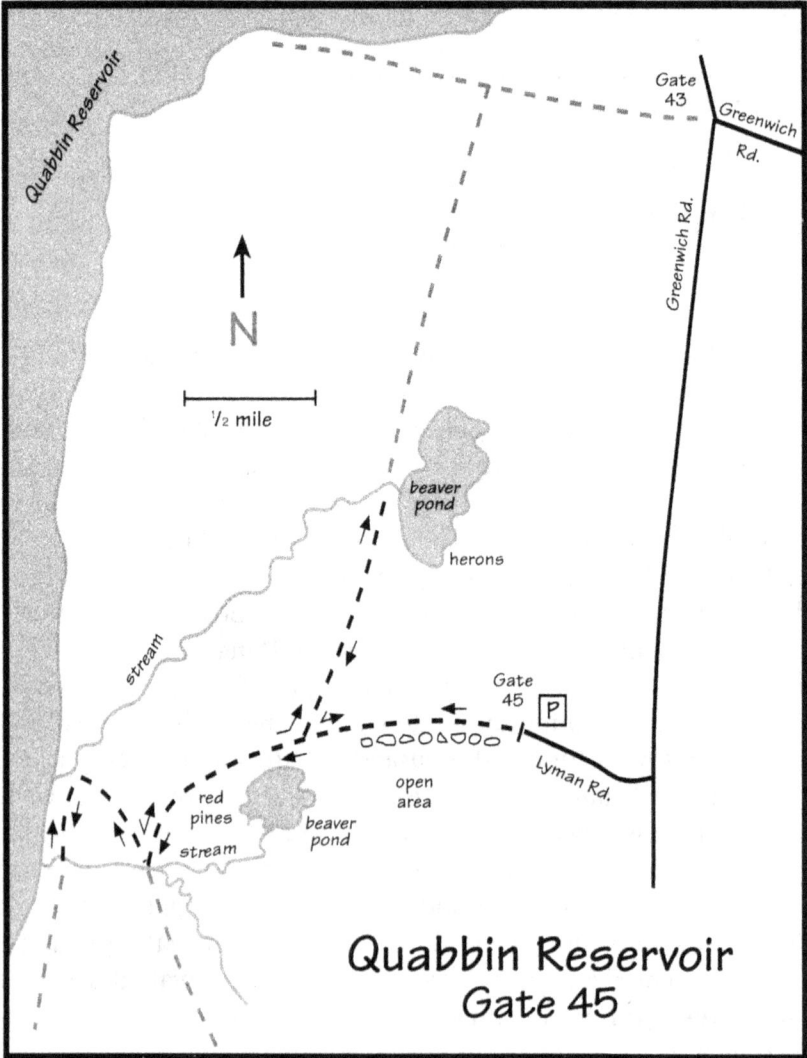

**Quabbin Reservoir
Gate 45**

Five minutes into the walk you will pass an open area on the left—a good spot to look for deer. (White-tailed deer were so numerous in the watershed that a limited—and controversial—form of hunting was recent-ly allowed.) The field is also a good place to spot **fox** hunting for mice and various hawks doing the same. Red foxes are bright yellowish red on the sides to deep yellowish brown on the back, with a long bushy tail tipped white. The best time to see them is at dawn or dusk, although sometimes, especially in the spring when mothers must hunt for food for their young, they are seen in the middle of the day. Besides fox, I often see ruffed grouse here (sometimes they will remain still as you unknowingly walk closer; then they suddenly spring up, scaring the wits out of you—it's happened more than once to me!).

After walking about 20 minutes, pass a road on your right, about three-quarters of a mile from the start of your walk. Keep its location in mind for the return walk from the reservoir. Proceed straight ahead through a wooded area with many white pines, and pass a **beaver pond** on the left. With the aid of binoculars, you might glimpse a beaver, but these fascinating animals are mostly nocturnal. Legend has it that beavers are smart enough to fell a tree in the direction they want it to go. In reality, the trees fall haphazardly, sometimes even crushing the beaver. An adult will cut down about one tree every two days (staying within 200 to 300 feet of the safety of water) and feed on the bark. In the autumn they stockpile green branches near the lodge to serve as a food cache through the winter.

Continue to follow the road in a westerly direction, first passing by a small plantation of red pine on the left. (Lots of red squirrels can be seen near these evergreens.) Soon the road arcs left and a **stream** rushes beneath the road through old stone culverts. Reach an intersection with another road and follow it to the right, downhill through a dense, **dark hemlock grove**. Hemlock has a more rounded top than spruces or firs, and its twigs and branches are more flexible. (You may want to first follow the brook upstream into the forest—this stream flows out of the beaver pond you passed, and you never know what wildlife you might encounter prowling the banks of the waterway.)

Walk downhill on the old road. The stream keeps you company, singing over small falls as it makes its way to fill the Quabbin. I've seen por-cupines feeding in the hemlocks near here. It is a good idea to glance upward into the trees occasionally for signs of these large prickly rodents. Porcupines consume a large amount of hemlock foliage, and oftentimes a particular hemlock will be completely stunted by browsing porcupine. Soon you will pass a few handsome white birch on the right and then you will arrive at the shores of Quabbin, roughly 50 minutes (two miles) after leaving your car. Follow the trail to the left, adjacent to the shore, and in a few hundred feet the stream appears again, cascading down the hillside and spilling into the Quabbin at a beautiful half-moon beach.

Quabbin is one of the few places in Massachusetts frequented by moose.

This is a wonderful spot to pause and rest your eyes on the blue waters of the reservoir. Directly across from you is an island—once a hilltop—called Mt. Lizzie, just one of 60 islands in the reservoir. Stretching in a north-south direction, Quabbin is almost 18 miles long and has a capacity of 412 billion gallons of water. (Just an inch of rainfall can add 750 million gallons to the reservoir.) The water is quite deep in spots, and the depth at the Winsor Dam is 150 feet, making this one of the premier cold-water fisheries in New England. (Fishing is permitted on much of the reservoir, but swimming is not allowed.)

Winter at Quabbin is an especially interesting time. Bald eagles and coyotes are sometimes seen out on the ice feeding on the carcasses of deer. Not only do eagles winter at Quabbin, but there are also nesting eagles here in the warm-weather months, a result of many years of effort to restore this magnificent bird to our state. Biologists brought six- to seven-week-old chicks to Quabbin and raised them on an elevated platform. When they were able to fly, they were released (with Quabbin imprinted as their home), and they later returned to build their own nests.

Although you might spot an eagle with the aid of binoculars from the shore, the best bet for observation is at the Enfield Lookout, near the dams. Usually someone is patiently waiting and watching with high-powered binoculars or a spotting scope, and most birders are happy to let you have a look. When the reservoir is not socked in by ice, the eagles soar over the water in search of fish, their primary source of food. With a wingspread of seven to eight feet and the unmistakable white head and tail on mature birds, a soaring bald eagle is one of the most impressive sights in the wild.

The fascinating **common loon** also visits and nests at Quabbin. Like the eagle, loons seek out the reservoir because of its vast expanse of open waters and the many secluded sections off-limits to the public. Both birds feed on fish—the eagle skims the surface to snatch a fish and the loon dives underwater and catches fish with its sharp beak. Cruising slowly on the surface, loons will stick their heads underwater looking for fish, then dive like dolphins, often chasing a fish for more than 45 seconds. Loons once nested throughout Massachusetts, but human encroachment led to loss of habitat and the birds were extirpated in the state by the early 1900s. Now there are a handful of nesting loons at Quabbin, and if the acid rain problem does not worsen, the outlook is considered good for increased numbers because large sections of Quabbin and other reservoirs are closed to boating. More than once I've heard their unmistakable, haunting cry rise over the waters of Quabbin.

You might want to walk the shoreline a bit, examining the smooth, twisted forms of driftwood and the many waterworn tree stumps that look like giant spiders. The patches of sand at the water's edge usually show the print of deer hooves and sometimes the tracks of other animals such as coyote, otter, raccoon, mink, and fisher. On two of my trips to the reservoir I've seen raccoons foraging among the rocks, presumably for mussels or crayfish.

When you retrace your steps to the car be sure to explore the side road mentioned earlier (as you return it will be on your left, just 20 minutes from Gate 45). This road leads to a large beaver pond after only a 15- to 20-minute walk. While the beaver engineers its surroundings for its own protection, a by-product of its work is a pond that becomes home to other wildlife such as otter and wood ducks. Perhaps the biggest beneficiary is the great blue heron, who uses the standing timber in the pond for safe and secure nest platforms. On my last visit, this pond had two heron nests. Nests are up to four feet wide and are made of sticks and branches. Although the nests look precarious, they hold up well year after year. In the springtime a heron rookery is an active place, with both parents feeding the young a diet of regurgitated fish and frogs twice a day.

Getting There

From the Massachusetts Turnpike take the Palmer-Route 32 exit. Proceed north on Route 32 through Ware, and then continue north on Route 32A into Hardwick. Across from the Hardwick town common on the left is Greenwich Road. Follow Greenwich Road 2.6 miles until you reach Gate 43. Bear left at Gate 43 (staying on Greenwich Road) and go 1.7 miles to Lyman Road on the right. Follow Lyman Road 0.7 mile to Gate 45 and park off the road. (Lyman Road can be slippery in periods of snow and ice. If conditions are bad, try Gate 43, Gate 40, or Quabbin Hill near the Winsor Dam.)

Open year-round, seven days a week, no fee, no rest rooms.

—M.T.

16 ✦ Rock House Reservation

West Brookfield
75 acres

❖ 1.5 miles

❖ 45 minutes

❖ easy

❖ great for children

Rock House Reservation is a "must see." On the property is a 20- to 30-foot **rock shelter**, known as the Rock House, that was used by Native Americans as a hunting camp in the cold-weather months. One look at this sloping ledge of rock and it's easy to see the advantages it offers—protection from wind and snow and a southeast-facing opening to catch the warmth of the sun. (The rock ledge could also have been used as a defensive fortification.) Because of the property's historical significance and the imprint left by retreating glaciers, the Rock House Reservation, managed by The Trustees of Reservations, is a good place to introduce children to New England heritage and geology. And the nooks and crannies within the rock shelter will delight little explorers!

The property's diverse habitats offer great opportunity for nature study. It has a pond, a pine and spruce stand, and upland woods of hemlock, maple, and oak, where glacial boulders are scattered over the hilly landscape. It is an especially interesting spot to visit in the winter because few people seem to hike beyond the Rock House, making **wildlife tracking** relatively easy along the reservation's many trails.

Begin your walk by following Inner Loop Trail uphill directly behind the signboard at the edge of the parking area. Within five minutes you will see the pond. Bear left along the edge of the pond, where the trail splits, and the Rock House will be on your left. Take a few moments to explore the shelter, and if it's winter, note how the ground immediately below the overhanging rock is free of snow. The shelter, probably formed by the glaciers, looks like a giant lean-to. It is surmised that Native Americans camped here over a 7,000-year period. An amateur archaeological dig in the 1930s revealed early tools, pottery, and bones from wolf, bear, and deer.

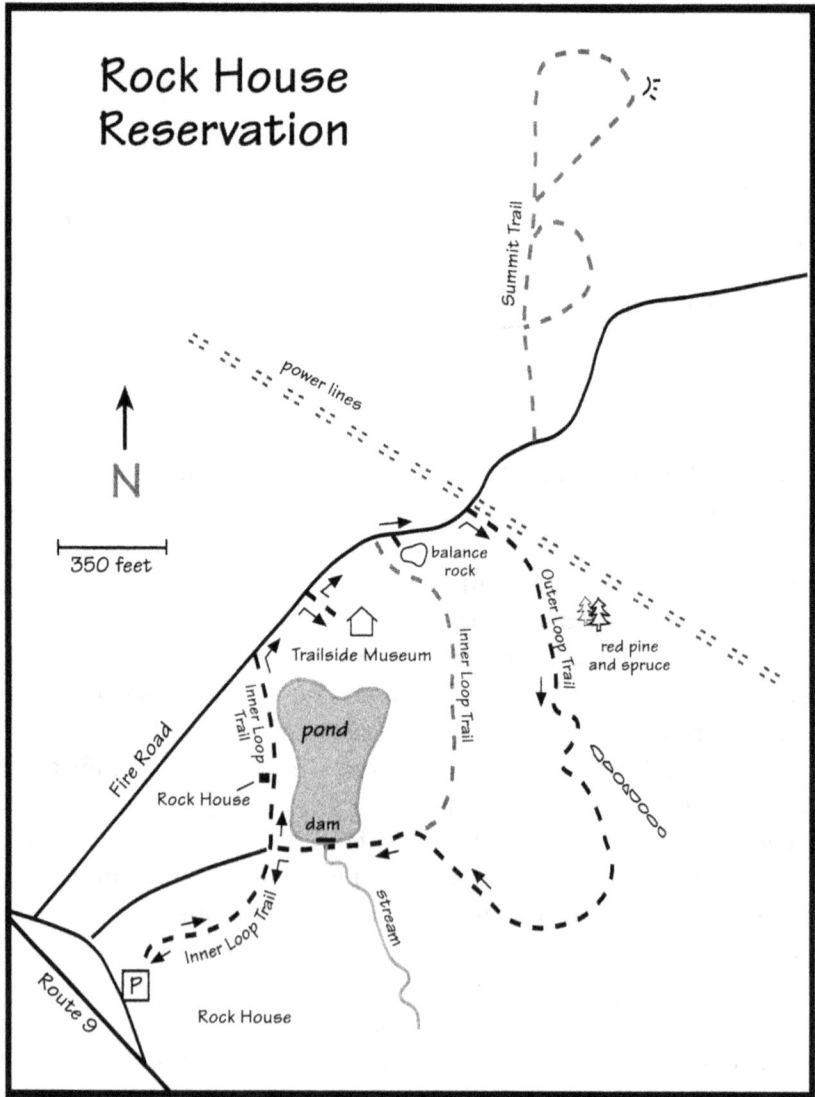

Rock House Reservation

Let your imagination picture the various uses of the Rock House by these early hunters. Perhaps they lit fires beneath the overhang, letting the rock walls reflect the warmth of the flames. Maybe logs and boughs were erected in the front of the shelter to keep out eastern winds or to serve as protection against wolves and enemy tribes. On one winter visit, I sat on the dry ground beneath the overhang and reflected on all the other souls that had rested in the same spot, wondering what kind of thoughts and dreams they had.

The **glacier** that covered New England formed as snow fell almost continuously to our north in Quebec. The snowpack grew over a mile high, and weight of the pile squeezed the snow at the bottom into ice. Then the massive pile of ice and snow began to slide south, smoothing northern sides of mountains as it advanced and leaving rougher surfaces and rubble when it retreated about 15,000 years ago. Note the smooth northern side of the granite hill of the Rock House and the rougher cliff face forming the shelter on the southern end.

After exploring the nooks and crannies of the Rock House, continue your walk by following the path along the **pond** in a northerly direction. The trail intersects with a fire road where you should bear right, following the road as it climbs above the pond. On your right you will soon see a small yellow cottage. Inside is a trailside museum (open year-round) where you can learn more about the property. From the porch of the cottage, look down upon the pond. This is a good spot to have a snack or, if it's autumn, admire the colors of the maples and oak that ring the pond. From this vantage point you might see beaver, wild turkey, screech owls, and fox.

When you walk back to the fire road, continue northeast passing the Inner Loop Trail, but keep an eye out to the right for Balance Rock. A five-foot boulder rests at the top of a rock ledge—yet another unique geological formation caused by glacial movement. (As the glaciers retreated, boulders were deposited haphazardly, like this one, and are called erratics.) Kids will love climbing to the top of the ledge to see this oddity. While my kids tried to push Balance Rock (no chance of moving the giant boulder), I admired the huge oak that grows directly below this craggy outcrop.

Back on the fire road it's only a five-minute walk farther to the northeast until you will see a power line ahead. Follow the trail to the right, called the Outer Loop Trail, just before the power line. If you were to continue on the fire road and then take a left onto the Summit Trail, you would reach a ridge with a vista within a 25-minute walk.

The Outer Loop Trail circles to the southeast, first passing through a plantation of **red pine**, **Norway spruce**, and **red spruce**. Red pine has four- to six-inch flexible dark green needles, and the bark has flat ridges and shallow grooves on it. Norway spruce has much smaller needles of a half inch to one inch and has drooping branches. The needles of a red spruce are smaller still, one-half inch to five-eighths of an inch long, and are often curved upward. The trail then passes through a wood of oak, white pine, maple, and a scattering of hemlock. Old stone walls lace the woodlands, indicating the farming activity here many years ago. Today the walls are home to chipmunks. I've also seen cottontails and porcupine tracks along the stone wall.

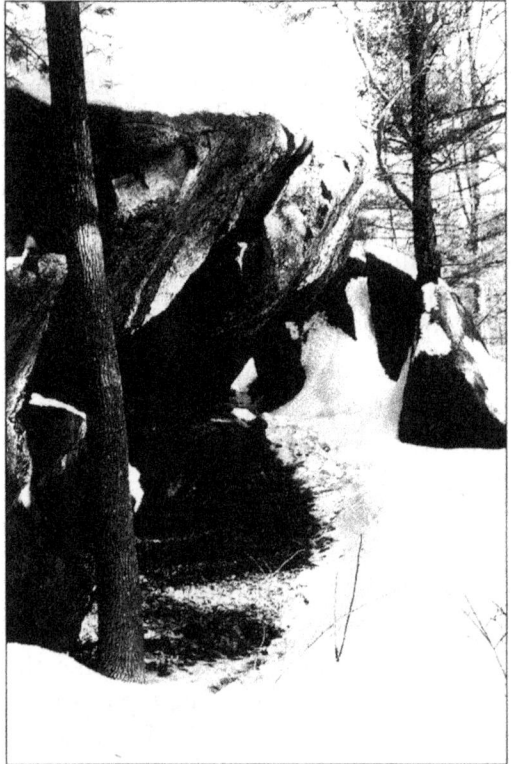

The large rock overhang keeps the snow from reaching the sheltered area below.

On one of my visits to Rock House I had the good fortune to meet Paul Gryzbowski and Dick O'Brien, who manage the Central Region properties for The Trustees of Reservations. They told me white-tailed deer, raccoon, coyote, and red fox have also been sighted on the property. One animal that few of us ever see but is likely to have hunted here is the **bobcat**, a secretive animal that ranges throughout the hills of the greater Quabbin area.

The bobcat is a solitary meat eater, active mostly at night. Its keen hearing and eyesight allows it to lie quietly in ambush until prey comes along. Cottontail and snowshoe rabbits are its chief source of food, although it sometimes eats mice, squirrels, grouse, muskrat, and birds. Occasionally a bobcat will take a young deer, either by stalking, lying in ambush, or even positioning itself in a tree above a deer run.

Bobcats den in rock crevices, hollow trees, or under fallen logs. They usually mate in February, and during this time they are known to make an eerie yowling sound. Their young are born in the early spring and are weaned when they are two months old, remaining with their mother through the summer before they go off on their own. If you should ever see one, consider it a special wildlife encounter.

Back on the Outer Loop Trail, it's only a half-mile walk from the start of this trail to its intersection with the Inner Loop Trail (turn left), and then another three or four minutes to the earthen dam at the base of the pond. Eastern water snakes and painted turtles sun themselves here. Be on the lookout for belted kingfisher and great blue heron hunting for small fish. A tiny stream leaves the pond here.

David Lahti studied the natural history of the property for The Trustees of Reservations and reported a beaver in the pond. He also spotted a mink running along the dam where you now stand. Many birds live on or pass through the 75 acres of Rock House Reservation, including red-tailed hawks, screech owls, scarlet tanager, downy and hairy woodpeckers, hermit thrush, and warblers.

From the pond, turn left at the end of the dam and retrace your original steps back to the parking area. If you visit in winter when the snow is deep, I recommend snowshoes rather than cross-country skis for the hilly, winding trails.

Getting There

From the Massachusetts Turnpike, take Exit 8 for Palmer. Go north on Route 32, into and through the center of Ware, where Routes 32 and 9 combine. When they separate, bear to the right and stay on Route 9 east for 1.2 miles to parking and entrance on the left.

Open year-round, seven days a week, no admission fee, no rest rooms.

—M.T.

17 Tantiusques Reservation

Sturbridge
55 acres

❖ 1.75 miles

❖ 50 minutes

❖ easy

❖ great for children

When one thinks of mining, the western United States usually comes to mind, but here at Tantiusques Reservation evidence of early **mining operations**, complete with a small mine shaft, is scattered throughout the wooded property. Since 1962 The Trustees of Reservations have owned and managed the property. Trails wind through the hills where white-tailed deer, raccoon, fox, ruffed grouse, and other animals make their home. You can either make a three-quarter-mile walk or extend your walk into the adjoining Massachusetts Wildlife Management Area.

The first excavation site for mining graphite is very close to the parking area. As you face the lone trail leading into the woods, an open cut into the rock is just beyond sight to your right, about 40 feet up a small hill, which can be easily climbed. Long before the white man arrived in the area, the local Nipmuck tribe chipped off the black ore to paint their faces for ceremonies. Later, when the settlers discovered the "black lead," they used metal picks and shovels to excavate the graphite sandwiched in the granite hills. (Graphite is softer than granite and could be excavated with simple tools.)

A trapper and scout named John Oldham first arrived at the site in 1633. Ten years later the property was acquired by John Winthrop Jr., son of the first governor of Massachusetts Bay Colony. But Winthrop's dreams of a lucrative operation never came to pass. In 1658 some black lead was extracted from the site, as told in this letter from the elder Winthrop to his son: "There is some black lead digged, but not so much as they expected it being very difficult to gett out of ye rocks...."

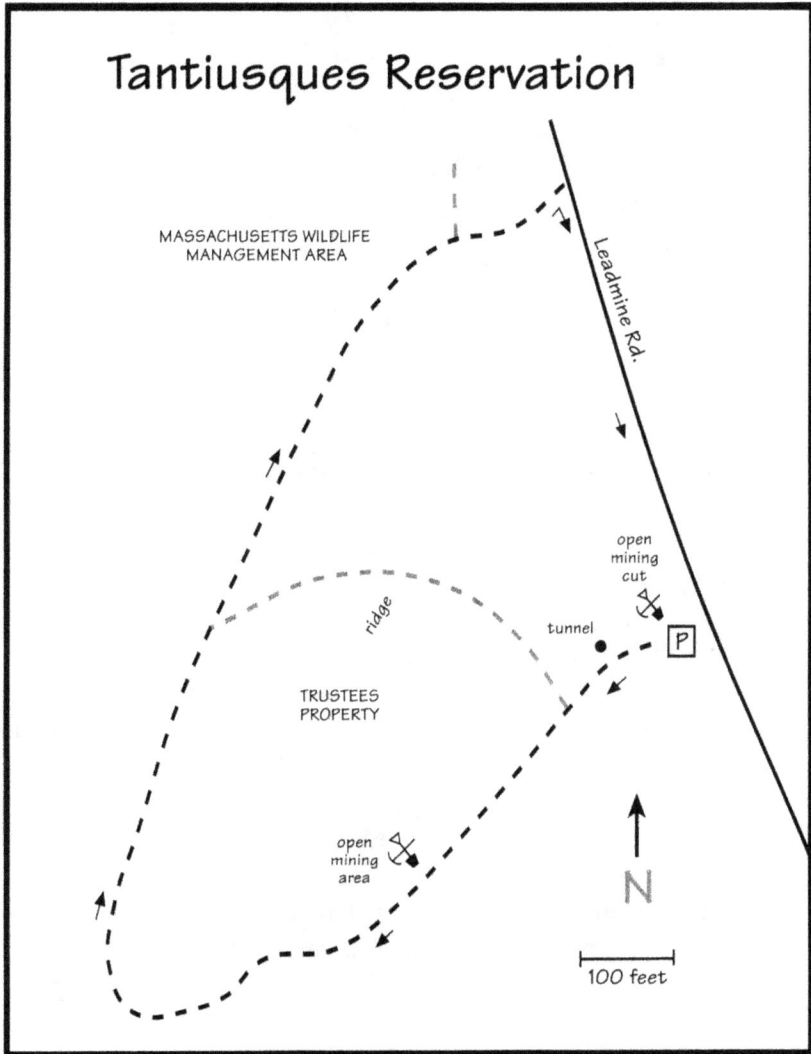

Tantiusques Reservation

After the property was sold by the Winthrop family in 1784, mining continued. Graphite was packed into barrels and taken to Boston on horse-drawn wagons. There it was loaded onto packet ships and sent to England. Operation of the mine ended in 1855.

A red fox kit plays near its den.

By following the main trail from the parking area it is possible to see a tunnel into the rock hillside just five minutes down the path. Its opening is about four feet by four feet, and it is particularly interesting to see in winter when strange **formations of ice** rise from the floor. Apparently the roof of the cave leaks water, and the falling drops freeze into something that resembles stalagmites. (It is dangerous to enter the small shaft.)

The trail angles off in a southwestern direction through oaks, maples, and an understory of **mountain laurel**. Autumn colors here are quite beautiful: the maples provide shades of crimson and gold, while the browns of the oaks contrast with the glittering green leaves of the mountain laurel. Another trail forks off to the right, leading over a ridge, but continue straight ahead.

Soon another mining area appears. This excavation is not a cave but instead is a cut into the rock hillside. You can walk into this one. It, too, has beautiful ice formations in the winter, with huge icicles hanging from the rock ledges. When you walk through the cut, it's like being in a miniature canyon with rock walls about 25 feet high.

Back on the trail, the path narrows a bit and hemlock trees are now mixed with deciduous trees. About 15 minutes from the start of your walk, the trail turns toward the north. The trail is fairly level and, with adequate snow cover, would make for good cross-country skiing. On my winter trip there were no human tracks in the snow, but it was easy to see the prints of deer and **fox**. The red-tailed fox is one of nature's most handsome creatures. Consider yourself lucky should you see one, for they are quite secretive. Thoreau admired the fox, writing, "His recent tracks still give variety to a winter's walk. I tread in the steps of the fox that has gone before me by some hours, or which perhaps I have started, with such a tip-toe of expectation as if I were on the trail of the Spirit itself...."

Fox are active hunters in the winter, following regular routes while searching for rabbit, partridge, and mice. They hunt alone, usually at night, and rarely range more than five miles from their home base. They use dens primarily for the protection of their pups, which are born in late March and April in litters of 1 to 10 pups. I recently came across a den that had 7 pups playing on the mound of sand in front of the den.

The trail now leads northeast, passing the connecting trail that climbs the ridge to the right. Continue on the main trail and, soon after passing the connecting trail, enter a Massachusetts Wildlife Management Area (be aware that **hunting** is allowed there, and if you are visiting in the fall wear blaze orange). I always love to walk on a straight, level trail like this because for a few minutes I can forget where I am and just let the rhythm of walking take over. The feeling of not having a care in the world and putting your body on automatic pilot is just one of the many reasons why I take a walk in the woods every weekend.

After walking toward the northeast for 20 minutes, you will reach Leadmine Road, though you may have to pick your way around a few trees that have blown down. Simply turn right and follow the road for about 10 minutes to reach your car. The total walk seldom takes me longer than 50 minutes.

Getting There

From I-84 west take Exit 1, Mashapaug Road—Southbridge. Turn right off the exit ramp and follow Route 15 south for 1.5 miles. Turn right onto Leadmine Road and travel 0.9 mile to entrance on left.

Open year-round, seven days a week, no admission fee, no rest rooms.

—M.T.

18 Cook's Canyon

Barre
47 acres

❖ 1.5 miles

❖ 1 hour

❖ easy

❖ great for children

Cook's Canyon is one of those little gems that somehow get overlooked in travel and outdoor guides. While only 47 acres, it has several points of interest beyond the forest, most notably a pond, Galloway Brook, and the canyon itself. The property was once owned by the Cook family, and in 1902 George Cook began planting thousands of trees, including pines, firs, elms, walnuts, birches, and maples, in the acres near the canyon. Massachusetts Audubon received the parcel of land around the canyon from Mrs. Cook in 1948, and it is now open to the public.

From the parking lot, our outing begins by walking through the grassy opening directly in front of the lot. A magnificent blue spruce is at the left of the opening and a white birch is straight ahead. Follow a wide, grassy path to the right and into a plantation of red pine. About 150 feet down the path it forks, and you should stay left. The trail is marked by blue paint dots on trees and follows a stone wall as it narrows. Walk on the carpet of pine needles, continuing in a southerly direction. About 10 minutes into the walk you pass a large oak that was spared when the original woods were cleared for farming. (If you're walking with children, see how many pairs of arms it takes to circle the base of the tree.)

On my last walk I saw only crows and red squirrels, but on a nearby road a coyote loped through a field. The coyote was about the size of a small German shepherd, and it stopped once to look back at me when I got out of the car. The eastern coyote is a relative newcomer to Massachusetts, having migrated into the state in the 1950s, and has been expanding its range ever since, even to Cape Cod. Here in central Massachusetts it is often seen in the woods, fields, and even out on the ice at Quabbin Reservoir, searching for prey. The coyote is an intelligent animal, and very adaptable, learning to live and even prosper alongside human development. Its normal diet includes small mammals, birds, fruits and berries, and just about anything else it comes upon. Coyotes often hunt and travel in packs, with a distinct pecking order among members, and coyote dens—which are sometimes the abandoned dens of other animals—are often located near rocky ledges (like the ones at Cook's Canyon) and may have more than one entrance. A mother coyote often moves newborn pups from one den to another for extra protection.

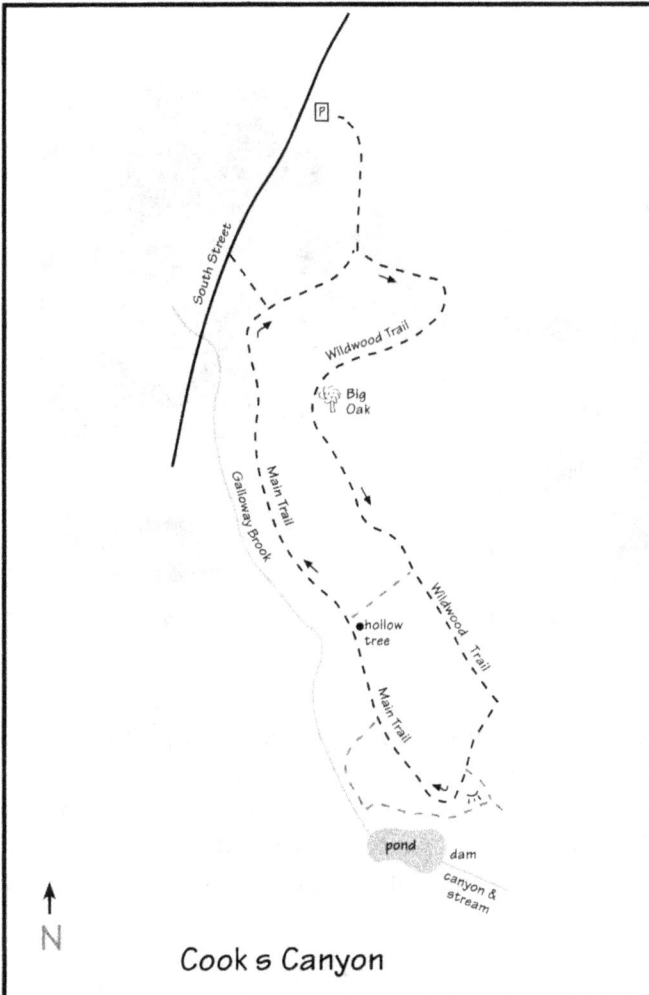

Cook's Canyon

Back on the trail, you pass a wet area on stone steps where red maples, which don't mind "wet feet," grow. About 10 minutes from the large oak, a side trail heads off to your right, but you should continue straight, keeping the stone wall to your left. In another six or seven minutes you arrive at a small pond. To view the gorge, simply follow the sound of falling water along the trail to the left of the pond near the small dam. The first waterfall into the canyon drops about 20 feet from the pond, but the water continues to cascade in other small falls for a total plunge of 100 to 150 feet into the hemlock-shaded ravine below.

There is a partial view of the Ware River valley from exposed rocks just to the northeast of the dam on a side trail. This rocky outcrop makes a good place to stop for a snack. (While the trail following the ravine downstream looks inviting, unfortunately it is on private land.)

The trail follows a stream at Cook's Canyon.

The next section of our walk is perhaps the most pleasant of all, as we head back toward the parking lot in a northerly direction on the Main Trail. The trail parallels Galloway Brook, and just a few feet up the trail you see a side path on the left leading down to a cluster of white birch next to the brook. It's a great place to sit and watch the clear waters of Galloway Brook flow by.

Back on the Main Trail, the next point of interest is a hollow tree, which will be a big hit with the kids because the opening is large enough for them to stand in. The tree might bring back memories of the classic young-adult book *My Side of the Mountain,* where a boy lives in a hollow tree.

Continue straight on the trail, passing a side trail on the right. Soon the stream curls to the left. Here the trail forks and you can choose which way to return the parking lot. If you go straight, you pass a small field where you might see bluebirds entering the birdhouses erected on posts. I prefer to turn left, which quickly leads you to South Street and a right turn to reach your car. Along the right side of South Street is the old town pound, a square holding area comprised of a high rock wall. When livestock got loose in days gone by, they were brought to the town pound for the owners to reclaim. From the town pound it's just a five-minute walk to your car.

You may have enough energy for another walk, and I'd recommend the Rock House Reservation in West Brookfield, which is also described in this book. Children will especially love the nooks and crannies in the rock shelter, and there is a relatively easy hike around the pond located there.

Getting There

From Barre center follow South Street to the south for 0.25 mile. The sanctuary and parking lot are on the left.

—M.T.

19 Harvard Forest

Petersham
3,000 acres

❖ 1.5 miles

❖ 1 hour, 15 minutes

❖ easy

If you can't tell a hemlock from a white pine, the Black Gum Trail at Harvard Forest is a great way to learn about tree identification. This loop walk has a number of markers which identify trees on a corresponding interpretive guide available at the signboard in the parking lot. Equally educational is the Fisher Museum (located at the parking lot) which features 23 three-dimensional models (dioramas) depicting the history of the New England forests and their management and ecology.

The walk begins by following the dirt road to the left of the Fisher Museum. The road cuts between the museum and a white farmhouse heading in a northeast direction, passing by the Torrey Laboratory (a brick building situated behind the museum). Within a couple minutes you enter a woodland of mixed hardwoods laced with stone walls. A few white pine, hemlock, and spruce grow alongside the hardwoods by a field that is reverting to forest. A quick way to distinguish between the three evergreen species growing here is to look at their needles: The white pine has long, slender needles in groups of five; the hemlock has flat, half-inch needles with blunt tips; and the spruce has stiff, pointed needles.

Five minutes from the parking lot a side trail goes off to the right, but our walk on the Black Gum Trail continues straight and is marked by yellow arrows and yellow disks. Red pine planted in the 1920s grow along the trail and can be identified by their four-to-six-inch needles growing in twos. The trail gradually climbs a small hill, passing more stone walls. These walls are straight and are most likely boundary walls, whereas walls that border fields sometimes zigzag and skirt wetlands. Another way of identifying the use of walls is to look at the size of the rocks. If the rocks are all large, the wall's primary purpose was to enclose livestock, but if the wall contains both large and small stones, it signifies that the farmer tried to remove all the stones from the field for better planting.

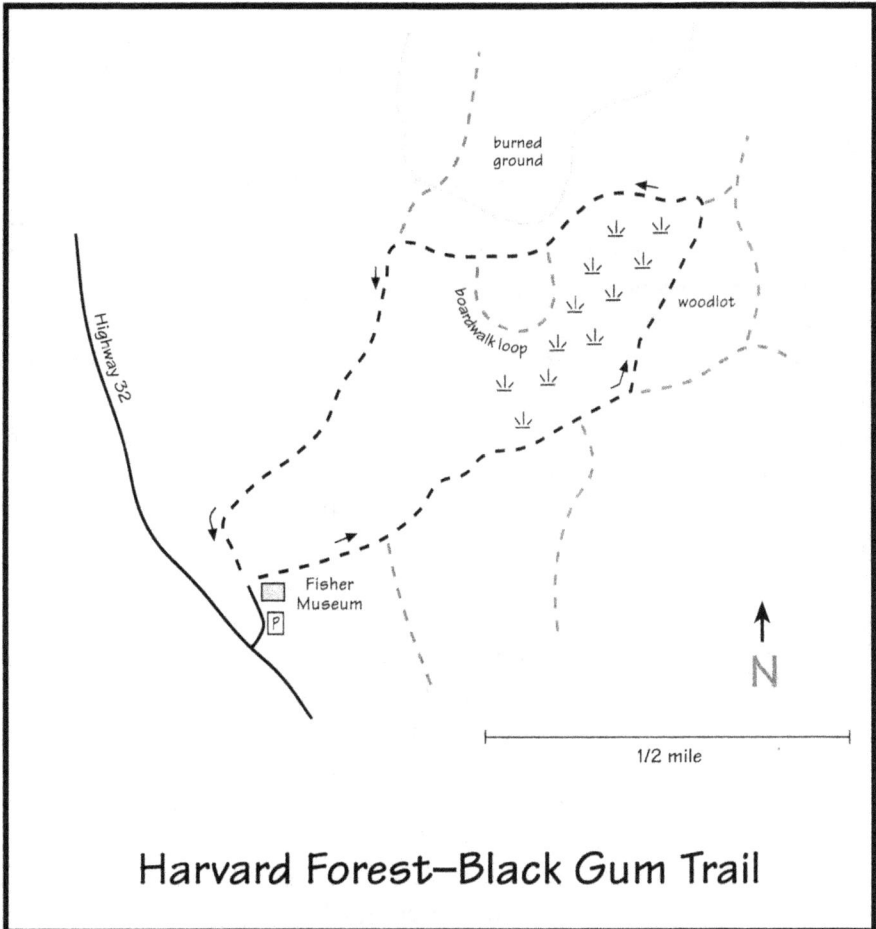

Harvard Forest–Black Gum Trail

Just about every species of wildlife native to New England is found in Harvard Forest. The woods in Petersham and the surrounding towns are of vital importance to wildlife because large tracts have been preserved by such groups as The Trustees of Reservations, Massachusetts Audubon, and Harvard University, which owns this forest. Wild turkey, deer, fox, coyote, beaver, and many birds of prey live here. One of the more fascinating creatures I've seen at Harvard Forest is the fisher cat, a large member of the weasel family. Its muzzle is pointed, its ears broad and rounded, and its legs and feet are stout. Its glossy coat is brownish black, with small white patches on the neck. (I've seen only a couple fisher in all my hikes because they are elusive.) A male can measure 40 inches long with a foot-long tail, although the maximum weight of a fisher is about 20 pounds. The fisher lives here because there is a good food source, including porcupines, which the fisher kills by circling the porcupine and nipping at its face, slowly tiring it before moving in for the kill.

While spotting a fisher is rare, seeing porcupines is rather common because they are fairly slow and do not always run from humans. If there is snow on the ground look for their pigeon-toed tracks with the quills from the dragging tail showing in the snow. Porcupines feed on buds, bark, and hemlock boughs, so it's a good idea to look upward occasionally into trees for their dark outline. Sometimes they feed so heavily on hemlocks that the tops of the trees are stunted. Few predators beside the fisher can kill porcupines because of their armor of quills. While porcupines cannot throw their quills, they can whip their tail around in a hurry and fill an intruder with the needlelike quills, which can be deadly if they work their way into a main artery.

Back on our walk, you pass markers #2 and #3 about 10 minutes into the walk, followed by a narrow trail to the right. You should continue straight, following the yellow disks. About five minutes later you will see a yellow arrow pointing left, and you should turn left off the road and onto a narrow trail that winds through a stand of mountain laurel. Other plants growing in the understory are Indian cucumber, hobblebush, winterberry, and an assortment of ferns. Seedlings grow in the moss-covered ground, which helps to keep the soil moist. Hemlocks tower above, blocking out most of the light. In 1989 lightning hit this section of woods, but most trees survived with only a strip of bark peeled off the trunk indicating where they were hit.

The trail heads through a swampy area where you pick your way over muddy sections on rocks, a good place to look for animal tracks. (John O'Keefe, the Fisher Museum coordinator, told me that he has seen many moose tracks and droppings here.) At marker #7, the trail splits and you should bear right, following the yellow arrow. Then you reach a **T** intersection (roughly a half-hour from the start of your walk) where you should turn left. Some of the hemlocks here are good size; try circling your arms around their trunks. Unless you have exceptionally long arms it's impossible to link your hands. The hemlocks in this area are being intensively studied and a platform tower was erected to provide access to their upper canopies.

Much of the ground on either side of the trail is wet, and several high-bush blueberry plants grow here. Marker #8 indicates a chestnut sapling growing from the base of an older tree that has died from the blight. The sapling will also die before it can become a tree. The blight manifests itself as an orange-red fungus seen along the cracks in the bark.

In 1957 seventy-eight acres burned here on the right of the trail at marker #10, and now the woods are comprised of only small trees such as gray birch, red oak, and red maple, many of them growing as clumps from fire-killed trees. The fire did not cross to your left because it is swampy ground where a truck with a water pump managed to beat back the flames. The swamp is home to some of the oldest trees in the forest, the black gums, identified by their shiny, egg-shaped leaves, which average about four inches in length. The fleshy fruit of the black gum (also known as sour gum) is relished by black bear, wild turkey, ruffed grouse, and many other species of birds. Black bear are rather uncommon in Petersham, but some residents have seen them. They are extremely wary, often venturing out only after nightfall. At marker #11 a boardwalk is being built that will extend 700 feet into the swamp and then loop back to join to the trail.

About 45 minutes into your walk you arrive at a green gate where the trail you are on intersects with a dirt road. Turn left to follow the dirt road, which is lined on both sides by stone walls and a few rather large oaks left as shade trees back when the land throughout the region was almost all farm and pastures in the 1800s.

After the near-total shade cover of the woodlands, this old country lane is a welcome change: sunlight filters through the mighty oaks, dappling the road. A few beech trees, identified by their smooth, gray bark, are scattered along the road as you walk in a southeasterly direction. In 10 minutes another dirt road heads to the left, but I like to continue straight ahead, where after a couple more minutes of walking you will reach an intersection and turn left, following a handsome fence along the edge of a field. From here you can see the Fisher Museum and reach the parking lot in a couple minutes.

Woodpecker holes in a dead tree at Harvard Forest.

Besides the trail described here, several other nearby tracts are owned by Harvard University. Data is gathered from the forest about tree growth and forest succession and ecology. One area of the forest consists of an experiment in which trees were intentionally knocked over (by marker #12) to replicate a blowdown and then research was conducted to see how the forest responds to such natural disasters. Among the researchers who have utilized Harvard Forest are ecologists, physiologists, soil scientists, microbiologists, and economists.

The Fisher Museum was named after Professor Richard Fisher, the founder of Harvard Forest, who conceived of the dioramas in the museum as a way to share the research findings of the forest with public. Arrangements can be made for use of the facility or daytime accommodation of large groups by calling 978-724-3302.

Getting There

From Route 2 take the Route 32/Petersham exit and go south on Route 32 for 3.0 miles to the entrance and parking on the left. The Fisher Museum is open weekdays 9:00 A.M. to 5:00 P.M. year-round; Saturday and Sundays noon to 4:00 P.M. May through October. It is closed on holidays. Hunting is allowed at Harvard Forest. For more information call 978-724-3302.

—M.T.

Crow Hill at Leominster State Forest

Leominster

❖ about 1.5 miles

❖ 1 hour, 15 minutes

❖ moderate

❖ great for kids

How did I overlook this place in the earlier edition of *Nature Walks in Central Massachusetts*? Maybe I'd been doing too many slide presentations about places to hike and not enough actual hiking! But at least I finally discovered Crow Hill. It's a perfect family destination where in the warm-weather months you can climb to the top of the cliffs at Crow Hill and then cool off with a swim at Crow Hill Pond.

This hike begins at the parking lot and makes a direct decent to the Crow Hill ridge line, with a short section involving a steep climb. (For a more gradual ascent, you could leave from the ranger station/headquarters.) Begin your outing by following the path from the parking area into a woodland of oak and maple. The trail heads in an uphill direction, and you must pay attention to your footsteps to avoid the numerous rocks and roots in the path. Thick stands of mountain laurel grow in the understory, so you might want to make a June visit when the white flowers of this bush are blooming. Another plant growing beneath the taller trees is the striped maple, a favorite food of moose—and there are moose here. In fact, a day after my first trip a female moose was hit by a car on Route 2 and then gave birth to her baby after the accident. The mother moose then died, but the baby lived and was taken to a wildlife rehabilitation center. No word on

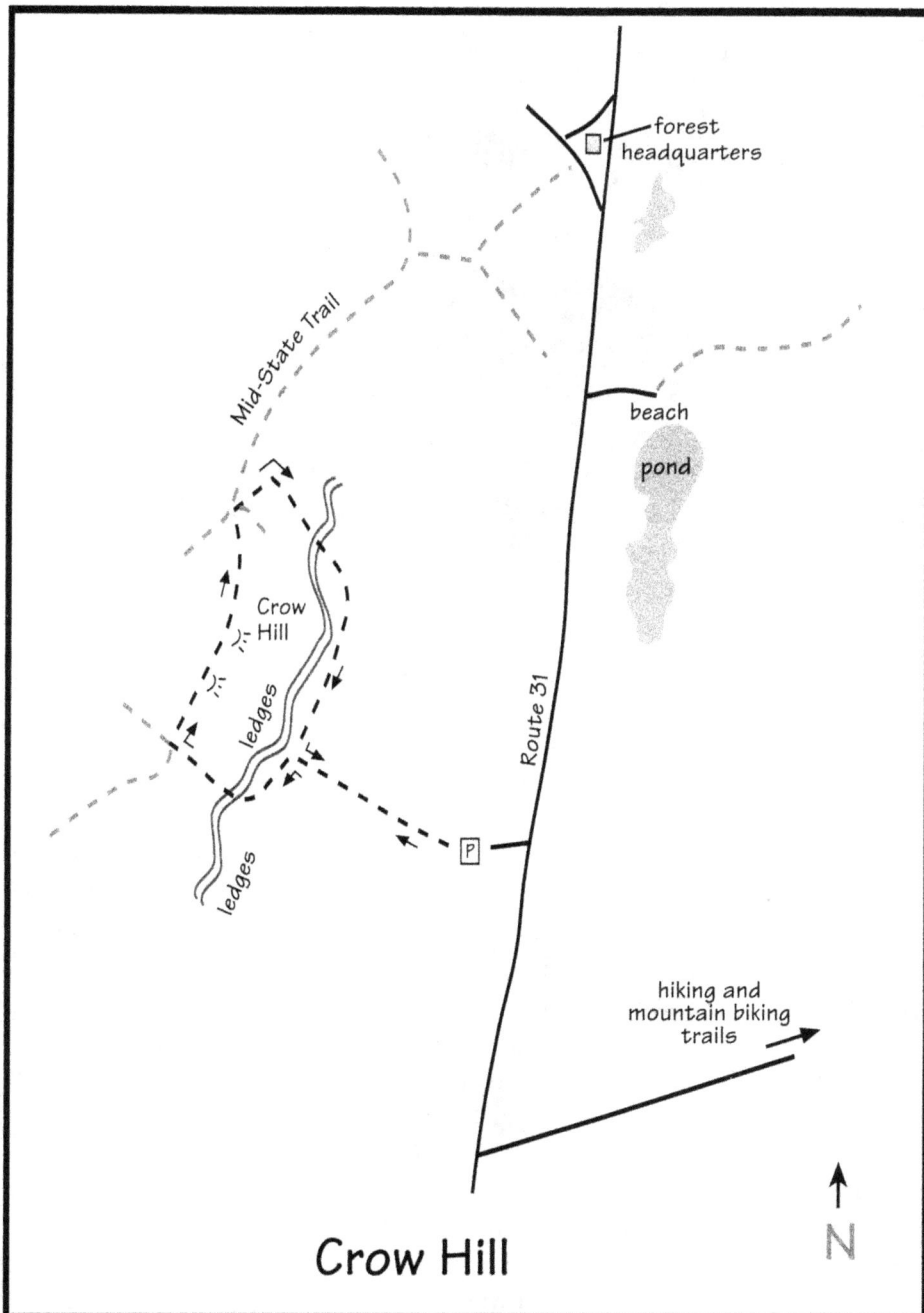

forest
headquarters

Mid-State Trail

beach

pond

Crow
Hill

ledges

Route 31

ledges

P

hiking and
mountain biking
trails

Crow Hill

N

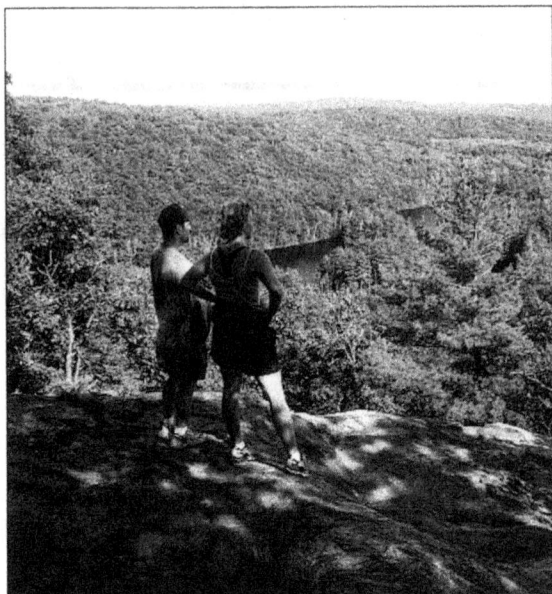

Looking eastward from the summit of Crow Hill.

what happened to the occupants of the car, but if they escaped injury, sure-ly their car did not! The moose is the largest land animal in New England and the ones that travel through Leominster State Forest are probably res-idents of Massachusetts, not transients from New Hampshire.

After about 10 minutes, the trail slopes downhill briefly, then back uphill, passing through an opening in a large stone wall. Look for chip-munks running in and out of the stone wall, where they make homes. Huge boulders are scattered in the woods amongst blueberry and lady's slippers. In 10 more minutes you will come to a cliff, where you can watch rock climbers scale the wall. (If you're with children, let them explore the base of the cliff, where overhanging rocks form little caves.) As you face the cliff, walk to the left and look for a break in the rock. This steep climb up the rocks will take you to the top of the cliff at Crow Hill. It's about a five-minute climb to a four-way intersection with yellow and blue markers on a birch tree to the left and an oak tree to the right. Go to the right, along the side of the ridge, following the trail as it passes through a tunnel of mountain laurel. In two minutes you reach fantastic views to the east-northeast. A gentle breeze often washes over this rocky outcrop, making it a fine place to stretch out and rest. The view in front of you is mostly rolling hills, with little signs of civilization.

On my last trip a **turkey vulture** swooped low on the winds, offering me a good view of this massive black bird with its seven-foot wingspan. Crows often harass turkey vultures, even though they look tiny next to such a massive bird. (Whenever you hear a bunch of crows cawing, have your binoculars ready—often it means they are mobbing or harassing larger birds such as hawks, owls, and vultures.)

The best time to see hawks at Crow Hill is in early September when broad-wing hawks start their migration southward. The number of hawks is highly dependent on weather and wind direction. Try to time your trip for a day without rain, as the hawks generally do not fly in the rain. They also ride the wind south, so pick a day when the wind is not coming from the south. They will not waste valuable energy fighting the air current. The summit of Mt. Wachusett is also a great spot for hawk-watching, and the access road is open for driving for those who do not wish to climb. One hawk you may see at any time of year in Massachusetts is the red-tailed hawk, which often lets out a high-pitched scream while it soars. The red-tailed hawk has adapted fairly well to man's presence; it can be seen sometimes along our highways, perched in trees and keeping a sharp eye out for any movement in the grassy strips along the roadways. One of the few birds that winters here, its hardiness was acknowledged by Thoreau when he wrote of "the hawk with warrior-like firmness abiding the blasts of winter."

When you're ready to walk again continue along the ridge-line path about five minutes to the next trail intersection, where you should turn right, following blue markers on the trees. The trail goes straight downhill, then curls to the right, where you pick your way down the ledge. You will pass a large oak tree growing out of the ledge, followed by a dozen rocks positioned like stairs. Stay right along the base of the ledge, heading in a generally southerly direction. Now the view is looking up at the sheer rock walls. Keep following the base of the ledge marked by blue arrows, and in three or four more minutes you will reach the intersection with the trail you initially walked when you first saw the rock ledge. Just turn left and retrace your steps back to the parking lot.

If it's summertime be sure to drive back to the Crow Hill Pond entrance for a dip. There is a wide sandy beach, as wll as picnic tables under the pines, and restrooms. In the cooler months try taking a side trip to Wachusett Meadows, detailed in *Nature Walks in Eastern Massachusetts*, or Wachusett Mountain, found in this book. For history buffs, try taking a spin south onto Route 140 to Redemption Rock near the northern end of Princeton. Redemption Rock is a huge boulder with a perfectly flat top, and it was here that Mary Rowlandson was released by the Indians during King Philip's War in 1676. Rowlandson recounted her six weeks of captivity in a diary, which has been published in the back of a book I recently co-wrote with Eric Schultz titled *King Philip's War*. Here is a passage from Rowlandson as she approaches Wachusett after weeks of hardship: "A bitter weary day I had of it, traveling now three days together without resting any day between. At last, after many weary steps, I saw Wachusett Hills but many miles off." Rowlandson then crosses a swamp where she slips and falls, barely having the strength to continue. A hand is offered her; it is King Philip (Metacom), who encourages her by saying, "Two weeks more and you shall be a mistress again." And within days Rowlandson was freed here at Redemption Rock. (The Midstate trail passes by Redemption Rock, and if you head north on the trail you can reach Crow Hill after a two- to three-mile hike.)

Getting There

From Route 2 take Exit 28 south (Fitchburg/Princeton) onto Route 31. Follow Route 31 south past the park headquarters. At two miles you will pass the main entrance to the swimming area road on the left; continue another half-mile to a dirt parking lot on the right where a sign says Crow Hill Trail. (If this lot is filled, park at the main-entrance lot.)

—M.T.

Franklin County

21 Bear's Den

New Salem
6.4 acres

- ❖ 3/8 mile
- ❖ 25 minutes
- ❖ easy
- ❖ great for children

Situated along a back road in the charming town of New Salem, the **waterfall** at Bear's Den should not be missed if you are in the area. Beneath towering hemlocks, the Middle Branch of the Swift River cascades over a 10-foot drop into small dark pools—a great location for photography buffs to capture the beauty of falling water. (Toward midday, the sun's rays hit squarely on the waterfall, making this my favorite time for picture taking.) Because the walk is a short one, a visit to this reservation is best combined with exploring other nearby natural areas such as Buffam Falls (see p. 175) or North Common Meadow (see p. 54). The name Bear's Den was given to the area by a settler who shot a black bear here. Black bear are now uncommon near Quabbin, but their numbers are healthy just to the west, on the other side of the Connecticut River.

From the roadside parking area, a rocky path follows the slope downhill toward the river. About 125 yards down the trail, on the right, you can see a rock foundation of an **early gristmill**. Just about every moving body of water in Massachusetts during the seventeenth and eighteenth centuries hosted either a gristmill or lumber mill. The textile mills of the 1800s tended to be on larger rivers, often built over the site of the earlier mills.

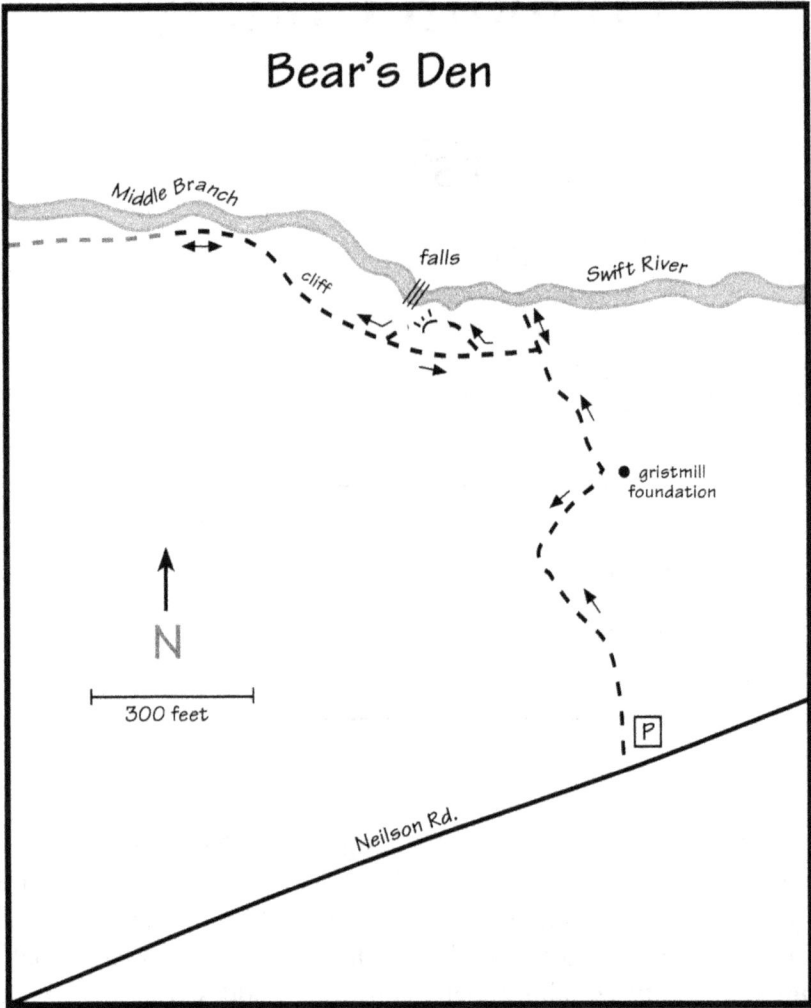

Bear's Den

Another 50 yards down the path will bring you to the river, which has carved out a small gorge through granite cliffs. The best view of the falls can be seen by following the trail to the left a few feet up a knoll. The water tumbles down either side of a rock outcrop, forming two falls, each perhaps 12 feet in height. Cool, damp air seems to have permanently settled over the falls, adding to the special feeling of this enchanting place.

Each season imprints its own distinct mood on Bear's Den. In the springtime, when the river flexes its muscle with snowmelt, the water roars over the jagged rocks, foaming white in the pools below. During summer the low water makes this the perfect spot to sit and cool your feet after a walk. Autumn's colors are somewhat muted by the ravine and many hemlocks, but small colorful splashes of deciduous trees can be as beautiful in their singularity as a whole forest ablaze. And winter's white blanket of snow and sparkling ice create a perfect contrast to the granite walls that rise darkly from the river's bottom.

You can climb the cliff above the falls, then follow a faint path alongside the river in an upstream direction. The stately **hemlocks** seem to grow right out of the granite, and **mountain laurel** is scattered in their understory. Fox, deer, wild turkey, raccoon, and fisher all live in these forested hills. **Fisher** do a good job of avoiding people—I've seen only one in all my hikes. They are deadly hunters, covering considerable ground, and in the winter it's possible to find their tracks and follow their trails as they search for mice, squirrels, rabbits, birds, and even porcupines to eat. Look for tracks that zigzag through the woods, stopping at rotten trees in search of rodent homes. Chances are, these are fisher tracks or those of another member of the weasel family.

A small waterfall is split by a boulder as it tumbles down.

The heavily forested land you are exploring is also good habitat for ruffed grouse, several species of owls, goshawks, and many smaller birds, such as thrushes, warblers, and many types of woodpeckers. **Ruffed grouse** prefer to winter in heavy conifers; they are a nonmigratory bird, 14 inches long, with rust and gray feathers with a black terminal band on the tail. When flushed they can burst into full flight (which can really startle you) but usually only travel a short distance before touching down again. The "drumbeat" you may hear in the woods is actually the male grouse beating its wings rapidly, trying to attract a female. As fascinating as this sound is, it is the female that is more interesting to me. More than once during a spring walk, I've come upon a female grouse that appeared to have an injured wing. The grouse was feigning injury to distract me from her tiny chicks, which blend in well with the brown forest floor.

The riverside trail is not long. When it peters out, retrace your steps back to the falls. It is said that during King Philip's War (1675–1676), the Native Americans under the leadership of the Wampanoag sachem Philip (whose tribal name was Metacomet) gathered here. Nearby towns such as Deerfield, Northfield, and Hadley were all attacked and put to the torch by Wampanoag and Nipmuck warriors during the first few months of the war. Later, when the war turned in favor of the colonists, it is possible warriors may have congregated here. They were driven from their camp along the Connecticut River after a battle with the colonists.

Today, this small reservation is the picture of tranquillity and open for all to explore. It is through the generosity of a Mrs. Grais Poole Burrage that we have this land to enjoy. In *Saving Special Places: A Centennial History of the Trustees of Reservations*, author Gordon Abbott Jr. writes, "It was her (Mrs. Burrage's) lifelong wish to have the Bear's Den remain as it had throughout the centuries, a magic and mystical place to be enjoyed by all."

Getting There

From Route 2 take Exit 16 to Route 202 south. Go 2.0 miles to the intersection of Routes 122 and 202 in New Salem, then take Route 202 south another 0.4 mile. Go right on Elm Street 0.7 mile, then left on Neilson Road 0.5 mile. Park on the roadside by the welcome sign on the right.

Open year-round, seven days a week, no admission fee, no rest rooms.

—M.T.

Mt. Grace
22 State Forest

Warwick
1,689 acres

❖ 2.8 miles

❖ 3 hours

❖ difficult

For exquisite fall foliage viewing, it is hard to surpass the **360-degree vista** from the tower atop 1,617-foot-high Mt. Grace in Franklin County, near the New Hampshire line. Thickly clothed in northern hardwoods, hemlock, and white pine, a sea of multihued woodland stretches for miles below you in all directions—northeast to Mt. Monadnock, south to Quabbin Reservoir, southwest to Mt. Tom, and west to Mt. Greylock. To obtain the views, however, you must climb the steel tower, which has been well maintained and is in good condition.

The elevation gain is a very respectable 1,047 feet—more than any other walk in this guide—but the Metacomet-Monadnock Trail (M-M Trail) is in fine shape, and you'll no doubt agree that the view is well worth the moderate exertion required. Allow about one and a half hours to reach the summit. Since this property is not much visited, you may even have it all to yourself!

After leaving your locked vehicle at a dirt pull-off on the west side of Route 78, walk south for about 0.1 mile to the M-M Trail crossing. Turn right onto the trail and follow it west across Mountain Brook. Continue straight up into the woods on the old woods road. Walking gradually uphill you'll soon cross another brook; on your left will be a tiny rock-lined pond built by the Civilian Conservation Corps (CCC) in the 1930s. The brook flows away to the right and the trail levels out, leading you to an Adirondack shelter. Eastern phoebes have nested inside the structure—look for the remnants of this flycatcher's moss-covered mud nest.

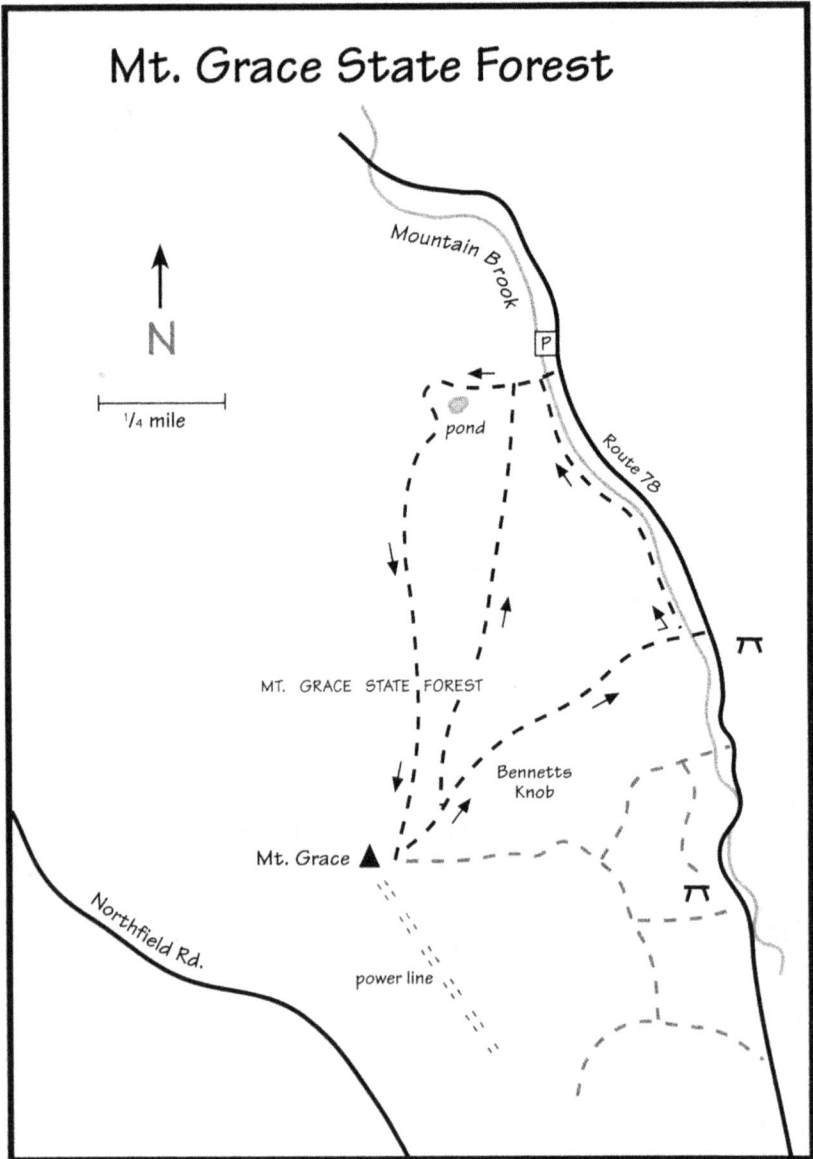

Mt. Grace State Forest

N

¼ mile

Mountain Brook

P

pond

Route 78

MT. GRACE STATE FOREST

Bennetts
Knob

Mt. Grace ▲

Northfield Rd.

power line

The M-M Trail now swings left and uphill—look for the trademark white paint blazes. Walk through lovely woods of eastern hemlock, American beech, and red maple. Some of the hemlocks are quite large, and there are many tiny trees pushing up from the forest floor; unlike many species, hemlocks are shade tolerant. There is not much ground cover here, but the twin coral-red berries and fingernail-sized leaves of creeping partridge-berry are numerous near the trail. Recross the small brook and continue to climb gradually over the wide track. Impish red-breasted nuthatches, sometimes tooting their tiny tin horns, reside and breed in the deep woodlands.

Cross another small brook and pass through a cool hemlock grove— the stream has cut a small gorge below and left. Continuing to climb steadily, the trail leads you through some rather large white pines. Energetic red squirrels gather the cones containing the delicious and nutritious winged seeds—some to be eaten now but most for future consumption. Mushrooms are also a favorite on the menu of this attractive tree squirrel. Red squirrels also eagerly seek out and eat birds' eggs, nestlings, and other high-protein animal foods. Farther up the trail you'll see a huge gray birch down to the right of the trail. At almost three feet in diameter, it may have been left to provide shade for livestock long ago. Gray birch superficially resembles white birch and many confuse the two species; **gray birch** does not peel as thinly or readily as white, and its whitish bark becomes increasingly gray and rough as it ages.

Terrestrial, sticky-skinned red-backed salamanders seek daytime refuge below the rotting logs of deciduous trees. By turning a few logs, you're sure to find some; be sure to carefully replace the log and salamander as you found them. In early October, the trail will be littered with the bright red leaves of red maple—a tree that can grow in wet, waterlogged soils as well as in dry ones.

Farther on, continue straight as a smaller, unmarked path enters from the right. The trail now becomes somewhat steeper and eventually swings to the left near the summit. Along this last section grow lots of **trailing arbutus**, the Massachusetts state flower. Mayflower, as it is also known, quite appropriately blooms in May. Both late low blueberry (about one foot tall) and early low blueberry (up to three feet tall, with larger leaves) are common along the trail. Dirt Fire Tower Road meets the hiking trail on the left just below the summit.

From the base of the tall tower the view is limited, but what a dramatic difference awaits as you ascend the eight tower levels for a completely unobstructed view in all directions. It's breathtaking. The fact that this area is quite thinly populated is readily apparent. Photogenic in any season, it peaks during the height of the fall foliage season in early October. If you're lucky and the winds are out of the northwest, you may also see large numbers of migrant broad-winged hawks and smaller, long-tailed sharp-shinned hawks drifting southward.

The sweeping panoramic view from the tower includes Mt. Monadnock in New Hampshire.

This is an excellent place to have lunch before heading back down the mountain. Little bluestem, a grass of the mid-continent tall-grass prairies, and bushy hair grass grow in the sunlight of the small clearing on the top of Mt. Grace. Blooming goldenrod attracts pollinating wasps, bees, and other insects to its yellow inflorescences in late summer and early fall. A bronze plaque commemorating the establishment of the state forest in 1920 was affixed to a granite glacial erratic on the summit by the Civilian Conservation Corps in the 1930s. The CCC completed a great deal of work in the forest, as it did on many of the state's other conservation lands. The boulder also holds the names of CCC employees who left their chiseled marks there some 65 years ago.

You have several options for the return trip. In addition to taking the most direct way—back the same way you came—you can follow a trail that leads east to a picnic area along Route 78 and then take a path from the picnic area back to your vehicle. The other choice is to follow a less easily found path that roughly parallels the M-M Trail on the opposite side of the ravine, back to the Adirondack shelter near the start of the route. In any case, retrace your steps back down the M-M Trail to start down.

If you do not wish to follow the M-M Trail down, take the narrow, unblazed trail that forks off of the M-M Trail less than 0.2 mile below the tower. Pass a lichen-covered glacial erratic on the left and come to another trail junction. The left path (orange paint blazes on trunks) leads down in a northeasterly direction, but the trail is not well maintained and it's easy to stray from the path. This path is not traveled much and the blazes, most low to the ground, are sporadic. Eventually it leads back to the Adirondack shelter and the M-M Trail.

Staying to the right at the trail junction will take you to the vandalism-plagued picnic area (no tables) that borders Route 78 along Mountain Brook, which flows through a nicely constructed CCC rock-lined channel. From here, it's approximately half a mile north to the parking area on a path that roughly parallels the west side of the highway.

Allow about one hour for the descent on any trail.

Getting There

From the junction of Routes 2 and 2A in Erving, take Route 2A east for 2.1 miles to the junction with Route 78 on the left. Take Route 78 north for 7.4 miles to the state forest headquarters—currently unstaffed—on the left just past the intersection of Route 78 and Athol Road. Continue north on Route 78 for 1.4 miles to a dirt pull-off on the left side of the road (approximately 0.3 mile before the junction with Robbins Road on the right).

Hours are dawn to dusk. No admission fee. No rest rooms are currently available. Motorized vehicles (except snowmobiles) are prohibited.

—R.L.

23 Northfield Mountain Recreation and Environmental Center

Northfield
2,200 acres

❖ 4.5 miles

❖ 4 hours

❖ moderate

Northfield Mountain is unique among properties covered by this guide. The 300-acre Northfield Mountain Reservoir—atop the plateau between the Connecticut and Millers rivers—is part of a Northeast Utilities pumped-storage facility that produces hydroelectric power during times of peak demand. Water is pumped 2.8 miles through a tunnel from the Connecticut River and up 800 vertical feet to the reservoir. When water is released, it drives the huge turbines of the subterranean power plant one-half mile below the surface. This process, which is capable of generating 1 million kilowatts of electricity, is explained by exhibits housed in the visitor center. Twenty-five miles of very well maintained and truly multiuse trails also set this operation apart.

Although significant portions of the property are in a highly altered state, there are ample opportunities here to explore extensive woodlands and to amble along scenic rock ledges with panoramic views. The property borders thousands of acres of forested lands, and thus virtually all the indigenous interior southern New England fauna is resident—from 0.15-ounce masked shrews to 300-pound black bears and even moose. The unvegetated banks of Northfield Mountain Reservoir are not a particularly attractive sight, but lovely Rose Ledge and Lower Ledge Trails will make getting there the best part of the journey.

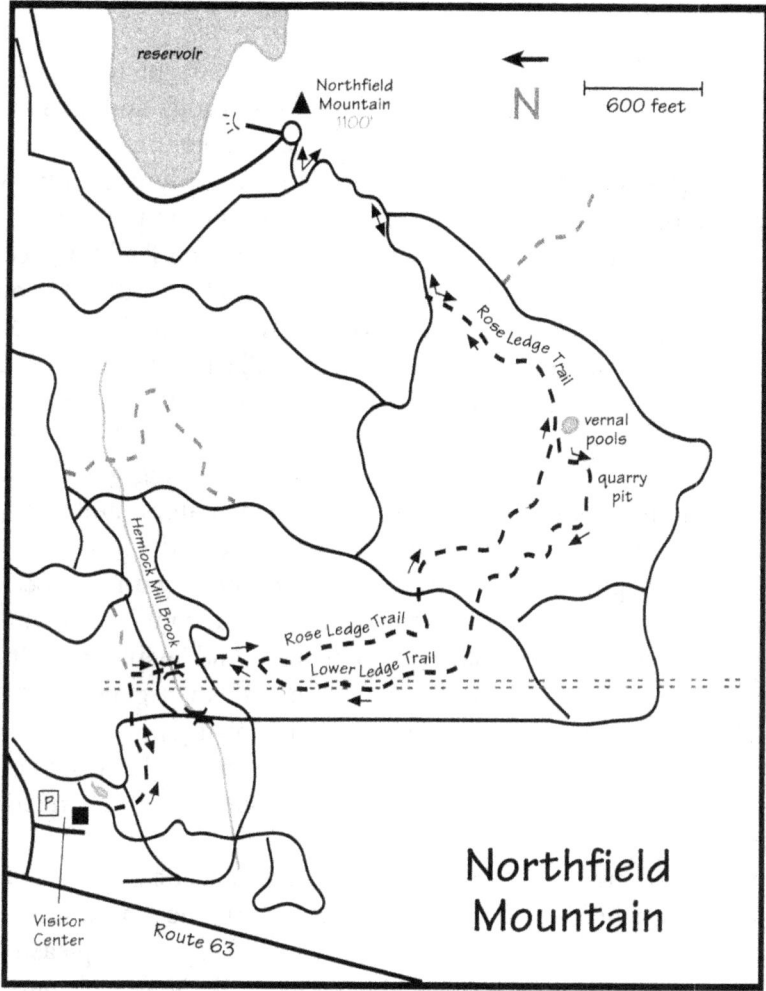

reservoir

Northfield
Mountain
1100'

N

600 feet

Rose Ledge Trail

vernal
pools

quarry
pit

Hemlock Mill Brook

Rose Ledge Trail

Lower Ledge Trail

P

Northfield
Mountain

Visitor
Center

Route 63

From the trailhead (elevation 283 feet) on the east side of the visitor center, where there is a large map of the trail system, walk toward the right around a small cattail-fringed pond, left. Light-green filamentous algae—*Spirogyra*—provides cover and sustenance to minute pond invertebrates, which in turn feed more complex creatures such as frogs and red-spotted newts. Continue across the mowed area and enter a white pine stand straight ahead. Watch for blue plastic blazes on the trunks. There is very little plant growth—starflower and Canada mayflower being the exceptions. Cross the cart road, swing left, and proceed under humming power lines past a restricted area on the left to the beginning of Rose Ledge Trail (orange blazes), right. Hay-scented and New York ferns are common along the trail.

Horizontally bedded **gneiss rock outcrops** begin to appear. Cross Hemlock Hill cart road. Enter shady hemlock woods and cross a bridge over a brook. Next cross Jug End cart road and continue through hemlocks. The character of the forest changes to drier oak/maple/pine with an understory of mountain laurel and American chestnut. After crossing a bridge over an intermittent stream, pass Lower Ledge Trail intersection on the right. Continue straight and proceed through woodlands composed largely of maple, birch, pignut hickory, and white pine. Tiny club mosses (princess pine) and ferns dot the forest floor. Black-capped chickadees are among the most abundant birds year-round. From fall to spring they travel in family groups with other year-round woodland residents—nuthatches, downy woodpeckers, and brown creepers. Flocking gives small birds like these some measure of protection from predators, and group effort makes finding food somewhat easier for all concerned.

Winding uphill, the trail traverses oak woods with a subcanopy of striped maple, a small but handsome tree with tight, white-and-green-striped bark, and a shrub layer of blueberry and maple-leaf viburnum. Look closely at the oak trunks for signs of the alien gypsy moth. Hairy, shed skins of gypsy moth caterpillars and brown, spindle-shaped pupal cases adhere to many oaks. Lacking natural enemies, this insect can defoliate large expanses of oak woodlands; the woodlands usually recover fully, however.

Soon you arrive at the first vista, albeit screened by vegetation. In early October, when I made one of my visits here, the scarlet foliage of red maple and the yellow leaves of black birch were especially pleasing as the sun's rays passed through and illuminated them like shards of stained glass. To the west are power lines that carry electricity south from the power plant.

After crossing Rock Oak Ramble cart road, follow Rose Ledge Trail uphill. Here especially notice the thin, stacked layers that make up the gneiss bedrock. Brown and dry, leafy lichens cling tightly to the rocks and absorb moisture during rains, turning green. There is another partially screened view toward the west coming up, but more evocative are the views back down the trail as you ascend. Your attention may be diverted to something closer at hand—at five inches long, black-throated blue warblers move through the foliage in search of moth larvae and other insects. These lovely summer residents must fatten up for their long migration to the tropics. The female, in contrast to the strikingly attired male, is a non-descript brown with a bright white wing patch.

As you reach the sunny fringes of the crest, the views become truly spectacular to the west and north—Mt. Greylock in the Berkshires and Mt. Haystack in Vermont are visible on a clear day. This is a fine spot for lunch and a great excuse—if you need one—simply to sit and enjoy the wonderful scenery. Such a perch is also an ideal site, especially in fall, to scan for raptors—hawks, vultures, and ravens. A flock of seven ravens—doing a lot more gliding than crows would have—passed by, as did a Cooper's hawk when we were there. The rock of Rose Ledge has a pink hue, and that perhaps is reason enough for this formation's name.

After leaving the vista point continue on Rose Ledge Trail past the Lower Ledge Foot Trail junction on the right, which goes downhill. Many low, flat ledge outcrops are covered by leafy lichens and surrounded by blueberries and oaks. Blueberries do well in the shallow, acidic soils and provide tasty berries for both wildlife and humans in August. Coarse bracken fern becomes more common as you proceed, and wintergreen is abundant. The trail descends gradually, passing knee-high patches of light-green sheep laurel. Although not nearly as imposing as its larger relative, mountain laurel, sheep laurel's smaller flowers—which also bloom in June—are a more intense pink. Laurels possess flowers with ingenious devices for depositing pollen on visiting insects. Spring-loaded stamens pop free, hitting the unwitting pollinator with a dose of pollen as it clambers about the blossom.

Upon reaching the Hill 'n' Dale cart road turn right. You soon reach the **T** intersection with 10th Mountain cart road, which is fairly level, wide, and manicured. Turn left and walk through oak woods to the intersection with Tooleybush Turnpike. Turn right and go uphill slightly to cross the paved Reservoir Road loop and walk to the observation platform overlooking the reservoir. Although this is the 1,100-foot summit of Northfield Mountain, the level plateau's setting belies the fact that you've climbed 817 vertical feet since leaving the visitor center. The southwestern end of the reservoir, its shores largely unvegetated, may host visiting common loons and bald eagles in spring and fall. Our best bird sighting here on the October trek was an American kestrel (formerly sparrow hawk), whose diet consists primarily of insects and mice.

To return, retrace your steps back down Ledge Trail to Lower Ledge Trail on the left. Just before the junction are two tiny ponds on the left side of the cart road—these pools may support breeding salamanders and wood frogs in early spring. Proceed downhill on Lower Ledge Trail past outcrops of layered gneiss bedrock. Some of the ledges are between 15 and 25 feet in height. Pass an old quarry site, left, with a pit some 20 feet across; this too might be a vernal pool. As you continue along the trail, the ledges become more impressive—eventually reaching a height of 50 or 60 feet. We encountered quite a large group of young rock climbers literally being "taught the ropes" by older, more experienced instructors. We watched their efforts with some fascination. This location was apparently almost directly below where we had stopped for lunch atop the ledges.

Horizontally bedded ledges of granitic gneiss are dominant features along the trail.

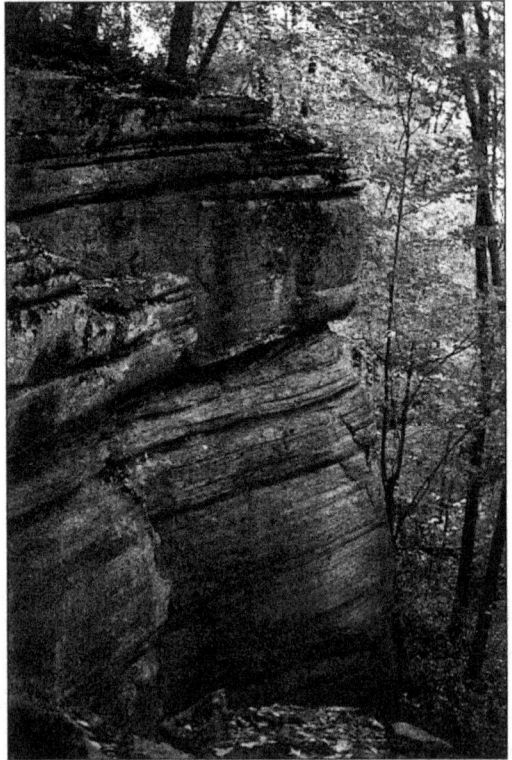

From the trail are nice, partially screened views through the trees of the formidable layer-cake rock wall. Fissured as they are with crevices, the outcroppings provide ideal denning sites for porcupines, which characteristically seek shelter in such locations. These plump rodents do not hibernate but instead gnaw the nutritious cambium, or inner bark, from trees during the winter months. Though they are despised by some as destroyers of timber, shade, and fruit trees, I unabashedly include porcupines among my favorite woodland creatures. They pose little real threat to the vast forested landscape of western Massachusetts.

The trail parallels the cliffs for quite a distance. Cross Yellowjacket Pass cart road. The orange-blazed Lower Ledge Trail descends through forest of oak and birch. Some of the red oaks are quite imposing. Pass into noticeably younger woodland of birch and maple, almost all the trees having a diameter of about seven inches—indicating a virtual clearcut in the fairly recent past. A few very large trees were spared—perhaps to provide shade for livestock; one red oak's blackish trunk is all of three feet in diameter.

After descending most of the way, walk a little bit uphill and through a stand of young white pines, paralleling the power-line cut you spied from above. The trail turns left and enters the cleared strip, and the edge of the cut provides an opportunity for a mostly unobstructed view of wooded hills and cornfields. After a brief ramble in the sun, re-enter the woods and pass through a hemlock stand where small flocks of three-and-one-half-inch-long golden-crowned kinglets search for minute insect prey in spring and fall. Males possess a central orange crown stripe, whereas females sport a lemon-yellow one. When you reach the junction with Ledge Trail, turn left and follow it downhill back to the visitor center.

Getting There

Take I-91 north to Route 2 east (Exit 27) in Greenfield. Follow Route 2 east for 4.6 miles to Route 63. From the intersection of Routes 2 and 63, travel north on Route 63 for 5.3 miles to the paved entrance road on the right, just before a cemetery on the same side. Follow the entrance road for 0.15 mile to the large public parking area just northeast of the visitor center. Trails are open every day, except during mud season in March and early April (call the visitor center for exact dates).

The center is open 9:00 A.M. to 5:00 P.M., Wednesday through Sunday, April through November, and daily during winter for cross-country skiing. Contact the center at 413-659-3713 for holiday schedule and hours.

No admission fees for hiking; there is a charge for cross-country skiing—rental skis and snowshoes are available. Rest rooms on the lower level of the visitor center; a pit toilet is at the trailhead. Picnic area is located at visitor center. Public programs are conducted throughout the year and many require preregistration. Mountain-biking (cart roads only—all bikers must register), rock climbing, orienteering, horseback riding, and hunting (except in no-hunting zone in the lower section of the trail system) are permitted. Dogs must be leashed at all times.

—R.L.

Erving State Forest

24

Erving/Warwick/Orange
4,479 acres

❖ 0.9 mile

❖ 1.5 hours

❖ easy

Imagine my surprise when I quite unexpectedly came upon a stunning view of Mt. Monadnock—its triangular mass rearing up stalwartly above the forested ridges. Even though more than 20 miles distant, the naked summit of this well-known peak seemed almost touchable.

This property possesses few bona fide hiking trails; a short, easy loop trail leads up a modest slope through a lovely hardwood forest with a shrub layer of thick mountain laurel and hobblebush. The views from an unnamed hilltop are very nice, and just beyond this vantage point you emerge into a small clearing with the stunning beauty of Monadnock looming in the distance. Dense forests of birch, maple, oak, and hemlock cover the hills and valleys, and Laurel Lake provides an interesting contrast. A fascinating community of bog plants exists at the far west end of the lake, where an active beaver lodge also allows close inspection.

After parking at the large paved lot just beyond the contact station on Laurel Lake Road, walk back up past the contact station (approximately 35 feet) to the trailhead, left. Follow the path into the hemlock forest opposite the lake. Cross a bubbling brook on a small, wooden roofed-over bridge. The woods are characteristically rocky, with many moss-covered boulders. Three-inch-long two-lined salamanders spend the daylight hours safely beneath flat stones along the brook margins, while more numerous red-backed salamanders can be found under rotting logs in moist woods.

Beyond the hemlocks the character of the forest changes. Increased sunlight supports tiny forests of princess pine (only inches high) on the forest floor, thick-leaved bracken fern, and the ground-hugging light-green leaves of trailing arbutus (also known as mayflower), the Massachusetts state flower. This species, with its white flowers and evergreen leaves, is quite common in the sunny margins along the path. A profusion of **mountain laurel** forms the understory. Its white-pink flowers add pleasing color in early summer, and the thick, shiny evergreen leaves offset the stark grays and browns of the winter woods.

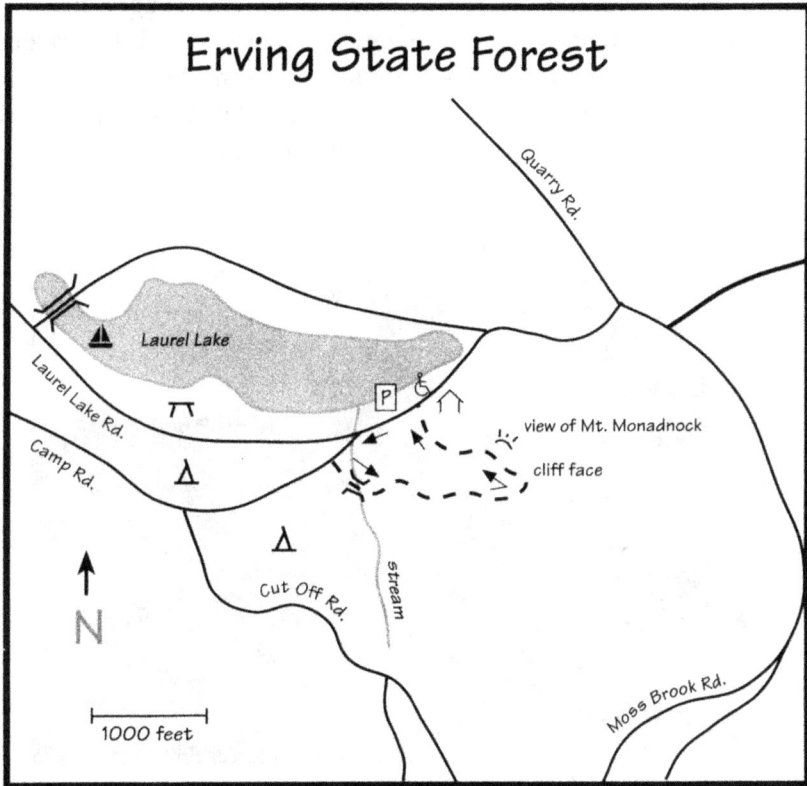

Erving State Forest

On the summit you'll find a few pitch pine. This tree often displays a picturesque appearance—gnarled and windblown. Its stiff needles, in bundles of three, sometimes grow directly from the trunk, distinguishing it from the more common white pine, which has five soft needles. Both grow on this exposed perch and combine to create a wonderful perfume. Rock-loving common polypody fern caps some boulders, and fleshy, evergreen marginal wood fern also favors these rocky sites. Silvery-green reindeer moss and other slow-growing, persevering lichens have colonized the bare rock. There is also a small patch of sheep laurel (said to be poisonous to sheep), decidedly shorter than its larger relative. Linger for the views of oak woods to the south; this and the next vista point are perfect for snack or lunch breaks.

Watch for migrant hawks passing overhead in September and October, or perhaps a common raven. I always feel fortunate to see and hear one of these impressive big, black birds. Fully four times the weight of the more familiar crow, ravens to me epitomize wildness. Their guttural croak speaks of vast, unbroken reaches of forest, steep cliffs, and rugged mountains. Absent from the commonwealth for some 100 years until 1983, ravens are again colonizing the maturing woodlands of western Massachusetts, and I for one am thankful. The virtual clearing of the state's forests for agriculture eliminated or greatly reduced woodland species, including the raven.

Lying beyond miles of nearly unbroken forest, the pyramidal mass of Mt. Monadnock looms into view as you round a curve in the trail.

Continue on down the trail through more hardwoods, including clumps of American chestnut (once a dominant tree until the chestnut blight of the 1930s made the species all but extinct), to the aforementioned view of Mt. Monadnock, 22 miles away to the northeast (as the raven flies).

Add some splendid fall foliage and you have the ingredients for wonderful photo opportunities. Behind you to the left is the broken cliff face, its outline softened by red maples and other plants.

To return to the parking lot and your car, continue on the gradually descending trail. In late summer and fall, the bright red berries of both creeping partridgeberry (small, paired, rounded leaves) and wintergreen (three leaves) dot the forest floor. Wintergreen contains a fragrant oil used for flavoring. White-breasted nuthatch and brown creeper diligently search bark crevices for insects and their eggs. Nuthatches generally descend trees while creepers ascend them. Eastern chipmunks scurry across the ground, sometimes giving a long series of high chirps that sound remarkably bird-like. Red squirrels, meanwhile, scamper from tree to tree recovering pine cones they've cut with their sharp incisors and caching the booty for later use. Both are hunted by coyotes—look for their hair-and-bone-filled scat along the trail.

At the terminus of the trail, walk down steps with railings to Laurel Lake Road. Turn left and walk approximately 250 feet back to the parking area and your vehicle. You might want to explore briefly the shore of Laurel Lake and scan the surface for waterfowl before leaving. A number of privately owned cabins are situated along the opposite shoreline.

By driving west on Laurel Lake Road, back the way you came, you'll reach the public boat ramp in 0.6 mile on the right. You may wish to park here and walk the short distance to the west end of the lake, where the bog vegetation and beaver pond are located. Wetland shrubs including bright-red-berried winterberry line this causeway. It's a native holly that loses its leaves in fall. On the left, notice a medium-sized beaver lodge against the opposite shore. In fall the industrious rodents add large quantities of mud from the lake bottom to the structure, insulating it against the elements. I also saw a dozen eastern painted turtles, our most common turtle species, basking in the bright sunlight of an early-October day here. They seemed to be soaking up sunlight before wintering at the bottom of the pond— their metabolic processes slowed to a point just adequate to sustain life.

A thick growth of sphagnum moss (the source of peat moss) borders the shoreline and the tiny islets. Bullhead lily leaves float on the surface, while the acid-soil shrubs **leatherleaf** and **sweet gale** grow in the developing bog—adding their decaying leaves to the mix. Within this moisture-rich yet nutrient-poor substrate thrive plants that have adapted by supplementing their diets with insects. **Pitcher plants**—almost otherworldly in their appearance—grow in clumps along the water's edge, trapping insects that wander down their open gullets. Stiff, downward-pointing bristles and sweet secretions lead the bugs in but prevent their escape. Enzymes dissolve them and the plant absorbs the goodies. This is one of the most accessible places to see these fascinating plants.

Getting There

From the intersection of Route 2 (the Mohawk Trail) and North Street in Erving (if coming from the east), Church Street (if arriving from the west—look for a state forest sign just before the fire station on the left), travel north on North Street (a right turn if coming from the east) to Swamp Road on the right. Turn onto Swamp Road, cross the brook, and follow the road northeast into the state forest. It is 1.7 miles from Route 2 to the state forest boundary. This road later becomes Laurel Lake Road, passes the entrance to the campground on the right, and in another 1.2 miles brings you to the contact station and parking area just beyond it on the left.

Hours are sunrise to sunset, unless you're camping. Parking fee is two dollars per vehicle. Roadside parking is prohibited. A modern brick rest room building (handicapped accessible) is located adjacent to the parking area and is open during the summer months. Swimming is allowed and changing houses are available. A pit toilet near the beach is also wheelchair accessible. Fishing is a popular activity on Laurel Lake.

—R.L.

25 Wendell State Forest

Wendell
7,557 acres

❖ 1.4 miles

❖ 2 hours

❖ easy

The largest beaver lodge I have seen in Massachusetts sits near the western shore of Ruggles Pond in the southwestern portion of Wendell State Forest. It must be 20 feet across at the waterline and eight feet high. The trail around the pond allows views from fairly close range. I did just that on an easy walk one bright early-October day—taking several photos of the lodge with a backdrop of fiery red maple foliage.

After parking in the lot at the picnic area on the north side of the road (opposite the pond), cross the road and walk to steps leading up into another picnic area along the west shore of Ruggles Pond. Cathedral white pines tower above the picnic tables. Follow the trail through the picnic area and come to a pavilion and playing fields on the right. Continue left along the pond shore. Blue plastic markers on the trunks and more recent white-painted blazes mark the trail.

Notice that the margins of the pond are spongy—thick with **sphagnum moss** which can hold 250 times its own weight in water. You are standing, in effect, on a waterlogged, floating mat of vegetation—a bog that will eventually increase its area concentrically until it covers the entire pond surface. Look closely to see a true bog plant—**American cranberry**—growing amid the sphagnum. Cranberry is a creeping plant with tiny, oblong, shiny green leaves. The fruits are small, red, and astringent—very high in vitamin C. Watch your footing and don't tramp around too much in this fragile bog environment, lest you damage it.

The **massive beaver lodge** is now close at hand. Its shape is pyramidal and it must weigh tons. Perched on branches at one end of the lodge during my visit was a rascally looking female belted kingfisher in the process of swallowing a small, silvery fish. Two grayish-brown eastern phoebes occupied the opposite end. Through my binoculars, I watched as one phoebe opportunistically picked an insect out of a spider web on top of the lodge.

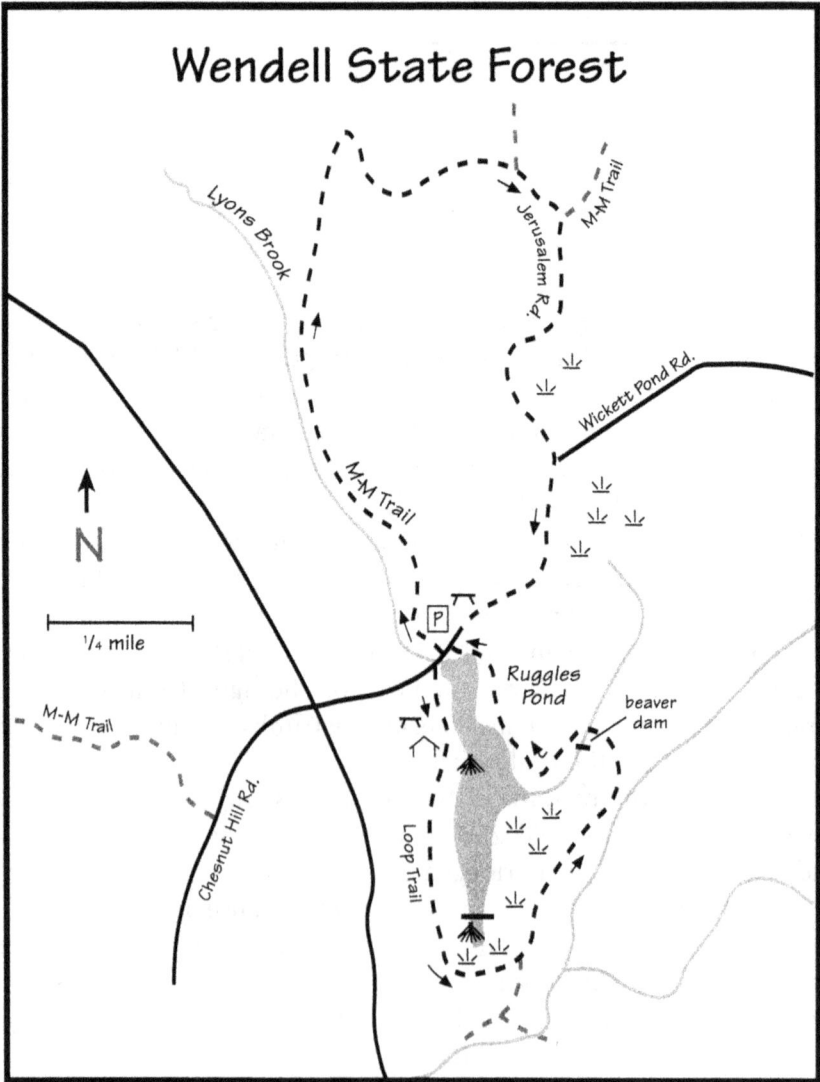

Wendell State Forest

Lyons Brook

Jerusalem Rd.

M-M Trail

Wickett Pond Rd.

N

¼ mile

M-M Trail

M-M Trail

Chesnut Hill Rd.

P

Ruggles Pond

beaver dam

Loop Trail

I imagined that inside the safety of their dark lodge, a beaver family rested. Perhaps two six-month-old kits lay with bodies curled together, touching their mother. The kits and their 50-pound parents, as well as two older siblings born 18 months ago, shared the big lodge. Much of each day now was spent cutting saplings and larger trees—mostly maple and birch—to reinforce the lodge and augment the family's winter larder. Under the cover of darkness, small trees were quickly cut and dragged into the water, where the nutritious inner bark was consumed. Debarked twigs were transported in the animal's mouth to strengthen the lodge walls, along with hundreds of pounds of rich, black mud brought up from the pond bottom by the beaver's front paws. Other unpeeled branches would be floated and forcibly jammed into the pond bottom, there to remain available under the ice until hunger prompted their retrieval.

Returning to the trail, swing away from the water. On this higher ground grow red maple, red oak, and considerable sheep laurel. Highbush blueberry is common too. A bit farther along, the much larger mountain laurel becomes common and a few large gneiss boulders dot the woodland floor. White pine then joins the mix of tree species; a few are large. On my visit, one fallen specimen—two and one half feet thick—had recently been cleared from the trail. The clean chain-saw cut revealed 90 growth rings; the last 30 were tightly packed—probably owing to competition with surrounding trees in the maturing forest.

At the southwest end of the pond the trail skirts a shrub swamp. Another beaver lodge is located here, and the multiplying beaver population has now dammed the entire width of Ruggles Pond. Follow the trail over a rocky area and then across a small stream that feeds Ruggles Pond—cross the wet spots on bog bridges. This area was loaded with robins during my early-October walk. Apparently the flock was feeding on the abundant winterberries and other foods to be had here. Go left when the trail splits. Cross a bog bridge and head toward the pond. To the left is a stand of white pines through whose swaying boughs the autumn winds blow to make that pleasant *whooshing* sound.

The trail skirts the shrub swamp again, and here a big black cherry tree, cut all the way around by beavers, still stands upright—at least for the time being. Cross more bog bridges and a gurgling brook with two large fallen trees across it—a hemlock and an oak. In this wet, rocky area eastern hemlocks become more prevalent. Soon the trail nears the pond with nice views of the water to the left.

While I was here, the melancholy screams of a **red-shouldered hawk** came to my ears. This large raptor, which feeds largely on reptiles and amphibians, is quite uncommon and found primarily in swamp habitats like this. A thick growth of two-foot-tall leatherleaf shrubs rings the pond margin. The thick leaves have undersides dotted with numerous tiny, cinnamon-brown scales. A luxuriant growth of emergent aquatic vegetation fills the lake. The leaves of yellow pond lily and the smaller water shield float on the calm surface. Beaver love to eat the fleshy roots of waterlilies and readily dig them up.

An impressive beaver lodge sits along the western shore of Ruggles Pond.

This is fine amphibian habitat too. Green frogs, spring peepers, and red-spotted newts are present. Listen for the amusing and distinctive plucked-banjo-string call of the green frog emanating from the pond, especially in summer. Frogs have existed for 350 million years, but scientists have noticed dramatic worldwide population decreases over the past decade. Several theories have been put forth and many causes may yet be found to explain this phenomenon. Painted turtles bask on logs in the pond well into fall. Like other turtles, they come ashore in late spring or early summer to lay their eggs in sandy, well-drained soils. The leathery eggs, if not found by raccoons or other predators, usually hatch in late summer. Temperatures within the nest determine whether all the embryos will develop into males or females!

After leaving the shoreline, you move away from the pond and enter a hemlock/white pine grove. The soils are saturated here, and the shallow-rooted hemlocks are easily toppled by wind. Over time this creates a **pit-and-mound topography**—pits left where the root mass of a hemlock was torn from the earth and next to it a mound created by the now decomposed roots and the soil once held in their grasp.

Follow the trail onto higher ground and cross a small knoll covered with hemlock and gray birch. Impish ruby-crowned kinglets, which nest farther north, stop off here twice each year, spring and fall. Kinglets are somewhat hyperactive and travel in small flocks. The male's red topknot is seldom visible. Descend from the knoll and walk along a hillside of hemlock on the right. The woods are again dotted with granitic gneiss boulders covered with the leafy brown lichens commonly known as rock tripe.

Follow the path sharply to the left and cross over stones under which flows another stream feeding Ruggles Pond. Even though you won't see the water, the sound of it beneath the stones is easily heard. A low beaver dam has backed the water up on your left. The trail turns sharply left again and enters red maple/white pine forest. Fallen needles form a soft, thick, comfortable cushion for your feet. Walk the short path to the water's edge. Small red dragonflies and large green darners hunt for mosquitoes and other flying insects and bask on rocks and logs with gauzy wings extended.

The main trail continues through a grove of large white pines. Look out across the pond toward the far shore and the large beaver lodge. Log bridges cover some wet spots. The trail follows the shoreline fairly closely back through pine/oak woodland to the public beach. Check the sand here for tracks of raccoon, opossum, Canada goose, and other wildlife. The picnic area and parking are across the road.

There are many other scenic trails in Wendell State Forest, including a portion of the Metacomet-Monadnock Trail (blazed with white rectangles). One very nice walk of about two miles takes you from the same parking area north and downhill along beautiful, cascading Lyons Brook. It then swings right, through attractive forest of northern hardwoods to Jerusalem Road. Across this road stands an imposing sheer cliff. From there follow the road south and west back to your car; turn right at the intersection with Wickett Pond Road.

Getting There

From Route 2 in Greenfield, drive 10.0 miles east and cross the Connecticut River over the French King Bridge. Continue east (south) on Route 2 for 1.0 mile to Route 63 in Millers Falls. Turn right onto Route 63 and follow it west and south across the Millers River for 0.7 mile. Turn right at the intersection (still Route 63) and drive west for 0.1 mile to where Route 63 bears left. Continue south for 0.3 mile on Route 63 to Highland Avenue on the left. Follow Highland Avenue for 0.5 mile to Wendell Road and turn right (a bridge that is out here necessitates this somewhat circuitous route). Follow Wendell Road for 3.1 miles to Chestnut Hill Road and turn left (forest headquarters are on your left). From the state forest entrance, drive 0.3 mile to the picnic area and parking on the left.

Hours are 10:00 A.M. to 4:00 P.M. weekdays, 10:00 A.M. to 5:30 P.M. weekends; summer (Memorial Day to Labor Day) hours are 8:00 A.M. to 7:30 P.M. daily. Parking fee is two dollars per car in summer; free in winter. Pit toilets and drinking water are available at the picnic area. Horses, bicycles, and snowmobiles are allowed on unpaved roads. Hunting is prohibited in day-use area.

—R.L.

26 Mt. Sugarloaf State Reservation

South Deerfield
532 acres

❖ 2.2 miles

❖ 1.5–2 hours

❖ moderate (steep section)

Lying parallel to the west bank of the Connecticut River at the southern terminus of the Pocumtuck Ridge is South Sugarloaf Mountain—a sandstone hill accessible both by automobile and on foot. The rust-colored mound lies along Route 116, only a mile east of I-91. Most visitors drive to the summit to enjoy the fine views of the broad Connecticut Valley and the Mt. Tom and Holyoke ranges, but the short (and in places steep) ascent on foot makes the vistas far more rewarding. True, the top is developed with paved parking, picnic area, and pavilion, and a multilevel observation building with modern restroom facilities, but these creature comforts may seem a just reward for the exertion. For a short hike to a great view, Mt. Sugarloaf State Reservation is hard to beat.

Aptly named, South Sugarloaf is composed of **tightly cemented sand (quartz grains) and pebbles** and shaped roughly like a loaf of bread (oddly, it was never glaciated). South Sugarloaf stands 652 feet above sea level, not enough to make your ears pop but certainly a fine perch from which to survey the countryside.

From the sandy parking lot, follow the path (red and blue blazes) beneath the large spruce tree to the power-line right of way and pass by a small cement blockhouse. Enter the woodland and walk between two sizable white oaks; the right one grew at an acute angle initially, before turning skyward. At the **Y** split, bear right to re-enter the power-line corridor. The first of several granite state forest boundary markers stands adjacent to the trail. The power-line cut is an artificial meadow habitat in what would otherwise be deciduous woodland. In late summer, the rusty-colored path leads through blooming white wood aster, tall goldenrod, and white snakeroot.

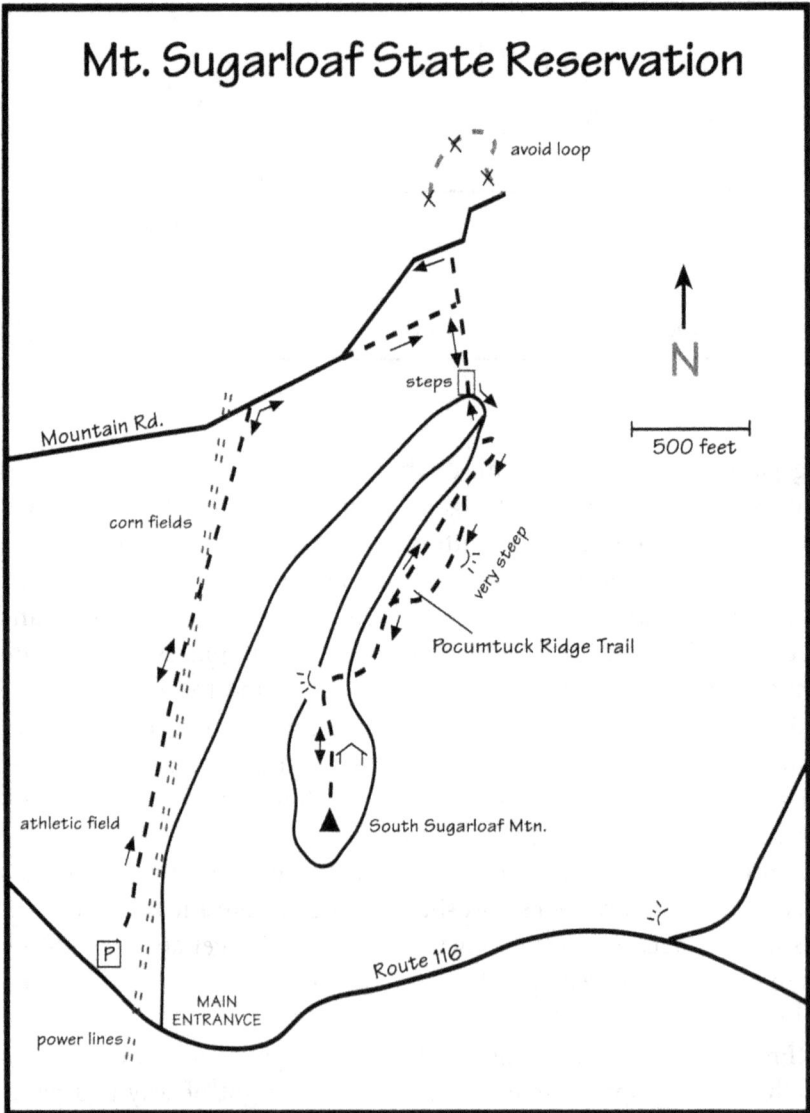

Mt. Sugarloaf State Reservation

avoid loop

N

500 feet

steps

Mountain Rd.

corn fields

very steep

Pocumtuck Ridge Trail

athletic field

South Sugarloaf Mtn.

P

MAIN
ENTRANVCE

Route 116

power lines

Before long turn right and re-enter forest; red blazes decorate some trees. The mountain rises rather steeply on your right. You soon reach the intersection with the extension of Mountain Road. Turn right to begin a gradual ascent through woods of birch and beech. The larger and higher mass of North Sugarloaf looms nearby on the left. Some of the black birches and oaks here are quite large. Sadly, sprouts and small trees are all that is left of the **American chestnut**, a former dominant tree species in these woodlands. The tree was all but eradicated by the chestnut blight in the 1930s. Chestnut leaves resemble those of beech but are much longer and more strongly toothed. A fungus attacks the plumbing system of nearly all of today's chestnuts before they can mature and flower, and thus regeneration of this once noble tree is limited to sprouting from old stumps. Hay-scented, Christmas, and evergreen wood fern constitute an attractive green layer between the shrubs.

Pass another small granite boundary marker, left, and continue straight. When the trail splits a short distance farther, you have a choice; both trails meet the old carriage road that leads to the auto road and summit. The right path is more eroded, exposing sandstone in places, and a bit shorter. The red-blazed right fork continues up under red oak; black, gray, and white birch; American beech; and red maple. Mountain laurel and blue-berried maple-leaf viburnum dominate the shrub layer. Striped wintergreen, pink lady's slippers, and wintergreen bloom here in late spring, while scarlet tanagers and red-breasted grosbeaks nest in the tall trees. At the old carriage road turn right and ascend for about 200 yards along a moss-covered bank on the left, where trailing arbutus (mayflower) grows, to a series of steep steps leading up to a hairpin curve in the summit road.

Step over the barrier and walk left along the road to where it forks. Enter the left, down only a portion of the road (note the Do Not Enter sign). The blue-blazed Pocumtuck Ridge Trail begins at the far end of the guardrail, turns right immediately, and ascends the hill by way of a some-times steep switchback. You emerge from a shady, damp hemlock grove into the light and warmth of a relatively dry oak hillside that offers screened views of the Connecticut River. A bit farther, take the left fork at the top of the hill toward the vista point (both go to the lower parking area). Lowbush blueberry is abundant in these acidic soils, and the raucous cries of acorn-eating blue jays fill the air. **Expansive southerly views** of the agriculturally rich Connecticut River Valley and ranges beyond soon appear. Watch for the blooming yellow trumpets of false foxglove in late summer just before arriving at an excellent vista point safeguarded by chain-link fencing. Follow the trail back into the oak/hickory woodland, level out, and arrive at the lower parking area, where portable toilets are located. From here it's just a few steps along the auto road (beware of traffic) to the picnic area on the summit—the perfect place for lunch or a snack.

Red and white oaks and red and white pines are the summit's dominant trees. The **stone observation tower** has three levels, each higher one affording a slightly better view of the broad, winding Connecticut River;

Wooded ridges rise beyond the fertile fields and settlements of the Connecticut River Valley as you gaze westward.

Amherst and the University of Massachusetts campus; and the Holyoke and Mt. Tom Ranges in their entirety in the far distance. You may even be able to make out the summit house on Mt. Holyoke, 16 miles away (see p. 197). From the top level a nearly 360-degree view is possible. If the day is a sunny one in September or early October, watch for butterflies, including southbound monarchs, and, of course, keep a lookout for migrant hawks. A photo exhibit at the tower's base relates the story of Granville Wardell's summit house, constructed in 1864 and destroyed by fire in 1966.

To return to your vehicle, retrace the same route. The lower portion of the steep, switchbacked trail can be tricky on descent. Alternatively, walk down the auto road to the hairpin curve and pick up the trail there. At the lower end of the old carriage road you may alter the route slightly by selecting the second (more level) path toward Mountain Road (turn left).

Getting There

From I-91 northbound, take Exit 24 (South Deerfield) and travel 1.1 miles on Route 116 south to an intersection just before the main entrance to the reservation, on your left. Turn left, pass the main entrance (auto road to the summit), and turn right instead, into the sandy parking area.

Hours are sunrise to sunset. No admission fee. Auto-road gates are locked at sunset. Horseback riding is allowed on woods roads. Motorized vehicles are prohibited except on paved road.

—R.L.

27 High Ledges Wildlife Sanctuary

Shelburne

570 acres

❖ 1.7 miles

❖ 2.5 hours

❖ moderate

Perched atop an exposed outcrop 1,000 feet above the scenic Deerfield River valley, High Ledges Wildlife Sanctuary on Massaemett Mountain offers magnificent views and wonderful wildlife-observation opportunities. On a clear day you can see the state's highest peak, Mt. Greylock, 25 miles to the west. Rocky woodlands of oak, birch, maple, and hemlock clothe the broad, mostly level summit. Old fields bordered by stone walls, brooks, and active beaver ponds add variety and interest to this picturesque and biologically diverse property. Established through land gifts to the Massachusetts Audubon Society in 1970 and 1976 by Ellsworth and Mary Bernard, the society continues to own and manage the property as an unstaffed sanctuary open to the public. Three additional parcels were added in the early 1990s, bringing the total acreage to 570.

The sanctuary's trail system is fairly extensive and quite well maintained, and it enables the visitor to enjoy the full variety of fascinating natural community types present. A map and compass are helpful, however. The recommended loop trail described below includes Lady's slipper and Waterthrush Trails. This loop will take you through a wide variety of habitats, including open fields, sunny ledges, birch groves, and an orchid swamp.

After stopping in the informal grassy parking area at the terminus of the entrance road, take a few minutes to explore the lovely open fields. On a sunny summer day butterflies are common (I noted tiger swallowtail, spring azure, monarch, inornate ringlet, and pearl crescent, to name a few), and bluebirds and tree swallows nest (May through August) in the wooden nesting boxes. The **eastern bluebird**, so beloved by many people, has made a heartening comeback over the past several decades, thanks in part to the installation of nest boxes like these. In this part of its range, the beautiful sky-blue, brick-orange, and white male and his duller mate usually raise two broods of three to five young over the course of the breeding season.

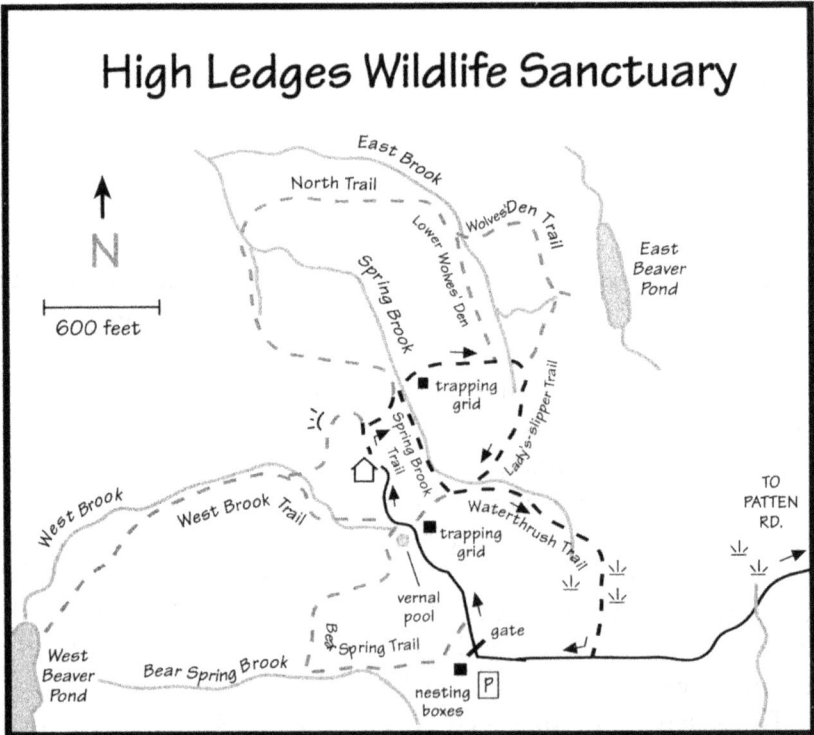

High Ledges Wildlife Sanctuary

To begin, proceed north around the gate and follow the road through a meadow regenerating to red maple, black cherry, and white birch. These pioneering species need large amounts of sunlight to prosper. Meadowsweet, lowbush blueberry, and thorny red and black raspberry canes—studded with white flowers in late spring and early summer—fill the area. Lichen-covered stone walls mark old pasture boundaries as you walk gradually downhill to a small **vernal pool** on your left, just off the road. The pool's water may be thick with the little black tadpoles of wood frogs. Vernal pools such as this are essential for the breeding success of wood frogs and Jefferson and spotted salamanders. Indeed, these creatures can breed nowhere else, and a primordial spectacle is played out each spring as the first rains bring the creatures out of their winter dormancy and urge them on to this, their ancestral breeding pool.

Return to the road and continue walking northwestward, this time uphill. Soon a cottage on the ledges will come into view. Flaky-barked red pines grow on the **promontory of bare rock** overlooking the valley. Settle down here for at least a few minutes to drink in the sublime panorama. Use caution, as the drop-off is abrupt and there are no railings to safeguard you! The towns of Shelburne Falls and Buckland lie close at hand, southwest on the banks of the Deerfield River, a major tributary of the Connecticut. Most of what you'll see between here and Mt. Greylock (elevation 3,491 feet) is covered in forest of varying shades of green. The 1989 landslide on Grey-lock's east face is still visible, even without binoculars. Listen for the evocative, flutelike songs of hermit thrushes and the sweet trill of the gray (above) and white (below) dark-eyed junco. The junco, usually more a bird of northern forests, apparently finds the 1,450-foot elevation and climate here to its liking.

Continue walking northward along the escarpment through thick growths of shiny-leafed mountain laurel that harbor the well-concealed nests of black-throated blue warblers to the beginning of Lady's Slipper Trail. Blue disks on tree trunks mark the trail (yellow disks on the opposite side of the trees signify that you are returning toward the trailhead). After a short distance heading downhill on a moderately steep trail, you come to a four-way intersection. North Trail goes left and Spring Brook Trail (red blazes) goes right. Continue straight on Lady's Slipper Trail across Spring Brook. Trail maps are affixed to tree trunks at most trail intersections, and small signboards on the trees also help you find your way.

On the right is a small-mammal live-trapping grid, the second of three located on the property. They are part of ongoing field studies designed to shed more light on the abundance and diversity of small mammals at High Ledges. The results of this and other research are used by the Massachusetts Audubon Society to craft an ecological management plan that will safeguard the interesting and sensitive natural communities while also allowing nonconsumptive use of the sanctuary by the public. One of the creatures found by using this technique was the big-eyed, nocturnal southern flying squirrel—not an animal you are likely to see during a daytime ramble.

Follow the trail eastward past the junction with Wolves' Den Trail (left), cross another brook and merge left with Gentian Swamp Trail. Here

Lady's Slipper Trail turns sharply south, right. Wonderful displays of **wild-flowers** are one of the highlights of High Ledges. In late spring watch for the blossoms of red columbine, whose drooping bells have five curved spurs, Canada mayflower; false Solomon's seal; and wild ginger, which hides its ill-scented, liver-red flowers under the leaf litter where beetles are sure to find and pollinate them. As you continue along, summer bird song, scampering eastern chipmunks, and red squirrels will lead you to the intersection with Waterthrush Trail at a damp, fern-covered spot. Among the nesting woodland birds you may see and hear along the way are the ovenbird (its loud *teacher, teacher, teacher* refrain is unmistakable) and the great crested flycatcher (a cavity nester with a yellow breast and rusty tail). In the wetland pockets look for Canada warbler, common yellowthroat (the male has a black mask), and chestnut-sided warbler.

Mt. Greylock, the state's highest peak, is visible through red pine boughs from the ledges, 1,000 feet above the Deerfield River.

Turn left onto Waterthrush Trail and follow it downstream along Spring Brook in an easterly direction to an orchid swamp, on the left where the trail turns abruptly right (southward). Golden ragwort is a tall composite with flowers the color of egg yolks. It favors wet ground and you'll find it blooming here in late spring and early summer. Continue south along the edge of the swamp, emerging into the sunny fields that red foxes and deer frequent at twilight. Turn right at the entry road and follow it for a distance of about 1,000 feet back to the trailhead and your vehicle.

Getting There

From the Greenfield rotary on Route 2 (also known as the Mohawk Trail), travel west for 5.4 miles into Shelburne and Little Mohawk Road on the right. Look for the tall white church steeple ahead on the right; watch also for signs to Davenport Maple Farm/Springbrook Campground. Turn right (north) onto Little Mohawk Road and follow it for 1.3 miles, turning left onto Patten Road at the large map sign. Follow Patten Road for just over 1.1 miles to a dirt road on the left where a small sign for the sanctuary is located. Note the stone wall to the right of the drive. Follow the dirt road for 0.4 mile to the parking area and trailhead just before the metal gate.

Hours are dawn to dusk; sanctuary road is closed winter and early spring. Limited parking. No rest rooms. Picking of flowers or fruit is strictly prohibited.

—R.L.

28 Bear Swamp Reservation

Ashfield
284 acres

❖ 2.5 miles

❖ 2.5 hours

❖ moderate

The rocky woodlands of Bear Swamp Reservation shelter seemingly incongruous stone walls, or, more accurately, stone fences—built some 150 years ago by farmers to mark property lines and confine livestock. This attractive, little-visited property is blessed with an abundance of spring wildflowers as well as a wide range of wildlife. It beckons nature-lovers to spend a few hours or a whole day enjoying nature's diversity.

You'll follow mostly well-marked trails through rich woodlands that are home to tiny short-tailed shrews, coyotes, and black-throated blue warblers; across fast-flowing brooks; past lichen-covered ledges and outcrops where porcupines find safe haven; and along beaver ponds hosting mink, dragonflies, red-spotted newts, painted turtles, and tree swallows. From Beaver Brook Trail you'll get a fairly close look at a small, active beaver lodge.

Lying for the most part above 1,500 feet, this property is defined by north-south trending ridges of metamorphic rock hundreds of millions of years old. More recently it was sculpted by ice as well. Alternating with the rocky folds are wet pockets—shrub swamps, beaver ponds, and ephemeral vernal pools. The cool, moist climate has favored the vigorous growth of northern hardwoods—birch, beech, and maple—as well as hemlock on the north-facing slopes. Red spruce, a boreal tree, imparts a somewhat wild, northern feel to the place.

The loop combination of Beaver Brook Trail to Fern Glade Trail to Bear Swamp Road to North-South Trail and finally to Lookout Trail will enable you to traverse communities from shrub swamps to forested ravines. These trails climb and descend several modest ridges with lookouts to the pond, cross babbling brooks, skirt a shrub swamp filled with lovely cinnamon ferns, and return to the beaver pond shore.

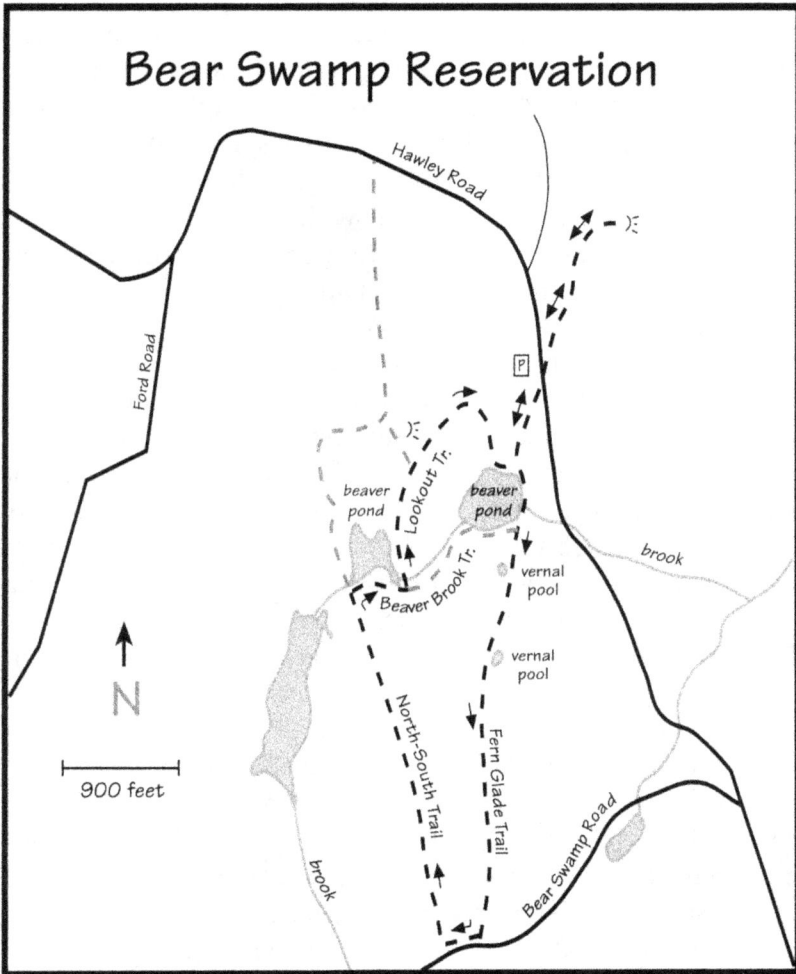

After parking along Hawley Road, proceed up Beaver Brook Trail and into the forest, past posts designed to deny entry to motor vehicles. The rather wide path (marked with painted white triangles and round green plastic disks) leads up through eastern hemlock, yellow birch, American beech, sugar maple, black birch, and moisture-tolerant white ash. Indian cucumber-root, creeping partridgeberry, false Solomon's seal, and wild sarsaparilla are the most abundant flowering herbs. You also see heart-leafed hobblebush and shiny, evergreen mountain laurel. Shortly, the trail crosses a small stream. Follow the trail to the left (this is the junction of Beaver Brook and Lookout Trails). You'll return to this spot later as you follow Lookout Trail back to close the loop.

Beaver Brook Trail passes stone walls to the right (just before crossing the pond's rock-lined outlet stream) and soon reaches the beaver pond— also on the right. A slight detour takes you to the shore, where, around to the right, you'll be able to glimpse an active beaver lodge situated along the edge of a small rocky island dotted with **red spruce**. Watch for leopard frogs, red-spotted newts, and green frogs, which often announce their presence with a loud shriek when startled. While relaxing here one June day I saw a huge great horned owl fly silently from its exposed perch into the seclusion of the bordering woodland. Our biggest owl, it feeds on large prey—rabbits, grouse, and even skunks.

Return to the main trail and continue right (south) along the eastern edge of the pond. A few hundred yards beyond the pond outflow, turn left onto Fern Glade Trail, blazed with blue crescents (Beaver Brook Trail continues toward the right around the pond). Mountain laurel is abundant here. Laurel produces clusters of showy white and pink, nickel-sized blossoms where it receives enough sunlight in late June and early July. A bit farther on, large yellow birches with peeling, brassy bark and red maples predominate.

The trail passes an isolated vernal pool on the right, where spotted and Jefferson salamanders and wood frogs breed. Cross a little, fast-flowing brook and head uphill through a small, darkened hemlock gorge where little is able to grow on the forest floor. Tiny, loudly singing winter wrens favor such moist, rocky ravines. After leveling out, the trail passes through young beech forest to another woodland pool on the left. Vernal pools are vital to the reproductive success of several species of amphibians, since these creatures can carry out early-spring courtship, mating, and egg-laying only in such ephemeral waters. In summer, the pool's most easily seen inhabitants are the small black tadpoles of wood frogs.

Fern Glade Trail continues southerly in a nearly straight line over level ground through broad-leaf woodland. In spring, look for red trillium (three petals) and sessile-leaved bellwort (a lily). The trail reaches paved Bear Swamp Road. Along the road's sunlit edges, watch for eye-catching, black-and-yellow tiger swallowtail butterflies feeding on orange hawkweed, and striking **black damselflies** fluttering near flowing water—the males have brilliant neon-blue abdomens!

Turn right onto the road and walk west less than 0.1 mile. Re-enter the moist woodland on the right where the North-South Trail is marked by a sign. Cross a small brook near the road and head north along the stream. Trail blazes here are blue bands around the trunks of small trees. Soon pass an extensive swamp, left, with a luxuriant growth of cinnamon fern—so called because its fertile fronds are an attractive rusty tan. These woods shelter an array of wood warblers: black-throated green in white pines, black-throated blue in laurel and hobblebush thickets, and black-and-white warbler creeping along the branches of maples like a nuthatch. Beautiful Canada warblers nest in cool, moist settings like this.

Beyond the swamp, the trail passes through woodland dominated by beech, northern red oak, birch, and black cherry (identified by its flaky, blackish bark). Soon you're heading gradually downhill to cross a stone wall. Eastern chipmunks are the most noticeable daytime mammals in these woods. In fall they're busy caching acorns and other goodies under logs and in hollows for the coming winter. The trail then makes brief east and north jogs and descends to a lovely cascading brook. North-South Trail blazes are blue arrows above a horizontal blue band.

About one-half hour after leaving Bear Swamp Road, you reach a trail junction. Turn right onto Beaver Brook Trail, marked by white triangles above a blue line, and continue downstream. At the site of an **enormous hemlock** the trail swings right, southeast. You see another beaver pond to the left and then reach and cross another stone wall. Follow a moss-covered ledge on the right and then cross a spring-fed brook.

At the intersection of Beaver Brook and Lookout Trails, turn abruptly left onto Lookout Trail over rock outcroppings, and climb a gradual slope to lichen-covered boulders on the right. At the second intersection turn right and walk up through a crevice to reach a sunny ledge overlooking the beaver pond. Re-enter the shaded forest of beech, black birch (smooth black bark), and hemlock by walking to the left. Here the ethereal sounds of hermit thrushes float through the air on late-spring and summer evenings. Crow-sized pileated woodpeckers are quite common. Look for their large, deep rectangular excavations—a sign that one of these red-crested birds has discovered and feasted upon a carpenter ant colony. The trail then follows along the base of a large ledge, right, and turns to the right. Note the **huge American beech** on your left. Beechnuts are much favored by wild turkeys, blue jays, squirrels, chipmunks, deer, bear, and other furred and feathered creatures.

Enter a maple/ash woods and go quite steeply downhill. The trail eventually becomes narrow, swings to the right, and follows along the edge of a small gorge. Here it is not well marked. Walk down along a rocky slope, with small cliffs to the right. Continue to within sight of the beaver pond and then curve left. This will take you to the pond, where the trail turns left again to roughly follow the shoreline east. A short, informal spur trail on the right will take you to the water's edge. Look for beaver signs—branches stripped of their bark and marked by the rodents' sharp, ever growing incisor teeth—floating in the water. In the shrubby wetlands nest alder fly-catcher (whose breeding song is *fee-bee-o*), common yellowthroat, and love-ly chestnut-sided warbler. Continue on the main trail past rock outcrops to the brook joining the trail. Continue left to return you to your car.

A black and yellow tiger swallowtail probes for nectar in an orange hawkweed along the sunny shoulders of Bear Swamp Road.

For a short, easy walk of 0.7 mile round-trip to an excellent overlook of Apple Valley, cross Hawley Road, walk left (north) about 150 feet beyond the reservation sign, and follow the wide four-wheel-drive track to the left up through hemlock woods. Where the road splits, stay right and proceed uphill. Soon you break out into a sunny clearing. The trail swings to the right and takes you to the top of a bedrock outcrop, where a plaque com-memorates the gift of this property by the Rev. and Mrs. Steinmetz. To your left the view extends beyond Apple Valley and all the way to Vermont. In fall, the brilliant golden foliage and bright white trunks of paper birch make for splendid photographic opportunities.

Getting There

From the intersection of I-91 and Route 116 in Deerfield, take Route 116 west for nearly 11 miles through the towns of Deerfield, Conway, and Ashfield to Ashfield center. Approximately 0.9 mile west of Ashfield center, Route 116 joins with Route 112 to form combined (briefly) Routes 116/112. Travel straight across Routes 116/112 onto paved Hawley Road and drive 1.7 miles to the reservation entrance on the left—look for the sign (you'll pass Bear Swamp Road on the left at the 0.9-mile mark, but continue straight on Hawley Road for another 0.8 mile).

Open sunrise to sunset. No admission fee. Parking along both sides of the road is limited. No rest rooms. Cross-country skiing is permitted. Camping, fires, and motorized vehicles are prohibited.

—R.L.

Chapelbrook Reservation

South Ashfield
143 acres

❖ along Chapel Brook, 0.75 mile

❖ 30 minutes

❖ easy

❖ Pony Mountain, 1.0 mile

❖ 45 minutes

❖ medium

❖ great for children

Small brook trout dart for cover in the aquamarine-colored pool. The sound of **falling water** is all around as the mountain stream known as Chapel Brook drops over a series of ledges. The first falls are 10 feet high, the next are 15, and then finally the stream tumbles 25 feet before continuing through a dark wood of hemlock. What a wonderful place to soak up the combination of woods and water! Chapel Brook is nestled in the foothills that ascend to the Berkshires near Route 9, climbing above the Connecticut Valley, also known as the Pioneer Valley.

The hiking here is terrific—one trail follows the stream while a second ascends nearby Pony Mountain. From the small parking area on Williamsburg Road, most visitors prefer to view the falls next to the road and then follow an old woodland road that parallels the stream in a downhill direction. Old stone walls and **wildflowers** are scattered beneath a canopy of large deciduous and evergreen trees. In the spring, look for pink lady's slippers and the delicate white flower of trillium. (The lady's slipper flower is a veined pouch, and it has two oval leaves at the base. The trillium has three broad leaves and three showy petals.) Deer use the trail between dawn and dusk—watch for their pointed hoofprints in the sand.

After about a 10-minute walk, you will notice that the stream flows closer to the trail and the rushing sound of water is your companion again. Look for the stone remains of what appears to be an old mill. With a little imagination you can picture horses hauling lumber or corn along this old road to an active little mill that used the stream as its power. The trail ends at private property, and you should retrace your steps back to the parking area.

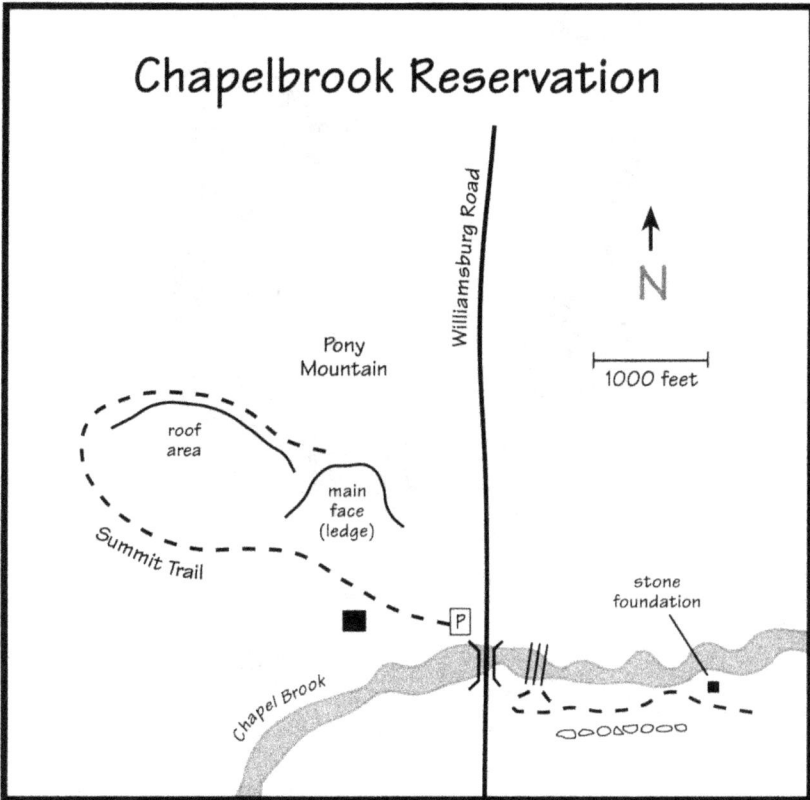

Chapelbrook Reservation

Williamsburg Road

N

1000 feet

Pony
Mountain

roof
area

main
face
(ledge)

Summit Trail

P

stone
foundation

Chapel Brook

The climb up Pony Mountain begins on the other side of Williamsburg Road and takes about 45 minutes round-trip. The trailhead is opposite the falls near a Trustees of Reservations sign on the north side of the stream. Follow the main trail, called the Summit Trail, as it first leads around the base of the mountain and begins a gradual climb that brings you to the summit. Although the trail is steep in spots, the sight of impressive **cliffs** near the summit can give you the energy to push on. On my hike

I heard the unmistakable sound of a ruffed grouse drumming its wings—first slowly, then building rapidly before its abrupt end. I never saw the grouse, but two ravens were perched at the top of a nearby tree calling out an eerie three-note *awk, awk, awk.*

A wide trail at Chapelbrook leads through a forest of maple and birch.

The forlorn cries of the raven made me think about another creature that is officially nonexistent here in Massachusetts—the mountain lion. If the state does have mountain lions, this is the kind of remote, hilly region where they just might roam undetected. Over the years, there have been plenty of mountain lion sightings in the Berkshires but no conclusive proof. Yet there are plenty of bears around, and in all my years of hiking I have seen only one. If bears can stay well hidden, is it possible that a few mountain lions have avoided humans altogether? (The mountain lion has a long tail and yellow-brown fur, and its chest and throat are white.

Females average 100 pounds and males average 150. Not including the two- to three-foot tail, a male mountain lion can measure almost eight feet long!)

On your way to the summit, pass through a beautiful beech grove. Their smooth gray trunks are a pleasure to behold, especially in autumn when their yellow leaves blanket the forest floor. Near the ridge top is an open field—it is private property but you can scan the edges of this open land for deer. Other creatures that live here but are rarely seen are coyote, barred owls, and the magnificent pileated woodpecker.

The trail passes through dense stands of hemlock as it turns to a southerly direction along the ridge top. Occasionally there are sections of exposed granite visible. Your pace will quicken when you see open sky ahead through the trees, signifying that you are near the summit. Spectacular views to the south, overlooking the quiet valley, await your arrival. Look down on a farm and tiny black dots of cows and horses in open fields. In the fall, enjoy a kaleidoscope of color, particularly from the treetops that are directly in front of the cliff. Sit here and rest to the murmur of the wind whispering through the evergreens before retracing your steps back to your car and civilization.

Getting There

From Ashfield center take Route 116 east 1.5 miles to South Ashfield. Where Route 116 turns left, continue straight ahead on Williamsburg Road (follow Williamsburg Road Route 9 signs) 2.2 miles. Entrance is on the right at the bridge.

Open year-round, seven days a week, no admission fee, no rest rooms.

—M.T.

D.A.R. State Forest

Goshen/Ashfield
1,536 acres

❖ 2.5 miles

❖ 2.5 hours

❖ moderate

Possessing great wildlife diversity, extensive northern hardwood forest, swamps, lakes, and ponds, D.A.R. State Forest is a wonderful place for a day of walking, nature study, and panoramic vistas. Because most of the area lies above 1,400 feet elevation, the growing season is curtailed; this has a profound influence on the plants and animals that live here. Stands of red spruce and bunchberry and boggy pockets give clues to the northern character of this forest. A lookout tower on high Moore Hill (1,697 feet) rewards you with a magnificent 360-degree view of the surrounding wooded ridges, including the nearby Chapelbrook Ledges (see p. 134).

Unmistakable evidence of earlier agriculture stands in the form of rock walls and old cellar holes found in this maturing beech/maple/hemlock woodland. The Massachusetts chapter of the Daughters of the American Revolution donated the property to the state in 1929. In the 1930s, the Civilian Conservation Corps (CCC) built roads, buildings, and other facilities, which remain in use today. A fairly extensive network of well-maintained and easy-to-follow (with a few exceptions) trails and dirt roads allows you to explore virtually every corner of this scenic forest. The walking is quite easy and the few hills are moderate.

Woodlands and wetlands shelter **black bear** (campers are advised to lock away their food) and bobcat, as well as the less glamorous but far more numerous red eft, a terrestrial salamander that becomes the aquatic red-spotted newt later in life. Signs of beaver and white-tailed deer are quite common along the wetland margins. Among breeding birds are the uncommon **Swain-**

son's thrush, as well as a dozen or more species of wood warblers, including black-throated blue, black-throated green, magnolia, and northern waterthrush (I found 33 species of birds on one early-July visit). Pink lady's slipper orchids, painted and red trilliums, Canada mayflower, and clintonia (a.k.a. blue-bead lily) brighten the woodlands in spring.

Your walk will take you from an observation tower where stunning views await, to hemlock and laurel-fringed Twinning Brook Pond on Long Trail, through woodland and wetland, to the eastern shore of lovely Upper Highland Lake, and back to the summit of Moore Hill.

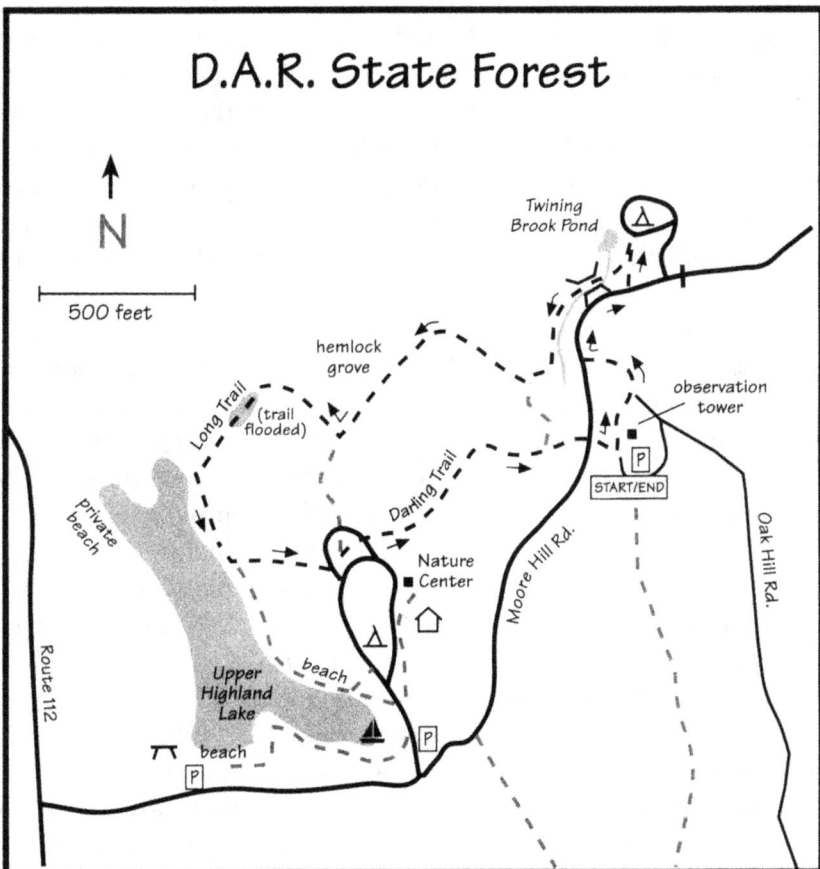

D.A.R. State Forest

N

500 feet

Twining Brook Pond

observation tower

hemlock grove

Long Trail

(trail flooded)

Darling Trail

START/END

Nature ■ Center

Moore Hill Rd.

Oak Hill Rd.

Private beach

Route 112

Upper Highland Lake

beach

beach

Climb the steps of the metal tower to obtain good views. Green ridges roll on into the distance with few signs of human habitation. Two miles away to the northeast, as the crow flies, sit the bare-rock Chapelbrook Ledges—looking here like a small, light-colored island surrounded by a sea of green. On a really clear day distant views of Mt. Greylock (northwest), the Holyoke and Mt. Tom Ranges (southeast), and even New Hampshire's Mt. Monadnock (northeast) are possible. After taking in the stunning vistas, descend and walk to the back of the tower (opposite the steps). An unmarked, and at first not easily apparent, trail descends to Moore Hill Road, crossing dirt Oak Hill Road in the process. Pick up the trail just slightly to the left after crossing the dirt road. After reaching paved Moore Hill Road, turn right and walk slightly downhill approximately 0.25 mile to a trail, left, leading to Twinning Brook Pond (stay right at the last junction) and the group campground.

Follow the Long Trail near the northeast end of the pond, closest to the campground, with an Area Closed (to camping) sign. Almost immediately cross Twinning Brook on a small wooden bridge. In early July, I was delighted to find a nest containing three large-mouthed, nestling robins in an arrowwood shrub near the pond's edge. The middle nestling, its head topped by a tuft of gray down, watched me through half-opened eyelids. The parent birds voiced their concern at my untimely arrival, so after a couple of quick photos I left the adults to the demanding business of rearing their hungry offspring.

Continue southwesterly past the pond and up a gradual incline as it roughly parallels a small brook. After approximately 0.3 mile, you reach a trail junction. Follow the Long Trail right and walk a short distance to another junction. A left turn would take you to the Darling Trail. Instead, continue on the Long Trail by turning right. The trail traverses beech woods, and there is rocky ledge to the left. After approximately 1,000 feet, the trail makes a broad swing left and begins gradually to descend. Pass through a dark hemlock grove and a swampy area on wooden footbridges and reach an intersection. Goldthread adds a bit of color to the dark, rather bare forest floor with its bright green leaves and white flowers. (Goldthread's name refers to the color of its roots.)

At the trail junction, where a sign reads 0.25 mile to Campground, turn right—away from the campground—to continue on Long Trail. The trail makes another broad bend and proceeds gently down through hemlock woods, and crosses a brook just before reaching the northern end of Upper Highland Lake (a portion of the trail may be impassable due to flooding by beavers). Note the No Trespassing sign on the right indicating the forest boundary. After reaching the lake (elevation 1,427 feet), the trail heads south along the eastern shore. From gaps in the thick shoreline vegetation, notice two beaver lodges—one on the far shore, the other on the near side of a small peninsula. A private camp is visible on the opposite shore.

A watchful robin nestling eyes an intruder from its nest in an arrowwood shrub.

Boating and fishing are popular activities. I saw fish jumping while I relaxed along the picturesque shoreline. You may wish to linger here awhile yourself. Notice the bur reed growing in the shallows. Its spiky, round flowers look like miniature medieval maces.

To continue, walk southerly on Long Trail to the Darling Trail junction, left. A sign here reads Campground 0.25 mile. Follow the Darling Trail away from the lake, proceeding gradually uphill. Listen for hermit thrush, veery, and little brown creeper, which creeps up tree trunks. The creeper's decurved, forcepslike bill is perfectly designed for removing insects, spiders, and their eggs from bark crevices.

Approach the paved campground road and notice the modern restroom building with a drinking fountain outside. Follow the paved road straight ahead through the campground and pick up the Darling Trail again, just left of another drinking fountain at campsite #49 R. The Darling Trail has no markers but is easy to find and follow. Scarlet tanager (the female is green), yellow-bellied sapsucker, and blue-headed and red-eyed vireos all nest in these woods.

After passing through beech/maple forest with an understory of mountain laurel, the trail leads uphill to a power-line cut. Just after leaving the woods, spot an old cellar hole to the left of the trail. Follow the power-line path about 200 yards to Moore Hill Road. The artificial "edge" habitat of the power-line cut enables gray catbird, chestnut-sided warbler, and many butterflies to find suitable living conditions. It also allows female brown-headed cowbirds access to the nests of interior woodland birds; the cowbird (a brood parasite) lays its eggs in the nest of another, generally smaller species.

Cross Moore Hill Road and follow the hiking-bridle trail immediately opposite up the slope to the observation tower, surrounded by tall trees including some sizable white pines, to where you left your vehicle.

Getting There

From the intersection of Routes 9 and 112 in Goshen, travel north on Route 112 for 0.7 mile to the well-marked state-forest entrance road on the right. Follow the entrance road (Moore Hill Road) to the visitor contact station, where fees are collected. To reach the trailhead at the observation tower, continue on Moore Hill Road for approximately 1.3 miles and turn right onto Oak Hill Road. The road splits at 0.2 mile; turn right and follow it to the tower parking area.

Hours are dawn to dusk, unless you're camping. Entry fee is two dollars per car. Rest rooms are available but not at the group campground. Camping, picnicking, swimming, boating, fishing, horseback riding, snowmobiling, and cross-country skiing are allowed. Gasoline-powered motorboats are prohibited. Public programs are conducted daily in summer. A tiny nature center building is located at the main campground.

—R.L.

31 Kenneth Dubuque Memorial State Forest

Hawley/Plainfield/Savoy
7,822 acres

❖ 4.5 miles

❖ 3.5 hours

❖ moderate

"Slightly off the beaten path" is surely one way to describe Dubuque Memorial State Forest. "Rugged," "rocky," and "remote" are other fitting adjectives for this large, rather wild property. Huge ancient sugar maples stand guard over old stone fences and former farm fields. The forest lies a long way from any population center and is little visited today, but 180 years ago this ground and its bubbling waters supported a thriving agricultural community.

In the early nineteenth century the town of Hawley had a population of more than 1,000 residents. Farms, sawmills, a stone charcoal kiln (still standing), and a successful tannery provided employment. Charcoal kilns had huge appetites for wood, and this land looked very different then than it does today. The farms were abandoned, though, and by 1970 only 224 people remained in Hawley. Some of the farmland was sold to the state early in this century, creating much of what we treasure as public conservation and recreation lands today. In 1980, Hawley State Forest was renamed to commemorate Kenneth Dubuque, a former forest supervisor who was instrumental in its establishment.

The land is reverting to northern hardwood forest, and in the process it is becoming a near-wilderness. Significant portions of the property lie above 1,600 feet elevation, with red spruce, balsam fir, and small shrub swamps imparting a distinct boreal character to the landscape. The hilly, glacially scoured terrain is dissected by clear, cold, high-gradient streams. Lovely Basin Brook bounces over dark-gray bedrock of folded schist covered with moss and lichens on its way to the Chickley River. Pure springs that once provided drinking water for the human inhabitants still percolate to the surface through glacial sands.

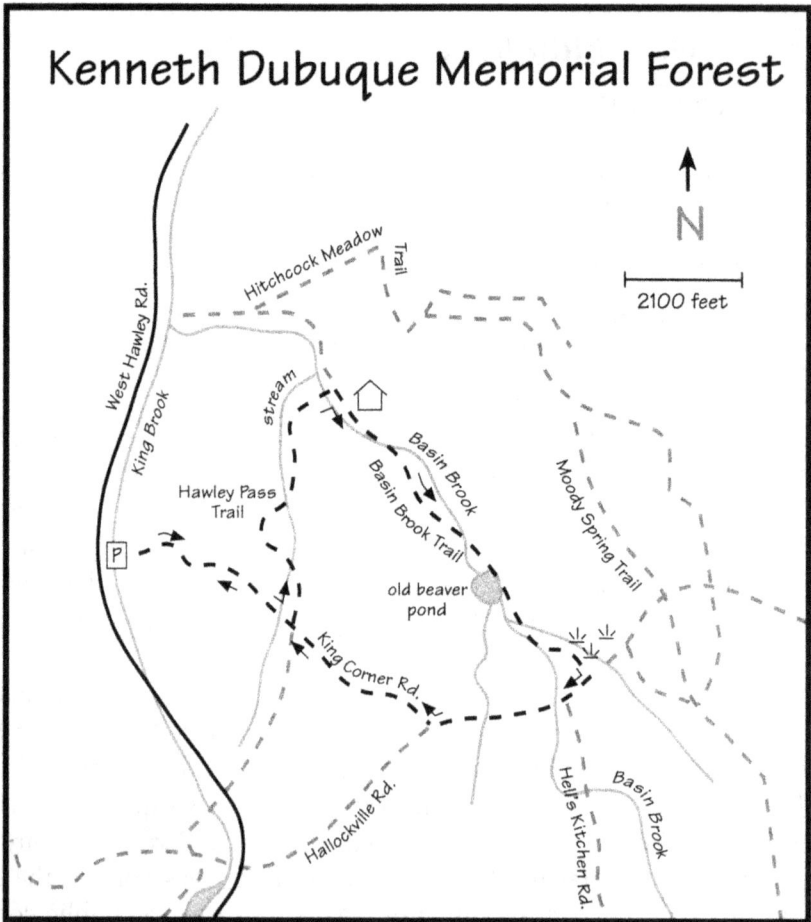

Patriarch trees of gargantuan proportions—spared long ago to provide shade or maple sugar—will catch your eye, but much of the forest is still quite young—new growth recolonizing land once cleared for pasturing or to make charcoal. That new growth now provides browse for white-tailed deer.

There are many miles of foot trails and former roads and other remnants of human occupation throughout Dubuque State Forest. The trails are in good condition, although some are not well marked. None of the hills are particularly strenuous. From the parking area to the high point on the trail described below is a vertical climb of 300 feet.

After parking in the dirt lot off West Hawley Road (elevation 1,350 feet), you might want to look at the painted forest map on the information kiosk situated on the left (a pit toilet is located directly behind it). Walk down the gated dirt King Corner Road—the settlement here is called King Corner—to start your hike. Cross wide King Brook and swing right, gradually ascending through woods of American beech (smooth, pale-gray trunks), **enormous sugar maples**, very large yellow birches, and eastern hemlocks. Among the blooming flowers of mid-summer you may see Indian tobacco (actually a lobelia with small, light-blue blossoms) and whorled wood aster. The delicate, light-green fronds of New York fern are numerous and easy to identify (note that both ends of the frond are tapered). You'll also find the similar hay-scented fern, which grows well in rocky, partially sunny sites. The odor of its crushed foliage has never reminded me of the scent of hay, but you may feel differently.

After about 20 minutes of walking on the broad former roadway, you come to Hawley Pass Trail, which crosses the road. Follow its blue-and-white painted blazes (some are faint) to the left. Unassuming greenish purple helleborine, an alien orchid, grows in the damp, shaded soils here. The trail enters hemlock woods along an unnamed brook that you just crossed. Walk through beech/hemlock woods and eventually pass a big, split glacial erratic. If the day is moist, watch the path in front of you for bright-orange red efts. Equipped with bright colors to warn potential predators of their poisonous skin secretions, red efts wander for up to seven years through woodlands prior to returning to the beaver pond environments where they hatched—to become aquatic red-spotted newts.

The last portion of Hawley Pass Trail descends gradually to rocky Basin Brook, which it crosses, and on to an Adirondack shelter and picnic table (in disrepair) near its junction with Basin Brook Trail. Not far from the shelter grow **American yew shrubs**; female plants bear unique translucent, fleshy red berries containing a single seed. Another name for this native shrub—ground hemlock—alludes to its resemblance to eastern hemlock. Yew needles, however, are longer and dark green on both sides. During an early-August walk, we took a few moments to rest here by the brook. In the small sunlit clearing several beautiful white admiral butterflies flew about. We relaxed watching the boldly patterned black, white, blue, and red insects.

A short distance beyond the shelter, the path crosses the brook and follows it upstream. About a mile away, Basin Brook enters the Chickley River, which flows northward to join the Deerfield. The Deerfield, of course, is a significant tributary of the Connecticut. Basin Brook almost seems to be more rock than water, as boulders and tilted bedrock layers—green with mosses and lichens—make up its channel in the small, narrow gorge. The setting is a lovely one and you'll enjoy your walk up along the gurgling stream. At a triangular blue marker, cross the brook again and continue to walk upstream along the opposite bank.

Soon you arrive at an old beaver pond surrounded by conifers. Old cuttings are still evident. (Beaver ponds gradually begin to fill with silt, are abandoned by the rodents, and eventually become wet meadows.) The trail then veers away from Basin Brook, through cool spruce woods where sweet-trilling dark-eyed juncos nest, to emerge from the forest onto Hallockville Road. The ground here is very sandy, a gift of the glaciers. Bracken fern grows along the sun-dappled roadsides. Predators like red fox often leave telltale signs of their nocturnal travels on paths and roadways. Tapered scats composed of fur, bones, and feathers are usually the only visual sign that a fox has passed by.

Basin Brook gradually tumbles 350 vertical feet over moss-covered bedrock.

Turn left at Hallockville Road and walk a short distance to a small shrub swamp on the left. In late summer the attractive globular white flowers of buttonbush decorate the wetland. We were fortunate enough to hear the screams of a red-shouldered hawk and then to see this uncommon bird. Adult red-shouldereds are slightly smaller and slimmer than red-tails, have horizontally red-barred breasts, and banded black-and-white tails. Look also for the chestnut-colored shoulders of a perched bird. This declining species favors wetlands away from settlements and preys upon reptiles and amphibians in addition to rodents. Mosquitoes and deerflies are also present.

Retrace your steps back along Hallockville Road, passing the junction of Basin Brook Trail on the right. Follow old roadways from here back to the parking area—a distance of approximately two miles. On the left are deep sand deposits which show signs of former mining. Trembling aspen, white birch, northern red oak, and lowbush blueberry grow in the sterile soils. Unfortunately, off-road-vehicle tires are hastening the wind and water erosion of these hollows. Continue down (west) along the road a short distance to a small pond on your left at the junction of Hell's Kitchen Road. Beautiful blue wild iris blooms in summer along the shore. Immediately beyond the pond, cross Basin Brook again.

Continue along the road, which borders beech/maple forest, for about 10 minutes past the pond and turn right onto King Corner Road. Male red-eyed vireos, colored olive green and white, sing incessantly in the woodlands, proclaiming the boundaries of their nesting territories. Roger Tory Peterson called this bird the most abundant bird of the eastern woodlands. The rich woodlands also contain perhaps our most beautiful and delicate fern—maidenhair. It's always a treat for me to find this attractive plant, which is not found in the acidic soils under evergreens. Climb gently now to the highest point along the route, reaching 1,660 feet above sea level about one-third of a mile past the turnoff from Hallockville Road.

After about 15 minutes of walking along the stone-wall-lined roadway, you come to Hawley Pass Trail again—but continue straight on King Corner Road, crossing the unnamed brook and heading back up and then downhill to the parking area. In addition to specimen-size sugar maple, yellow birch, and hemlock trees, there are also some very big white ash here—the tight-fitting bark of its long, straight trunk characteristically crosshatched. Ash seeds resemble canoe paddles, and the tough wood is used to manufacture ax handles and baseball bats, among other things.

Getting There

From Route 116 in the center of Plainfield, take Route 116 west (and north) for 2.5 miles to its junction with Route 8A. Turn right onto Route 8A and travel north for 2.3 miles to a driveway on the right (opposite Stetson Road) leading to a dirt parking area adjacent to a state-forest maintenance shed.

Hours are sunrise to sunset. No fees. Horseback riding, cross-country skiing, and snowmobiling are permitted on some trails. A pit toilet is situated at the entrance.

—R.L.

32 Mohawk Trail State Forest

Charlemont/Savoy/Hawley
6,457 acres

❖ 4 miles

❖ 3 hours

❖ difficult

Following the slow retreat of the mile-thick glacial ice sheet that gouged out much of the dramatic topography visible today, the swift-flowing Deerfield and Cold Rivers continued to cut through the uplands of western Franklin and eastern Berkshire Counties to produce spectacular narrow valleys and steep ridges. The Deerfield, a popular whitewater stream, originates in the Green Mountains of southern Vermont and flows southward into Massachusetts, feeding the mighty Connecticut. The smaller Cold River has its source closer at hand—in the Hoosac Range of Berkshire County, just to the west. Their clear, cold waters intermingle at the northeastern edge of Mohawk Trail State Forest, producing a land of spectacular beauty and numerous opportunities for varied outdoor adventures. Whitewater rafting and kayaking are very popular activities.

The forest trails wend steeply up the mountainsides but reward the hiker with sublime views of the Deerfield River valley. The steep slopes of Todd Mountain and nearby locations within the state forest contain some of the last vestiges of fabled old-growth forest remaining in the state. Black bear, bobcat, river otter, fisher, coyote, porcupine, and many smaller creatures inhabit this rugged terrain.

The region has a long and storied past. Route 2, today's principal east-west highway through northwestern Massachusetts, is known as the Mohawk Trail because it closely follows what was once the major trading route for peoples of the Iroquois nations between the Hudson and Connecticut Rivers. The path between the summits of Todd and Clark Mountains—still known as

Indian Trail—is a surviving portion of the original trail used by Native Americans. Mohawk Trail State Forest was established in 1921.

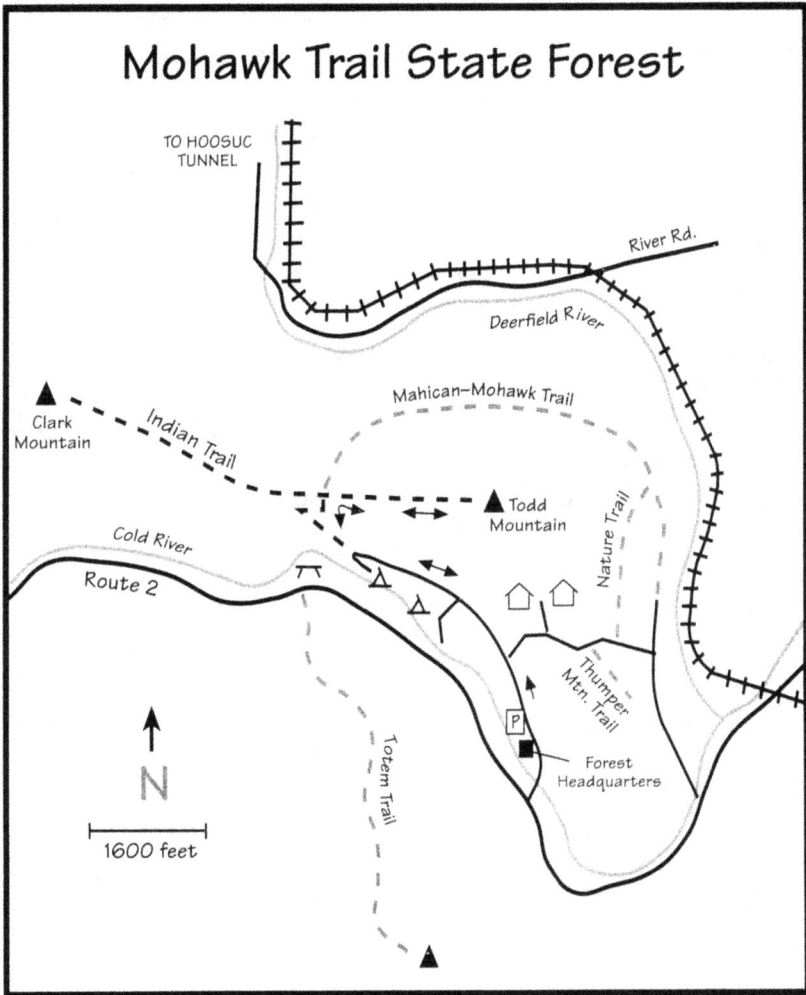

Mohawk Trail State Forest

TO HOOSUC TUNNEL

River Rd.

Deerfield River

Mahican–Mohawk Trail

Clark Mountain

Indian Trail

Todd Mountain

Nature Trail

Cold River

Route 2

Thumper Mtn. Trail

P

Forest Headquarters

N

Totem Trail

1600 feet

After passing the contact station, park next to the headquarters buildings, immediately to the left near Cold River. In summer, nest boxes not far from the buildings often house blue-green and white tree swallows. Watch for adults arriving with crops full of insects for their ravenous young. On summer weekends, when the popular campground is usually full, walk along the paved road to the campground and trailhead. It takes about 15 minutes to reach the Indian Lookout trailhead, on the right just before the road makes a sharp curve downhill to the left. Drinking water and restrooms are available at the campground bathhouse.

Although it is only 1.25 miles from the trailhead to Todd Mountain Lookout, the trail is very steep for the first half-hour or so until you reach the crest. Go slowly, take it easy, and enjoy the abundant plant and animal life along the way. At the lower elevations, russet-headed wood thrush and olive-green red-eyed vireo provide musical accompaniment. Gorgeous **black-throated blue warbler** is one of the most common of its family in these woodlands. The male is deep blue and black above and clear white below, while his mate is drab brown but with a distinctive bright white wing patch. The abundant laurel and hobblebush thickets here provide them with ample nest sites. Listen for their distinctive, buzzy *beer-beer-beer-bee* songs.

On the dry, sunny, south-facing slopes of white and red oak and abundant witch hazel, trailing arbutus (mayflower)—the Massachusetts state flower—blooms in spring. Wintergreen produces white, bell-shaped flowers in summer. Both are low growing. One of the tallest and most noticeable summer wildflowers of the gravelly slope is downy false foxglove, which sports large yellow, funnel-shaped blossoms. Interestingly, it is parasitic on oak roots.

After an elevation gain of almost 700 feet, you reach the ridge crest, which connects the summits of Todd Mountain and Clark Mountain. Clark Mountain (1,920 feet) is heavily wooded and, although 200 feet higher than Todd, offers no clear views from its top. This is the original **Indian Trail**, traversed by countless feet over the last three-plus centuries. Turn right to reach the summit of Todd Mountain. The crest trail passes through an abundance of mountain laurel, short red oak, and lowbush blueberry, which ripen in August. Early azalea bushes are fairly numerous in the rocky soils between the two peaks; the gorgeous pink and very fragrant flowers appear in May.

Although the ridge trail won't take you through old-growth forest, the adjacent northern and eastern slopes of Todd Mountain are a sort of time capsule. **Four-hundred-year-old eastern hemlock trees** stand high above the Deerfield River valley—a reminder of what this portion of western Massachusetts may have looked like before colonial settlement. These trees were spared largely because harvesting on these extremely steep slopes was deemed uneconomical. After less than one-half mile of very pleasant walking on the ridge crest, you reach the rocky, partially open summit of Todd Mountain—more than 900 vertical feet above the trailhead.

I was thrilled to find rather fresh bear scat on the trail in the woods near the edge of the clearing. **Black bear,** the largest native mammal of our woodlands, is making a strong comeback as the state's forests mature. Consider yourself extremely fortunate if you happen upon one of these magnificent animals—something that's not likely to occur given their keen sense of smell and acute hearing. Black bears, despite their considerable size (adult males often weigh more than 300 pounds), are actually reluctant to make contact with humans—fleeing at the first sight, odor, or sound of you; the only exception being a mother bear and cub(s) that feel cornered and thus threatened.

The view from the Indian Trail atop Todd Mountain is one of the most scenic in the region.

Have a seat on the exposed bedrock and survey the splendid scene— from the southeast to the southwest the view is superb. Sitting in the sun on this lovely summit is an exhilarating experience, and you probably won't want to rush back down the mountain unless you have an urgent appointment to keep. **Indian Lookout**—from where Native Americans are said to have viewed the advance of colonial settlement up the valley—is situated a short distance farther; there the trail ends.

While returning along Indian Trail, listen and watch for the many species of birds that breed in these woodlands. I counted 33 species on an early-July visit, of which seven were colorful, active wood warblers. In an uncharacteristic moist tangle on the otherwise dry slope, I saw and heard two beautiful male Canada warblers as well as several fledglings. These birds usually inhabit wet, boggy sites. On my way back down the mountain I also encountered a very annoyed female ruffed grouse and her brood of fairly large chicks. Female grouse, in protecting their young, often make odd mewing sounds and sometimes even boldly charge the intruder—a behavior that startled me the first time I experienced it.

Be sure to turn left upon reaching the connecting trail to the campground rather than continuing straight on to Clark Mountain. Take your time: going steeply downhill can put a strain on the knees. After reaching the campground road, turn left and walk back to headquarters and your vehicle on the right.

For a slightly less strenuous walk with a nice view at the end, you might want to take Totem Trail to the 1,584-foot summit of an unnamed promontory due south of Todd Mountain. The trail begins on the opposite side of Route 2, just past a picnic area between the Cold River and Route 2, one mile west of the entrance road. Look for the Entering Pioneer Valley sign along Route 2 if you're arriving from the west. Park at a pullout just west of the picnic area on the north side of the road. A bronze plaque commemorating the establishment of the state forest in 1921 is situated at this trailhead.

The round-trip distance for this trail through richer northern hardwood forest of birch, maple, beech, and hemlock is three miles. The rocks on the trail may be very slippery on a damp or humid day, so watch your footing. Allow about one and one-half hours for this walk. Many ferns, especially spinulose wood fern, club mosses, mosses, and fungi cover the floor of this damper, more shaded forest. The overlook, which is not as open as that on Todd Mountain, has views east into Trout Brook Cove and toward Hawks Mountain, the Deerfield River, and Route 2, which parallels it. During my July visit a red-tailed hawk soared over the ravine and two turkey vultures—quite close at hand—made several passes, riding the rising thermals of a mid-summer morning.

Getting There

From the east: From the I-91 rotary in Greenfield, take Route 2 west for 19 miles to Charlemont. From the center of Charlemont, continue west on Route 2 for another 3.9 miles to the state-forest entrance road on the right. Cross the Cold River and follow the road left to the contact station. Parking is just to the left, adjacent to headquarters.

From the west: From the junction of Routes 8 and 2 in North Adams, take Route 2 east for 14.1 miles to the state forest entrance on the left.

Hours are 9:30 A.M. to 8:00 P.M. for the picnic area. Access to the parking area near headquarters is always available. There is no parking fee for hikers; a $2 fee is collected for picnicking; camping fee is $6 per night; cabins may be rented for $8–$10 per night (minimum stays required, reservations strongly advised). Rest rooms and water are available at campground. Motorized vehicles are prohibited from trails; pets must be on a leash.

—R.L.

Mt. Toby Forest

Sunderland
755 acres

❖ 4.2 miles

❖ 2.5–3 hours

❖ moderate

Although designated on most maps as Mt. Toby State Forest, this property is not part of the Department of Environmental Management's (DEM) state forest system as such. Rather, since 1916, the University of Massachusetts has owned and managed it. The Massachusetts DEM and the Division of Fisheries, Wildlife, and Law Enforcement also own a small number of additional acres. Mt. Toby Demonstration Forest, as it might more accurately be called, provides an outdoor laboratory for foresters, biologists, and other scientists studying various aspects of forest ecology, as well as a place where the best forestry practices can be brought to the public's attention.

For the hiker and nature enthusiast, Mt. Toby represents a wonderful place to walk under towering hemlocks and along a clear-flowing brook to the 1,269-foot-high wooded summit of Mt. Toby. Here, an excellent 360-degree panoramic view awaits those who climb the additional 70 feet to the top of the mountain's fire tower. The nearly 900 feet of vertical elevation gain provides exercise for the body, while the verdant woodlands provide plenty of stimulation for the senses.

Walk from the small dirt parking area back along Reservation Road a short distance to a metal gate across a forest road. A brown wooden sign identifies the Mt. Toby Forest Management Area. The Robert Frost Trail heads immediately uphill on the right, but continue straight instead. Note that timber has been harvested on the left as you walk under tall, straight white pines, an indication that they grew up hemmed in by others of their kind. Partridgeberry and, later, shinleaf both produce white flowers in early summer along the roadway, while blue-headed vireos sing from the trees.

New York, hay-scented, and Christmas ferns are among the first ferns you'll encounter; a considerable variety of these ancient, nonflowering plants grace these woodlands. Dark-green hemlocks, certainly one of our loveliest conifers, appear; you'll see many more, but not all are green and healthy.

Mt. Toby Forest

Listen for the little tinhorn notes of the impish red-breasted nuthatch as it creeps down the rough trunks of massive white pines in search of crevice insects. The loud reverberating *teacher, teacher, teacher* of the ground-nesting ovenbird rings through the summer woodlands (I counted 23 on one June afternoon), and eastern wood pewees sing a melancholy *pee-a-wee* song. A rock outcrop appears on the right, upon which are perched hemlocks, evergreen wood fern, and common polypody fern (the little one). Note that it is sunnier and warmer to the left of the road, under the pines. Bracken ferns thrive in such situations. A bit farther on the right, a sign reads: Favorable Soil and Site Conditions for Mixed Hardwoods. Re-enter shaded woods. American redstarts, red-eyed vireos, and black-throated green warblers are among the many neotropical migrants that breed here but winter in the tropics. Red and black oaks join the pines, hemlocks, and red and sugar maples now as you pass by an old assemblage of big concrete culvert sections at a bend in the road. False Solomon's seal is abundant; its tiny white flowers are clustered at the tip of the stalk in spring. In June the little paired white trumpets and deep-green, fingernail-sized leaves of partridgeberry form a lovely ground cover beyond the stream bed. Common wild sarsaparilla, which somewhat resembles the rare ginseng, crowds the road shoulders. The fragrance of warm pine resin wafts to one's nostrils on a warm sunny day just before you reach a small grassy clearing, bordered by pines and oaks, on the left. Wild roses produce two-inch pale-pink blossoms in June which delight the eye and nose. Spittlebugs, the nymphs of a leafhopper, take refuge in the frothy white spittle they produce from plant sap.

Re-enter shaded woods of white pine, red maple, and hemlock on the darker slope. To your right stands a rock outcrop well camouflaged by moss and other greenery. Remain on the roadway where lesser paths intersect. An especially fertile natural fern garden at the base of the slope holds silvery spleenwort, maidenhair, and interrupted ferns. As nutrients continually wash down the slope, they fertilize this garden. In a depression to your left a bit farther along is a stand of ostrich fern (often found in rich river flood plains). The roadway begins to climb gradually as you pass over culverts and through deep shade cast by imposing hemlocks, tall and straight. A tiny gurgling brook parallels the roadway. Some trees about to be cut are marked with paint, and a young grove of planted red pines, with scaly bark, stands on the left.

Red maple, black birch, gray birch, hemlock, and red oak make up the forest as you reach a sunny junction with a less-traveled woods road. The power lines you have been following also turn right here. You will return to this spot after your descent from Mt. Toby. For now, bear left and descend gradually in shade. Continue straight ahead as you encounter additional trails on the left. Note the white birches that display thin peeling bark which reveals tan beneath—quite different than the bark of gray birch. Shrubby striped maple joins the understory layer in these rich woods. White snakeroot, which blooms in late summer, is ubiquitous; its deep-green leaves are heart shaped. You'll also find sweet cicely, white baneberry (doll's eyes), tall meadow rue, and red trillium in addition to lots of false Solomon's seal. As the slope becomes steeper, yellow birches appear. The high-pitched, sibilant songs of black-and-white warblers drift down from the trees. Steep outcrops rise up on your right. This rock is a conglomerate, a metamorphic rock made up of angular, mostly one-to-

Purple-flowering raspberry blossoms in June and July and produces tart red fruit.

three-inch long chunks of varying composition. The boulder wears a toupee of emerald-green mosses. Delicate maidenhair fern decorates its base and purple-flowering raspberry shrubs add color to the roadside.

Peering through the screen of trees to your left, where there is a steep drop-off, yields views of a wooded ridge beyond. A steep blue-blazed trail goes left downhill, but stay on the road as it levels out. Soon you hear and then see Roaring Brook, 25 to 30 feet below in a small ravine. Fiery orange, black, and white Blackburnian warblers sing their thin, lispy refrains from high in the hemlocks and pines. Soon reach a boulder with the inscription Arnold D. Rhodes Natural Area est. June 1974. No timber harvesting is permitted in this area named for Dr. Rhodes, a former University of Massachusetts forestry faculty member. The brook is nearly at road level here. An odd sight indeed is a foot-thick yellow birch that has grown around a foot-long stone three feet above the ground. How the rock came to this elevated position is open to conjecture. In a small pool under a fallen hemlock we delighted in watching a red-eyed vireo, a female redstart and a female scarlet tanager, bathing, each in turn, in the cold water. Each bird shook off the excess fluid while perched in the overarching hemlock. Continue uphill along the hemlock, birch, and maple slope on the left; on the right grow white, gray, and black birches. A scarred, graffiti-covered American beech tree here will carry its black "tattoos" until death. In this stretch, you'll cross the rocky Roaring Brook three times within a short distance. A patch of wild ginger thrives in the rich soil between brook and woods road. Its liver-red spring flowers lie hidden beneath the leaf litter, where beetles find them. Red squirrels scamper over the forest floor, race up hemlock boles, and chatter from their boughs, while wood thrushes and rose-breasted grosbeaks add their sweet notes to nature's music. Hemlocks dominate the shady left slope, where the paucity of undergrowth permits views 200 feet into the woodland. Birches and other broad-leaved trees dominate the sunnier right side of this shallow ravine.

As you cross the brook again, note the impressive columnar white ash, black birch, and eastern hemlock specimens in the damp soil. Red-backed salamanders spend the daylight hours safe and moist beneath fallen logs. Here we listened attentively to the loud, exuberant song of the diminutive winter wren emanating from beside the brook. Another crossing and the path's incline increases. Continue straight as a blue/red-blazed trail goes right. Patches of light-green hay-scented (boulder) fern line the roadway through this deciduous woodland. The evocative woodwind performance of a hermit thrush added greatly to the atmosphere as we walked steadily uphill under hemlocks, maples, and birches. Another graffiti-scarred beech, a 78 clearly visible on its trunk, displays the lasting damage done to it.

Reach a major road intersection and turn right, toward the summit, along a steady, easy grade. This forest is noticeably younger, the trees much smaller. Mountain-bikers enjoy riding this gravel road, and its ample width makes amiable coexistence with hikers possible. Gray birches, a species that colonizes open ground, become more numerous. Many leaning trees show signs of "soil creep" on the steep slope. Intermixed with the oaks, maples, and beeches are scattered dead hemlocks that have fallen victim perhaps to the woolly adelgid, a minute sap-sucking insect wreaking havoc on southern New England's hemlocks. Appearing very vibrant in contrast are blooming wild roses and wild geraniums, both pink hued in June. Along this rather level north-south ridge, the oaks and hickories are of lesser stature. Lowbush blueberries produce ripe fruit in midsummer beneath them. Even white oaks, whose acorns germinate in autumn, appear. This is a very different forest indeed from that through which Roaring Brook flows.

Grasses and sedges thrive in this sunnier exposure. Rattlesnake weed resembles yellow hawkweed, but its larger leaves appear to have blood-filled veins, while the pubescent leaves of trailing arbutus, or mayflower—the Massachusetts state flower—border the woods road to your left. Soon the road curves left and you emerge into a small clearing dominated by a nine-section steel fire tower. You must ascend the steps to a point above the treetops to gain the splendid 360-degree view, but it's definitely worth the climb. Sandy fields lie inside a bend of the Connecticut River just three miles north, while the tall buildings of the University of Massachusetts–Amherst campus stand seven miles away in the opposite direction. Between these cardinal points are Mt. Tom and the Sugarloafs, the latter merely three miles distant.

To begin your descent, follow the power lines behind the tower steeply downhill. Watch your footing among the loose stones and gravel. Hay-scented fern thrives in this rocky, sun-dappled soil. A thick coppice (sprout) growth of red maple indicates fairly recent brush-clearing under the power lines. To the northeast, the verdant hills are a pleasant sight, but better to keep your eyes on the footing in this steep section. If your knees are problematic, you may prefer to hike up this orange-blazed section rather than descend it. In early summer the tubular yellow flowers of bush honeysuckle add a nice bit of color along with the pale-pink of mountain laurel shrubs. Most laurels are now too shaded to produce the extravagant floral displays this species is famous for. Almost all of the woody growth, at least near the right of way, is less than four inches in diameter, which is periodically cleared to a width of about 75 feet.

At a trail split, take the left fork. Listen in late spring and early summer for the lazy *beer-beer-bee* song of the exquisite black-throated blue warbler, a bird partial to laurel thickets. One young trailside black birch has been polished a rich mahogany by the many hands that have gripped it for support. The young growth attracts feeding wood warblers and other insectivorous birds. The trail splits again; stay left on the wider, orange-blazed path into pines (the paths reunite farther downslope). A lush growth of big cinnamon ferns receives necessary moisture from trickling water on the left. Cross a couple of seepage flows where green frogs find suitable quarters. A thriving stand of purple-flowering raspberry puts forth numerous two-inch magenta blossoms in early summer. This member of the rose family is one of our showiest shrubs. A pair of agitated common yellowthroats voiced their displeasure at our passage.

Continue straight, under the power lines, as the trail levels out and a blue-blazed path joins from the left. Soon you'll come to the main woods road that you walked south over toward Roaring Brook. Turn left to retrace your steps to your vehicle, approximately one mile distant.

Getting There

From the intersection of MA 63 and MA 47, travel west on MA 47 for 0.2 mile and turn left (south). Continue south on MA 47 for another 0.8 mile to Reservation Road on the left at the site of a horse farm. Turn left onto Reservation Road and follow it 0.5 mile to a gravel parking area on the right.

—R.L.

34 ❋ Sachem Head

Greenfield
156 acres

- ❖ 1.8 miles
- ❖ 1.5 hours
- ❖ easy, with one moderate slope

Sandwiched between the Connecticut River, at its confluence with the Deerfield River, on the east and the town of Greenfield on the west, lies the basalt ridge known as Rocky Mountain. This two-mile traprock ledge, born of volcanic eruptions some 190 million years ago, is anchored by two promontories that are popular hiking destinations—Poets Seat on the north and Sachem Head on the south. A network of parallel and crossing trails connects Highland Park, Temple Woods, and Rocky Mountain Park, all municipal parklands. Because a paved auto road leads to Poets Seat, it hosts many sightseers, while significant portions of the foot trail leading to the tower are within sight and earshot of busy Greenfield streets.

The walk to Sachem Head, in contrast, will take you deeper into the forest and farther from the hubbub of daily life. The views from Sachem Head are excellent, and the 200-foot elevation gain is confined primarily to one moderately steep stretch. If you don't have a great deal of time but want panoramic views for a moderate amount of effort, this may be the walk for you.

After parking in the small lot at the base of the auto road to Poets Seat, walk back down (south) on Mountain Road whence you came for 0.4 mile. Be careful to walk facing traffic—the shoulder is narrow and caution is urged. Cross Mountain Road at the sight of a yellow metal gate at the entrance to Bear's Den Lane. A stone monument informs one that the 56-acre Temple Woods property was donated to the town by the Women's

Club of Greenfield in 1984. Be sure not to park here. Follow the wide woods road rather than the steeper trail on the right; both are red blazed. Although the din of traffic is still very evident just below you, it will soon fade. Oaks, maples, black birches, and eastern hemlocks cast a welcome shade on a warm summer day as you listen to the music of tufted titmice, red-eyed vireos, ovenbirds, and veery. To the right rises a **basalt** slope where Christmas and evergreen wood ferns are common.

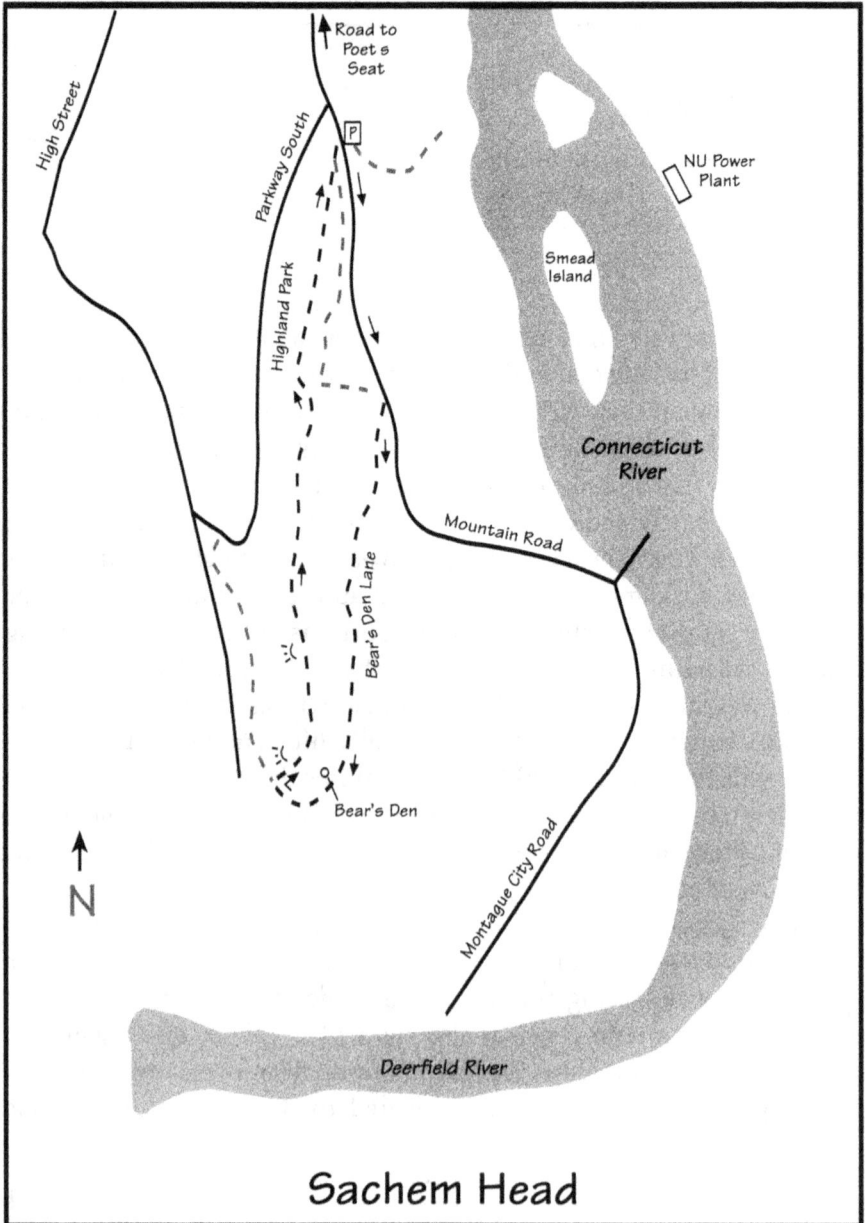

Sachem Head

Pass a yellow-diamond-blazed trail on the right. Another trail, this one marked by yellow rectangles, goes off to the right a bit farther as the road curves left and climbs gradually; remain on the woods road. Wood thrushes, scarlet tanagers, black-and-white warblers, ovenbirds, and eastern wood pewees fill the woodland with a cacophony of song as they advertise for mates and guard their territories. Three-leafed tick trefoil and wood aster form a nearly solid green margin along the roadsides. Pass on the left an appealing 10-foot-diameter growth of **partridgeberry**, with its twin white trumpet flowers in June and creeping foliage. The path goes very gradually downhill now as an unblazed trail wanders off to the left; remain on the road. As the forest deepens, hermit thrushes and brown creepers add their voices to the avian chorus of spring and early summer. The brilliant red fruit clusters of elderberry shrubs enliven the otherwise nearly all green scene. In these moist, rich woods, two-inch long red-backed salamanders remain ensconced under damp logs by day and search for insect prey by night. Lungless, they breathe directly through their mucus-coated skins, which is why they venture out when the atmospheric conditions are more benign.

The blue-blazed Pocumtuck Ridge Trail enters from the right at a sign; this is the steepest route to the top. Remain on the woods road, however. The trail is named for the **Pocumtuck people** whose homeland, for hundreds (and perhaps thousands) of years was centered in what is now the town of Deerfield, just three miles to the south. Intersect the Pocumtuck Trail again a bit farther along on the left. In June and July, the big, showy pink blossoms of purple-flowering raspberry line the moist swales along the road. Reach the basalt cliff that holds **Bear's Den** on the right. A narrow trail leads up through shrubbery a short distance. It is refreshingly cool inside this cleft in the basalt bedrock. Its roof has been blackened by many a campfire, obscuring the normal reddish brown hue of the rock. Return to the road and turn right.

Stay right where the roadway splits and follow the red blazes. Poison ivy is a roadside plant you want to avoid, while sugar maples, white pines, and oaks are the dominant tree species above you. Stay to the right again as a green-blazed trail enters from the left at a curve. The sweet trilling songs of five-and-one-half inch **pine warblers** drift down from high in the conifers; being yellow and green, they are very hard to pick out of the foliage. More brightly colored orange, black, and white American redstarts are common among the broad-leaved trees in these woods. On the right, beneath the tall boles of impressive white pines, are the stone remnants of a picnic area. Reach two more trails on the right, close together. Turn onto the first, which has a series of wooden steps made of former railroad ties forging up the slope. A low rock wall indicates that livestock once pastured on this now wooded incline. Should you walk forcefully, without a pause, you will get a brief but strenuous workout.

Reach a false crest where parasitic wood betony produces its unusual hooded yellow flowers in spring. At a large white pine turn sharply left and climb up over the angular traprock (the geologists' name for basalt) to the ridge top and its attendant views among oaks and pines. Here you're treated to views on both sides, as well as straight ahead to some extent. Re-enter woodland on the blue-blazed Pocumtuck Ridge Trail. Here we observed a **red squirrel** retrieve an acorn and then quickly scamper up a hemlock with its prize. The deep shade of the hemlock grove is also home to the **hermit thrush**, which sings hauntingly beautiful music as if through an enchanted reed.

Arrive at another exposed summit framed by wavy-leafed **chestnut oak** (its bark is deeply furrowed and blocky) and shrublike scrub, or bear, oak; white pine; and small hemlocks. **Lowbush blueberry** thrives in the nutrient-poor, acidic soils. An episode in the lives of a family of black-capped chickadees, our state bird, played out just over our heads as we watched two full-grown fledglings chasing one of their parents mercilessly about, begging for food.

You soon reach the **Sachem Head** summit (*sachem* means Native American chief), where a wooden platform roughly 15 feet square forms a nice perch from which to bird-watch or simply enjoy the scenery. Due south, three miles distant, is the Pocumtuck Range, capped by radio antennas. To the west, gaze out upon flowing green ridges. Just beyond and below the escarpment's edge stand many tall white pines. Farm fields and a few tobacco barns lend scale to the near scene. Two miles away to the southeast, a railroad trestle spans the Connecticut. On an early July day we watched soot-brown chimney swifts hurtle over the promontory in their odd, alternating-wing-beat flight in pursuit of flying insects. These tiny, cigar-shaped birds winter in Peru! A bit farther north along the trail is an outcrop that with a bit of imagination resembles a **bear's head** and forequarters, but you have to look back over your left shoulder to see it, as it will be behind you. Here, perhaps appropriately, grows the creeping **bearberry** "shrub" with its shiny green foliage.

Continue walking downhill through hemlocks, oaks, and black birches. When you reach a fire ring of stones under the hemlocks at a split in the trail, bear left to regain the high ground and continue along the blue-blazed Pocumtuck Trail. You reach another in a series of exposed vista points. The tough traprock provides good footing, but watch your step. Begin a gradual descent and then walk up again over rock. **Huckleberry shrubs** (the leaves are distinguished from blueberry by the minute resin dots on both surfaces) and lowbush blueberry provide delectable fruit for numerous mammals, including humans. Pass an informal side trail on the right. More panoramic vistas appear as the trail skirts the exposed ridge top. One morning in early July, raucous yells alerted us to the approach of **common ravens**. As we gazed skyward, a family flock of five birds shot along the escarpment together.

At a blazed intersection, turn left. The trees growing on this volcanic ridge are short for the most part, owing to the scant soil. The voices of territorial yellow-throated vireos can be heard emanating from the taller woodland below. A few red cedars, trees that germinate in abandoned pastures, dot the ridge top. Soon the buildings of Greenfield come into view again. Enjoy the lovely, nodding flowers of **harebell** in summer, when the whining drone of dog-day cicadas is synonymous with summer heat. From here the descent occurs in stages, alternately dropping and leveling out. Two-foot-tall maple-leaf viburnum shrubs are common along the rocky path. Their foliage turns an interesting rosé wine color in autumn. Occasional taller mountain laurels put on a floral display in June, while witch hazel delays its blooming until fall. Pass another trail on the right, but remain on the blue-blazed trail. Gray squirrels, rather than red squirrels, inhabit this drier, more deciduous woodland. More numerous than either is the ubiquitous eastern chipmunk, the familiar ground squirrel that is almost as much at home in the branches as on the forest floor, and, of course, beneath it.

The sound of traffic from Mountain Road indicates that the end of your walk is nearing. The trail has left the open escarpment. Although you'll seldom be fortunate to see one, 16-inch-long, red-crested **pileated woodpeckers** leave obvious signs of their presence throughout maturing woodland in the form of deep excavations in trees infested by carpenter-ant colonies; note the deep borings in the dead pine. At the trail junction continue straight rather than right. Trailing arbutus, or mayflower, flourishes along the path, but its small size and creeping habit cause it to be easily overlooked. You are now walking over fairly level, less rocky ground on an old woods road. Continue straight where the Bear's Den path enters from the right. Just ahead is Mountain Road (a sign here tells you that Sachem Head is 0.9 mile back the way you came); cross it cautiously and walk back to your vehicle, about 150 feet to the right.

Getting There

From I-91 interchange 26, the junction of I-91 and MA 2A in Greenfield, travel east on MA 2A (Main Street) from the bottom of the exit ramp for 1.1 miles to downtown Greenfield. Turn right at the traffic light onto US 5/MA 10 (Deerfield Street). Drive 1.1 miles south on US 5/MA 10 to where Montague City Road and US 5/MA 10 diverge (Routes 5/10 cross the Deerfield River almost immediately). Do not cross the river, but bear left instead onto Montague City Road. Drive for 1.1 miles to another divergence; here Mountain Road turns left (Montague City Road continues over the Connecticut River to the right). Follow Mountain Road for 0.9 mile across level ground and then steeply uphill to the parking area for Poets Seat on the right. Note that this parking area comes into view quite suddenly.

—R.L.

35 Dunbar Brook

Monroe/Florida
6,457 acres

- ❖ 5.5 miles
- ❖ 3 hours
- ❖ moderately strenuous

Immense trees and a bubbling trout stream create a setting with nearly magical properties. From time immemorial flowing water has had an inherently soothing effect on people, and so it has here. Although this walk's midsection boasts an 800-foot elevation gain, much of the trail leads one downhill under towering trees and alongside Dunbar Brook.

This part of Monroe State Forest, which borders Vermont, is a relatively wild place but one where the remains of water-powered industry are still visible. The massive trees are survivors from a time when virtually all this region was cut over for lumber, charcoal-making, and grazing. Only the precipitous slopes, which made harvesting timber uneconomical, saved what are now forest giants.

Dunbar Brook is a cold-water tributary of the Deerfield River. After snowmelt and spring rains merge their flows, the brook is a raging torrent capable of transporting large boulders. But even during dry summers, its cold, crystal-clear waters sustain native brook trout, spring salamanders, and a host of other aquatic creatures.

From Upper Dunbar Parking Area along Main Road, walk from the map kiosk down gravel Raycroft (South) Road through mixed northern hardwoods toward cascading Dunbar Brook. A blue-blazed trail begins on the left just before you reach an auto bridge over the brook, which you'll cross at the conclusion of your walk. Soon, rushing water and massive gneiss boulders create a photogenic sight. The rocks extend into the woodland of yellow birch, eastern hemlock, American beech, and red maple. The powerful roots of some birches hold boulders tightly in their grasp. Soon arrive at the **ruins of a former mill** for which the brook provided power— two parallel walls of stones stacked some 12 feet high.

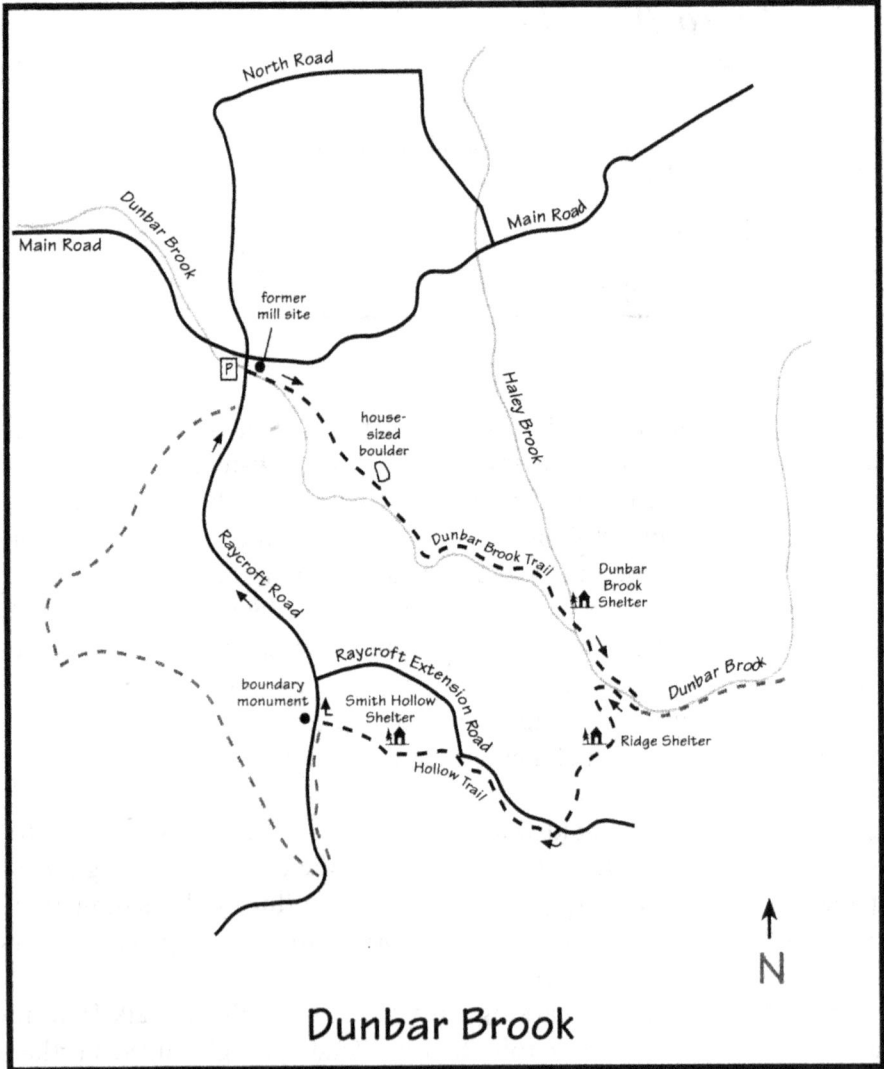

Dunbar Brook

American yew, a low-growing, spreading evergreen; hobblebush; and striped and mountain maples add visual charm to the woodland, while the aroma of conifer needles stimulates another sense. Enter a hemlock stand after crossing an intermittent cataract on angular boulders. As you walk uphill, note that with the exception of spinulose wood fern, little else can survive in the deep shade. The trail bears left, away from the brook, at a blue blaze and then uphill; a few railroad ties serve as steps. Black-throated green and Blackburnian warblers nest in the tall evergreens above and sing sweetly, but the sound of occasional traffic from Main Road is still also evident.

The needle-cushioned path reaches an angled **T** intersection with a wider trail; turn right onto the rather level old woods road. New York fern and shining club moss, which resembles green bottlebrushes, grow on the forest floor as well as on the numerous rocks. Rough yellow birches more than two feet in diameter appear. They are a dominant northern hardwood forest tree. In May, red trillium (wake-robin) and clintonia (blue-bead lily) flower beneath them. A house-sized boulder on the right, large enough to have small trees growing on top of it, catches your eye. Some rocks show milky-white quartz intrusions. Re-enter shaded hemlock woods where blue-headed vireo, brown creeper, and hermit thrush dwell. At a **Y** junction (both sides blazed blue) take the right fork. A striking mahogany-and-cream-colored **bracket fungus** on a hemlock snag caught our attention. This is but the organism's fruiting body; a vast threadlike fungal network draws sustenance from the decaying wood.

Six-inch-tall patches of **shining club moss** under the beeches and hemlocks appear as a green shag rug. This nonflowering relative of ferns thrives in moist, rich, acidic soil and propagates by subsurface runners. In contrast, **columnar hemlocks** (nearly three feet in diameter) and beeches (nearly as large) make one feel insignificant. Both species tolerate shade well. Hobblebush forms chest-high "thickets" which, as its name indicates, can be difficult for human or beast to walk through. Many beeches unfortunately show the effects of disease. A minute scale insect creates points of entry in the bark of a healthy tree for a fungus that goes on to disfigure it. Walk easily downhill and re-enter a dense young hemlock grove, then climb. Pink lady's slippers (moccasin flower) bloom in the acid soil in late spring. Wood sorrel (its leaves resemble clover) sports delicate white and pink blossoms. In the trees above, black-capped chickadees, red-breasted nuthatches, red-eyed vireos, and black and white and magnolia warblers search for insects.

The shiny, scalloped leaves of goldthread reflect sunlight in the light gaps, and marbled gneiss boulders protrude from the forest floor. Walk steadily downhill on the cushioned path, then level out. Some black birches, red maples, and red spruces appear. Seedling red spruces originated from seeds missed by red squirrels. Note the screened view of the verdant ridge beyond the brook. The trail turns right and brushes by a **looming cabin-sized boulder** capped by mosses and polypody fern. There is virtually no moss on this shaded flank. Pass another big outcrop topped by the little ferns and then descend between boulders and bear right. Hemlocks and birches perch on other smaller rocks. One sports its own miniature forest of two- to three-foot tall hemlocks. Continue downhill in the shade cast by hemlocks and birches. The rocky stream bed soon comes into view. A yellow birch (young trees have brassy, peeling bark) two feet in diameter and a red spruce 20 inches across constitute large specimens for this region.

Turn left at a **T** intersection just above the brook and parallel its crystalline waters. Naked two- to six-foot-long boulders demarcate its bed. A **massive, blackened old yellow birch** measures fully 31 inches in diameter along the bank. Indian cucumber-root blooms along the trail in early summer. Its flowers are small, pendant, and yellow; its small tuber is edible. Cross a seep where frogs find refuge, and walk under a canopy of young hemlocks. To your left is a boulder-strewn slope. Six- to eight-inch-long **brook trout** patrol the sun-flecked pools of Dunbar Brook, easily spotted in the clear, oxygenated water. Even on a hot day, air temperatures are comfortable. While you linger and cool off, listen for the loud, exuberant song of the tiny winter wren above the steady roar. For the most part, though, the brook drowns birdsong. A wreckage of weathered logs and debris along the bank testifies to the water's power, notably after vernal deluges.

Pass another huge yellow birch (with three trunks) soon after resuming your walk. Hobblebush with its large, heart-shaped leaves is abundant along this pleasant stretch. Cross another rill, the first of several that carry runoff from the steep slope on your left. Christmas fern and a few long beech ferns grow here. **Dusky and two-lined salamanders** live in wet places like this, where predatory fish are absent. Cross a log bridge over a drainageway and enter birch, beech, hemlock, and maple woods, with a few white ashes. Here we enjoyed the ethereal song of **Swainson's thrush**, a seven-inch-long olive-brown bird of spruce forests; we were to be treated to two more that June day.

Cross Parsonage Brook flowing in from the left on a log bridge. There are some fine hemlock specimens here, and their accumulated dead needles provide soft footing. The forest is red maple, yellow birch, and red spruce (one is more than two feet in diameter) as you bear away from the stream slightly. Early yellow violets, with heart-shaped basal leaves, bloom in early spring as you walk, higher above the brook now. On the right rests a boulder with a thick, milky-white quartz intrusion. Quartz is one of the hardest minerals and the main ingredient in sand. Cross a **power-line cut** where species preferring edge habitats, such as chestnut-sided warblers and some butterflies, find conditions to their liking. The cut is growing up to spiraea, white pine, birch, maple, raspberries, and ferns.

Re-enter cool mixed woods where blue-headed vireos and black-throated green and Blackburnian warblers breed. Large trees continue to impress, including a white pine on your right almost three feet in diameter. The rushing brook is audible below the fairly steep slope as you descend. Hermit thrushes vocalize as you make your way down through birch/beech woodland; a big twin-boled beech stands on the right. Ovenbirds and American redstarts join the refrain. Haley Brook joins Dunbar Brook from the left; continue straight ahead where an ORV trail crosses Haley Brook. Reach **Dunbar Shelter,** the first of three. The adjacent pit toilet is in disrepair. Walk by the shelter, turn left, and very soon cross a wooden bridge over Haley Brook. Partridgeberry and shinleaf grow where an ORV track joins the trail from the left. Yellow-bellied sapsuckers, wood thrushes, and **black-throated green warblers** (we recorded 18 along the

*Most of the first portion of the walk follows
Dunbar Brook's boulder-strewn channel.*

trail) advertise their presence as you cross a short wooden boardwalk. Plenty of white snakeroot, which contains a toxic alcohol, lines the path. In earlier centuries, many people died from drinking milk produced by cows that had eaten the plant.

At the **Y,** bear right toward the brook. The trail can be easily overlooked and you may well be tempted to continue straight on the unblazed old woods road, but don't. The shiny, heart-shaped leaves of little Canada mayflower carpet the forest floor; a spike of tiny white flowers appears in spring. Reach a junction with an old woods road on the left, and then continue straight ahead on the level trail along Dunbar Brook. Pass another enormous white pine and then another. Clumps of leafy green sedges grow on islets in the stream. Watch for an **old millstone** that lies along the edge of the brook just before you reach a fire ring and a picnic table which indicate a tenting site amid the pines. Turn right and descend stone steps toward the brook. This is a nice location to rest and reflect upon the awesome power of flowing water. When you start again, you negotiate the **50-foot-long wooden span** across Dunbar Brook and begin an 800-vertical-foot, switchbacked ascent on the other side.

Soon after crossing the stream come to a **T** intersection, both directions blazed blue; turn right (left will take you to Lower Dunbar picnic area). Proceed uphill rather steeply. Foamflower, clintonia, and Indian cucumber-root help hold the soil in place. Yellow birch is abundant and red maple and a shrub layer of hobblebush grow on this northeast-facing slope. A massive sugar maple is on the right and an equally impressive white ash stands on the left. A tiny tree frog known as a **spring peeper** hopped about on the forest floor, cryptically colored to melt into the faded tan beech leaf upon which it sat. Had it not moved, I would never have seen it. Proceed up the steep slope via switchbacks where a 31-inch-diameter old-growth yellow birch stands guard over the rocky trail. Steps have been cut into two birches lying across the trail. Here a mound of bear scat which appeared to be at least several days old briefly halted our progress. Wildlife officials now estimate that some 1,600 black bears reside in our four western counties.

Plump, three-inch-long American toads betray their positions with hops. These amiable amphibians search for insects and slugs on the forest floor. Walk through a small hemlock stand, where one of us spied a hen turkey, and level out. All three club mosses—princess pine, cedar, and especially shining—grow here along with Indian cucumber-root. Birch and maple become dominant again as you reach the **Ridge Shelter**. Here the blue-blazed trail, actually a woods road, bears left. Smooth-trunked American beech joins the mix as the path winds past a few rock outcrops. Hay-scented, or boulder, fern colonizes the glades where sunlight reaches the forest floor. Come to a boggy spot on the left where sphagnum moss, cinnamon fern, sedges (which look like grasses but have triangular stems), and red spruce thrive. Look for the tracks of white-tailed deer in the moist soil of the woods road.

Pass the remains of an old wooden gate, with only the posts still standing, and soon reach gravel Raycroft Extension Road at a **T** intersection; both directions are blazed blue. This is a wider version of what you've just walked. Turn right and pass a good-sized red oak on the right. This pleasant, level roadway passes through red maple, beech, gray and white birch (the latter's bark peels more readily), and hemlock woods. Chipmunks scamper and chirp below the understory of striped maple or moosewood. **Impressive red oaks** too become commonplace as caterpillar-consuming red-eyed vireos sing up a storm all day long, regardless of the temperature. Sessile-leaved bellwort, Canada mayflower, false Solomon's seal, and cedar club moss line the gently undulating treadway. At an overgrown woods road to your right, continue straight ahead.

Just past a jutting boulder, come to a narrow woods road on the left (blazed blue) and turn onto it. Descend gradually through similar woodland where blue-headed vireos and black-throated green warblers nest. Reach a trail on the left where a sign reads Trail and includes a directional arrow and blue blaze. Turn left onto it, noting the remains of stone walls that once kept livestock out of crops. Walk downhill beneath beeches, maples, and birches (including black birch, a tree that avoids fire-scorched earth) and reach **Smith Shelter**, the third and final one. A family of wood thrushes fussed and scolded as we ambled through their haunts. Walk down a steeper hill, passing a two-foot-diameter yellow birch in the process. Where two signs mark the way, the path turns sharply right and leads you uphill through hardwoods. A **venerable old sugar maple** some 40 feet off the trail to the right measures 38 inches in diameter. Left to provide shade for livestock and maple syrup for humans, it was spared the ax long ago. Beech's propensity to sprout is illustrated by roots crossing the trail.

Reach the power-line cut again. The trail's location on the opposite side is difficult to locate; it commences a bit farther upslope. Re-enter beech woods containing spruce and maple on a narrow and less traveled path. These woods are home to many species of colorful wood warblers, sometimes called the "butterflies of the bird world" for their bright colors and flitting movements. Ones to listen and look for here include black-throated blue, Blackburnian, and magnolia. Pockmarks in the path indicate where chipmunks have retrieved acorns. Seedling spruces thrive along the path, and a few scaly hop hornbeam trees make an appearance. Sun-dappled fern glades add beauty to the woodland scene as you walk on a wider trail now. White birches become numerous. Continue gradually uphill to reach Raycroft Road.

Your route turns right, but first walk left for approximately 100 feet to examine a **stone boundary monument** between Franklin (right) and Berkshire (left) Counties; the year 1900 is engraved at the top, followed by a series of subsequent years. Continuing left would eventually take you to the summit of Spruce Mountain. Turn right instead to follow Raycroft Road 1.5 miles back to your vehicle. Ignore a variety of other tracks that enter from both sides along the way. Walk up a gradual hill flanked by light-green hay-scented fern. **Whorled wood aster,** which blooms in late summer, is ubiquitous. White ash joins other northern hardwoods as you pass through a Depression-era red pine plantation. Raycroft Road Extension merges on the right, but continue straight. In summer, red-berried elder shrubs are loaded with clusters of bright red fruit. This gentle rise constitutes the height-of-land (2,000 feet elevation) along your route today.

Young trees indicate fairly recent clearing of some stands of trees, while in contrast a sugarbush of ancient maple lines the roadway. A large beech on the right displays the telltale **claw-mark scars of a black bear** that climbed this tree to feast on beechnuts one autumn, years ago. Ovenbirds, American redstarts, and other birds are more plentiful woodland inhabitants. Walk down a gentle hill past ferns, hobblebush, raspberries, wild sarsaparilla, and tall Indian cucumber-root. Cross a couple of small feeder streams as the road becomes rougher. A boulder to your left is covered with polypody fern and what's left of a one-foot-diameter yellow birch that once was perched atop it. More angular gneiss boulders capped with ferns appear. Lovely pink **ragged robin,** wood sorrel, and meadow rue bloom on the roadside in June. Just ahead you soon hear the pleasing roar of Dunbar Brook. Bear left at a small parking area; cross the small auto bridge to walk uphill back to your vehicle.

Getting There

From the intersection of MA 2 and MA 8 in North Adams, follow MA 2/8 north 1.3 miles to where MA 8 turns left at a flashing yellow light. Continue straight (east), however, on MA 2 for an additional 2.9 miles, ascending the steep slope to the hairpin curve. After rounding the curve (Golden Eagle Restaurant on the left), continue sharply uphill, cresting at West Summit. Continue straight on MA 2 and soon cross the Florida town line; from here drive 1.45 miles to Tilda Hill Road on the left. Turn onto Tilda Hill Road, which becomes Main Road at the county line, for a total of 4.2 miles to a small gravel parking area on the right, immediately beyond a sign for the Monroe State Forest Recreational Trail System.

—R.L.

Hampshire and Hampden Counties

36 Buffam Falls Conservation Area

Pelham
65 acres

❖ 1 mile

❖ 30 minutes

❖ easy

❖ great for children

Buffam Falls Conservation Area is one of those lesser-known gems, far off the beaten path, worth the effort to find. Two small streams, Buffam Brook and Amethyst Brook, meet here in a woodland of tall hemlocks. The walk is short, relatively flat, and nice for children.

The entrance to the conservation area is about 400 feet north of the parking area on North Valley Road, just opposite the first house. A sign welcomes you to Buffam Falls Conservation Area and a small footbridge spans Buffam Brook. When you cross the footbridge, turn right. The path follows the brook downstream through shaded forest where mountain laurel grows in the understory beneath hemlocks and a scattering of pines.

It's only a 10-minute walk to the confluence of Buffam Brook and Amethyst Brook. The largest of the many **waterfalls** (all are relatively small) will be on your right, on Buffam Brook, just before the two brooks meet. Just beyond the falls, steps lead down to the confluence of the two brooks. This is a nice spot for photography, especially near noon when the sun is overhead and lights up the white cascading water and surrounding evergreens. The shaded waters stay cool even in the summer, and small brook trout hide beneath rocks near the riverbank.

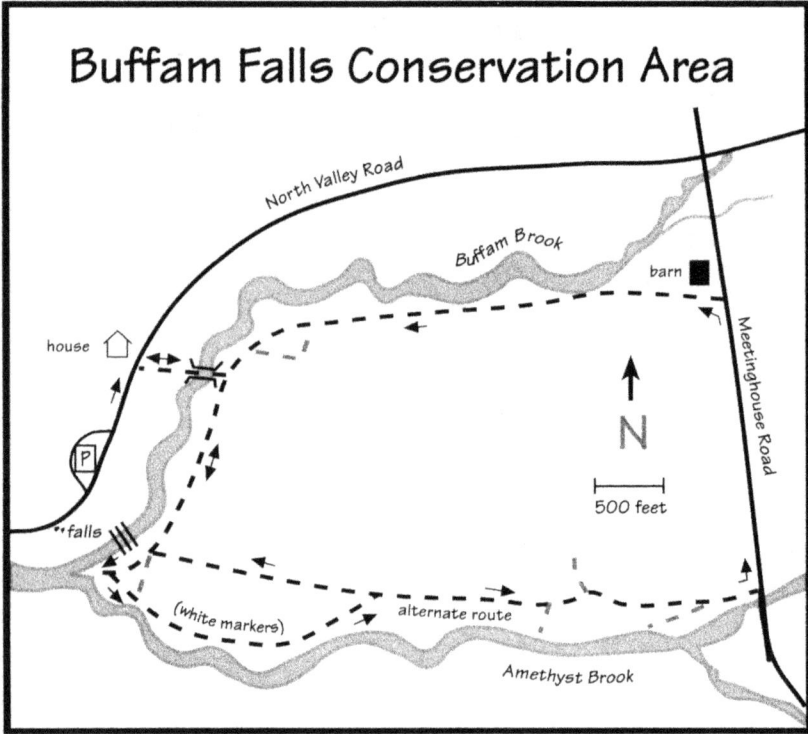

Buffam Falls Conservation Area

In periods of low water it's possible to cross Amethyst Brook and follow another network of trails; however, this trail stays on this side (north) of the brook. Retrace your path back up the steps and then take the trail with the white paint markers following Amethyst Brook upstream. (It will be on your right after climbing the steps.) The trail stays close to the stream, and as you pass through this dark ravine, the sound of flowing water mixes with birdcalls from the forest.

Much of this section of Pelham and the western portion of Amherst have been left in their natural state to protect this important watershed, and the diversity of wildlife is rich. Deer, wild turkey, raccoon, and otter are just some of the animals seen on the property. Although once abundant when Europeans first settled in New England, **turkeys** were wiped out in Massachusetts by 1851 from overhunting and destruction of the birds' hardwood habitat. Through a program of trapping wild turkeys in New York and transplanting them in Massachusetts, beginning in 1972, their numbers are now increasing throughout the Bay State.

Hemlocks shade the cool waters at Buffam Falls.

In spite of their increasing numbers, they are difficult to see in the woods. Generally, they see you before you see them, and their coloring blends in well with the woods. One time I came upon a flock of wild turkeys and was amazed at how fast they could move, silently weaving through the undergrowth. They look similar to the barnyard turkey but have a rusty (not white) tip to the tail and are a bit slimmer.

Turkeys feed on acorns, wild turnip, jack-in-the-pulpit, and early buds of hardwoods. In the springtime the male "toms" try to attract females by strutting with tail fan erect. Toms weigh an average of 16 pounds and females about 9 or 10 pounds. And unlike the domestic-bred turkeys, which are too heavy to fly, these wild birds can take to the wing at 35 miles per hour!

As you walk along Amethyst Brook, the **hemlock** needles that cushion your steps also serve to keep the undergrowth down, thus allowing you to scan the woods for wildlife. Hemlock trees block out much of the sun, and their acidic needles also help to keep vegetation from growing beneath their sweeping branches.

After you've walked about 10 minutes down this streamside trail, it climbs to the left a bit, rising away from the stream, and connects with another trail. By turning left the trail forms a loop, leading back toward Buffam Brook.

More ambitious hikers may want to turn right and explore the trail to the east, which leads through a pine grove. The trail roughly follows Amethyst Brook upstream for about half a mile and then crosses Meetinghouse Road. Leave the trail and turn left (north) and go along the dirt road for 0.4 mile to an old barn on the left. To the left is a path; follow it westerly. This will lead you downstream along Buffam Brook and back to the entrance at the footbridge.

(There are additional interesting trails to explore nearby at the Amethyst Brook Conservation Area. The parking lot for this area is found on Pelham Road, roughly one mile west from where it passes North Valley Road.)

Getting There

From the junction of Route 202 and Amherst Road (at the Pelham Town Hall) take Amherst Road west about 2.0 miles to the United Church of Pelham (where Meetinghouse Road and Enfield Road intersect with Amherst Road). From this intersection continue west on Amherst Road exactly 1.2 miles to North Valley Road on the right. Turn right on North Valley Road and go 0.6 mile to the pull-off on the left under the power lines.

From Amherst take Main Street east to where it crosses North East Street and continue 1.7 miles (Main Street turns into Pelham Road). Turn left on North Valley Road and go 0.6 mile to the pull-off on the left under the power lines.

Open year-round, seven days a week, no admission, no rest rooms.

—M.T.

William Cullen Bryant Homestead

37

Cummington
195 acres

❖ 0.9 mile

❖ 1 hour

❖ easy

This little rill, that from the springs
Of yonder grove its current brings,
Plays on the slope awhile, and then
Goes prattling into groves again,
Oft to its warbling waters drew
My little feet, when life was new.

So begins William Cullen Bryant's "The Rivulet," written in 1823 at his home, now a property of The Trustees of Reservations. This poem is one of many written by the poet and newspaperman during his long and productive life. In 1799, as a child of five, Bryant moved to the then two-story home on the hill, now a National Historic Landmark, where he spent the happiest days of his youth. Years later, after gaining fame and fortune as poet and editor of the *Saturday Evening Post,* he returned to his boyhood home amid the rolling, wooded hills of rural Hampshire County. He lived out his later years tending orchards—he and his brother planted 1,300 fruit trees and rows of now massive sugar maples paralleling the stone walls—and walking the woods and fields until his death in 1878 at age 84.

From the small gravel parking lot (elevation 1,560 feet) across from the homestead, walk back down the road 300 feet. Walk through a gap in the stone wall to the left and cross the pasture to West Cummington Road. In late summer, insects abound in the grass. Field crickets chirp endlessly on warm days as butterflies seek nectar and mates. Watch for fritillaries, monarchs, red-spotted purple-white admirals, viceroys, large wood nymphs, inornate ringlets, sulphurs, and whites. Rivulet Trail begins on the opposite side of the road. When crossing the pasture is not advisable due to the presence of dairy cows, walk to the intersection of Route 112 (Bryant Four Corners), turn left, and walk north on West Cummington Road for approximately 300 feet to the trailhead on the right. Yellow circular paint blazes mark the trail route.

The forest floor is cushioned with decaying pine needles, providing the perfect seed bed for **Canada mayflower** and other acid-tolerant wildflowers. Rivulet Brook, which is spring fed, flows year-round, tumbling along, twisting and turning. In summer listen for the songs of wood warblers and scan the tree branches for American redstart, Canada warbler, rose-breasted grosbeak, red-eyed vireo, and tiny red-breasted nuthatch. Besides sugar maple and white pine, white ash and black cherry are fairly numerous; some are quite large. As the trail descends gradually through a small hemlock gorge, notice that many of the hemlocks are sizable, creating thick shade below. The bark of very old hemlocks tends to become a reddish cinnamon color. Where the stream has cut deeply—leaving high banks—the exposed roots of hemlocks are clearly visible. In the stream itself, flat, moss-covered stones harbor dusky salamanders. Spinulose wood fern (an evergreen), shining club moss—which looks something like a green bottlebrush—and numerous fungi protrude from the moist soil. Red squirrels eat the abundant toadstools.

I counted the growth rings of one hemlock that had been cleared from the trail and found 85—a mere youngster amid these towering giants. Where more sunlight is available here, **yellow birch**, one of the northern hardwood forest codominants, has grown to truly unusual size. Nowhere else in western Massachusetts have I seen such large specimens. In spring the woodland floor brightens with the three-petaled blossoms of painted and red trilliums and violets (which Bryant mentions in his poem). Christmas fern, long beech fern (whose bottom leaflets point downward), and New York fern grow in the rich soils below the big trees. The songs of wood thrushes resound through the woodland at dusk and at dawn.

Progress down along the north side of the brook. The ravine becomes deeper; its clay banks have been eroded and exposed by powerful flood waters. Rivulet Brook flows into the Westfield River just 0.7 mile north of the trailhead.

At the lowest point on the route (1,390 feet) cross a wooden bridge. The trail turns left to begin the return just before reaching two very large white pines near the trail—look for double yellow blazes. These trees are so large, I photographed them with a friend standing alongside for scale.

Although not shown on the official Trustees map of the property, the trail now makes a loop at its terminus and rejoins the main trail near the brook. Red-backed salamanders and red efts patrol the moist woodlands looking for insects and other small invertebrates to eat. Red efts are bold enough to be abroad in daylight, especially if it's raining; they are poisonous to predators. Beechnuts litter the trail below the smooth, light-gray-skinned trees in late summer. Wild turkeys, bear, squirrels, and other wildlife are fond of the nutritious nuts.

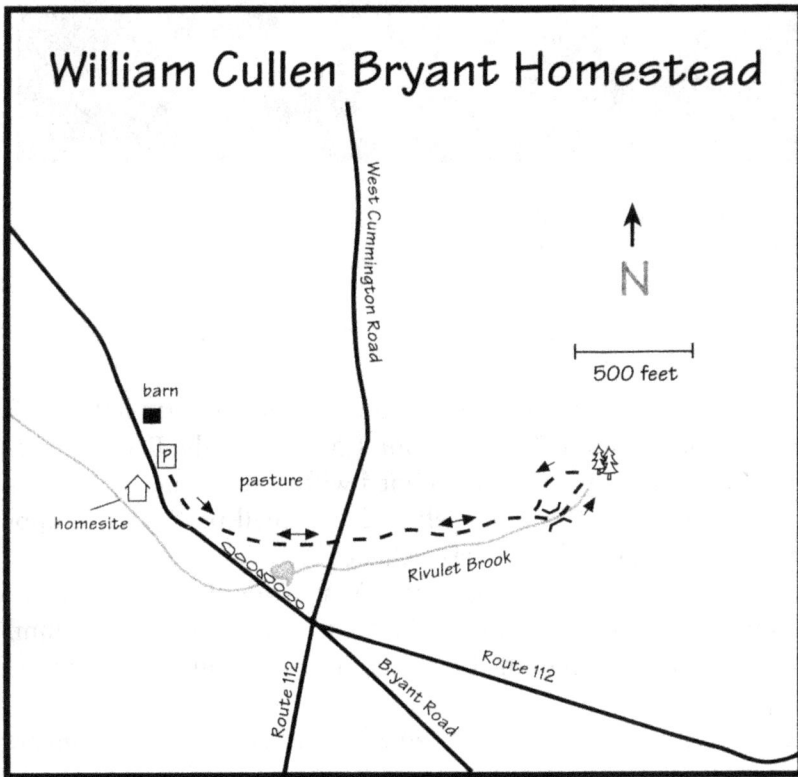

William Cullen Bryant Homestead

Work your way slowly uphill and back to the trailhead, and think about how these woods may have changed since Bryant's youth. Some of the trees are much older and much larger, to be sure. The landscape, rather than predominantly farmland as it was in his day, is now largely wooded. In many ways, however, probably little has changed in this rural setting— something that would no doubt please the poet were he alive today.

An inherent tranquillity overhangs the pasture and woodland as seen from the homestead.

Getting There

From the east: Take Route 9 west to Cummington and turn left onto Route 112 south. Follow Route 112 south for 1.5 miles to the Bryant Four Corners. Continue straight on the road lined with maples and stone walls that leads to the homestead on your left and the small parking area opposite, which can accommodate about six vehicles.

From the west: Turn right onto West Cummington Road in West Cummington just before it crosses the Westfield. Follow West Cummington Road west and south to the Bryant Four Corners and turn right to enter the property.

Reservation closes at sunset. No admission fee. House hours are Friday, Saturday, and Sunday, 1:00 P.M. to 5:00 P.M. Admission fee to house. Rest rooms are located inside. Picnic tables are available across from the parking area.

—R.L.

38 Chesterfield Gorge

Chesterfield
166 acres

❖ 3 miles

❖ 2 hours

❖ easy

You will find no other place in Massachusetts quite like this one. Chesterfield Gorge has that kind of primeval beauty embodied by solid rock and flowing water. The corrosive power of water and glacial ice are clearly evident in the sheer, gray granite chasm; gouged and sculpted bedrock bears the legacy of grinding glaciers followed by millennia of polishing by water. The margins of this lovely, fast-flowing stream—designated a National Wild and Scenic River in 1994—are lined with smooth, oval granite cobbles. The shallow, rocky bottom makes this ideal habitat for cold-water fishes such as brook, brown, and rainbow trout and newly restored Atlantic salmon.

Stately white pines and hemlocks line the east side of the narrow gorge. Oaks, birches, and beeches thrive in the sun on the opposite side. Interrupted fern, sedges, horsetails, and willows grow in the moist flood plain slightly downstream of the chasm.

At the upper end of the gorge—the "narrows"—stand the stone abutments of the **historic High Bridge**. Built circa 1770, the bridge enabled the Boston to Albany Post Road to span the Westfield. British troops crossed the bridge retreating to Boston after their defeat at Saratoga in 1777. A tollgate was erected on the opposite (east) side of the river in 1779, and the remnants of the gatekeeper's house and the surrounding small community are all that survive. This Trustees of Reservations property was acquired in 1929 in a successful attempt to prevent it from being logged. Additional parcels were added later, and the reservation is bordered by the 2,000-acre Gilbert Bliss State Forest.

This is a rather flat, easy walk. From the parking area, a short trail skirts the top of the bluff above the river, affording wonderful sights and sounds of the gorge and river. Continue to walk downstream and slightly downhill where the path rejoins River Road to the right. Beyond the gorge you can reach the rich natural community along the river by many short, informal trails leading from the road.

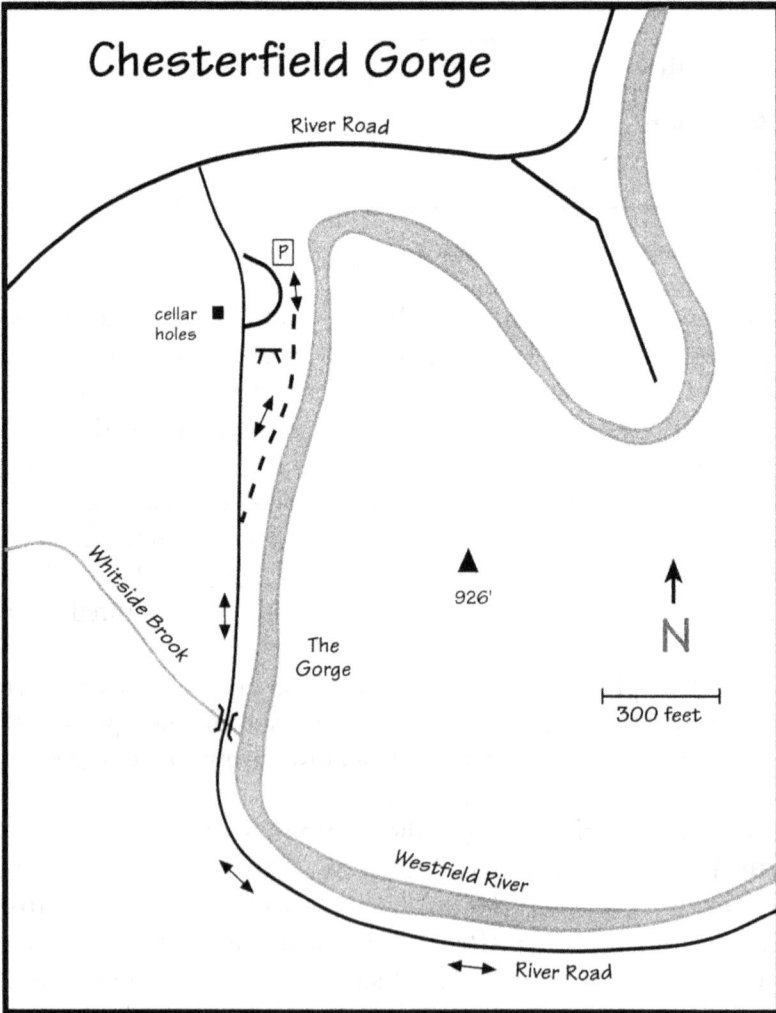

Chesterfield Gorge

River Road

P

cellar holes ■

Whitside Brook

▲
926'

The
Gorge

N

300 feet

Westfield River

◄► River Road

After parking and reading the notices on the visitor information board, where a map is posted, proceed directly to the gorge overlook area. Be aware that **poison ivy** grows abundantly in the reservation. Walk down through the grassy, well-kept picnic area on the right, to the trail leading to the edge of the defile. Metal railings provide a measure of safety. From here, gaze southward (right) and downstream through the narrows. The view is truly inspirational and you may want to capture it on film. (Relatively high film speeds are recommended.) The **sheer granite walls** are topped by a thick growth of eastern hemlock. The ground beneath your feet is spongy with the accumulated layers of decayed and decaying needles. Little else can grow in this acidic soil, so rich in tannin.

After you've enjoyed the views, continue to where the trail intersects River Road and turn left onto the road. Follow the gurgling river downstream. Across the river are forests of beech, birch, and maple. Mountain laurel, which blooms beautifully in late June and early July, provides an evergreen shrub layer. Hobblebush, another understory shrub, produces large clusters of white, hydrangea-like flowers in May. Ferns and little club mosses grow on the forest floor. Spring's wildflower extravaganza yields such finds as Solomon's seal, with white flowers hanging in pairs along the stem; false Solomon's seal; Canada mayflower (all three are lilies); wild sarsaparilla, which has round heads of modest yellow flowers on long stalks; red trillium, or wake-robin; and white starflower.

About 700 feet beyond the end of the reservation trail on the right, you'll pass Whitside Brook, a modest but lovely cascading stream that flows over moss-covered boulders on its way to the Westfield. The steep slopes beyond the brook are clothed by hemlock and pine. Impish red squirrels bound across the forest floor or chatter at an intruder from above. You may also see smaller striped eastern chipmunks.

The river makes a swing to the east. Beyond the gorge, the flood plain widens. Explore the rocky riverbanks in late spring and early summer. Among the colorful wildflowers blooming in the sunny but moist river corridor are pink wild geranium, golden alexanders, robin plantain (actually a daisy relative), tall buttercup, and pretty marsh blue violet. When you look back upstream to the north you'll see the rounded green mass of Smith Pyramid—500 feet above the river. At 1,185 feet, it is the highest point in the area.

During a visit in early June, I was fortunate to see a female **common merganser** and her seven ducklings. This large fish-eating duck is a rare breeder in Massachusetts. The female, with her soft gray body plumage and slightly crested, rust-colored head, made loud barking sounds while half swimming, half running over the surface of the water, urging her young to follow her, which they did. In seconds, they were out of sight. Common mergansers have serrated bills well designed for gripping slippery fish.

Here they feed on common shiners and other small fishes. You're more likely to find the blue-and-white, shaggy-crested belted kingfisher hunting here. The female is the more colorful of the pair, with a chestnut "belt" across her abdomen as well as a blue one.

The 100-foot-deep chasm bears witness that even granite is no match for the gouging action of flowing water over the eons.

Continue down the dirt road, passing a huge fern- and moss-covered boulder on the right. Listen for the songs of such forest-dwelling birds as eastern wood pewee, veery, wood thrush, and rose-breasted grosbeak. Mosquitoes are numerous in late spring and summer, so you may want to bring repellent. Far more welcome are the beautiful butterflies that bask, feed, and puddle in woodland clearings and along the riverbanks. Big yellow and black tiger swallowtails were in the process of emerging from their pupal cases during one of my late-spring visits. The sight of a dozen of these gorgeous insects probing for mineral salts on a gravel bank was a memorable one indeed.

If you look carefully into the shallows you'll see inch-long caddis fly larval cases constructed of sticks by these insects. Watch closely and you may see the animals crawling slowly about, dragging their homes with them. Larger aquatic invertebrates in the river include three-and-one-half-inch-long crayfish. Emerging mayflies provide food for trout. Fishing here is by artificial lure only and strictly catch-and-release. The state Division of Fisheries and Wildlife has posted many fishing-access sites along the river, and trout fishing is, as you might expect, a popular pastime.

Proceed another few hundred yards (1.45 miles from the parking area) to a closed iron gate at the state forest boundary. A small feeder stream flows under the road near this point. Bronze-colored **two-lined salamanders** spend their days under flat stones along the wet margin of the brook.

Retrace your steps back to your vehicle (about 1.5 miles) to explore the historic, human-made features of this property, or continue walking along River Road to the Knightville Reservoir in Huntington—a distance of 6.0 miles.

After returning to your vehicle at the lot (parking is not allowed along River Road), continue north approximately 200 feet beyond the parking area on informal trails to a vantage point on the west side of the river, opposite the High Bridge abutment. You can get a nice view of the native stone structure from this spot. Continuing to the left down to river level, see examples of **sculpted bedrock**, left of the abutment. The Westfield makes another 90-degree turn here to the east. When you're ready, head back toward the parking lot, and cross the road to view cellar holes remaining from the early settlement. In early May, a thick stand of lovely bloodroot carpets the edge of the clearing with delicate white blossoms.

Getting There

From Route 143 in Chesterfield, travel 2.0 miles to West Chesterfield, cross the Westfield River, and turn left onto Ireland Street (no sign) opposite Cummington Road. Travel 0.8 mile down Ireland Street to gravel River Road on the left. You'll see the green and white Trustees of Reservations sign for the gorge here. Drive down River Road for 0.2 mile to the parking area on your left.

Hours are sunrise to sunset. Entry fee is two dollars for adults; children under age 12 are free. Pit toilets are available. Dogs allowed on leash only. Swimming, bathing, and wading are prohibited.

—R.L.

39 Glendale Falls Reservation

Middlefield
60 acres

❖ 1.2 miles

❖ 1.5 hours

❖ moderate

Clear and cold, Glendale Brook flows headlong over polished **granite ledges**, forming gleaming white cascades and root-beer-colored pools as it rushes toward the Middle Branch of the Westfield River. Pleasantly out of the way, Glendale Falls is actually a series of picturesque cascades, more than 150 feet high in all. The volume pouring over the rust-stained ledges is quite considerable—especially in spring—and a visit is well worth your while at any time.

From the top of the falls (1,060 feet) is a beautiful view eastward of the wooded ridges on the far side of the Middle Branch—some reaching 1,600 feet above sea level. All three branches of the Westfield were declared a National Wild and Scenic River in 1994. Eastern hemlock grow on the north-facing slope right of the falls, while birch, beech, and maple stand on the sunnier opposing side. Mountain laurel and hobblebush grow beneath the dominant trees. The only way to view the falls themselves is to walk down the rather steep, rocky hill to a point below the cascades, stopping quite often to take in the photogenic scenes above.

Native stone foundations of two buildings, one possibly a former mill house, stand on the northern shore, and a big **granite mill wheel**—looking like a huge doughnut—lies abandoned along the edge of the cascades. Upstream of the falls are wetlands and upland meadows that in the 1700s were part of the Glendale Farm. Now The Trustees of Reservations owns and manages this lovely property.

From the parking area you can walk along the south side of the stream or alternatively cross the brook above the falls on steppingstones and proceed downhill through the deciduous forest on the north side of the cascades. **Witch hazel**, a small tree from which the astringent of the same name is derived, is quite abundant. Unlike most plants, this tree blooms in late fall, producing somewhat straggly yellow blossoms. Its leaves are wavy toothed and have uneven bases. Other understory trees you'll see include the aptly named ironwood (also known as musclewood); striped maple, or moosewood (green-and-white-striped bark); the scaly barked hop hornbeam; and the white-flowering Juneberry, or shad. The name "shad" refers to the fact that gizzard shad (a herring relative) make their spring migrations up streams from salt water at the time, when this tree flowers.

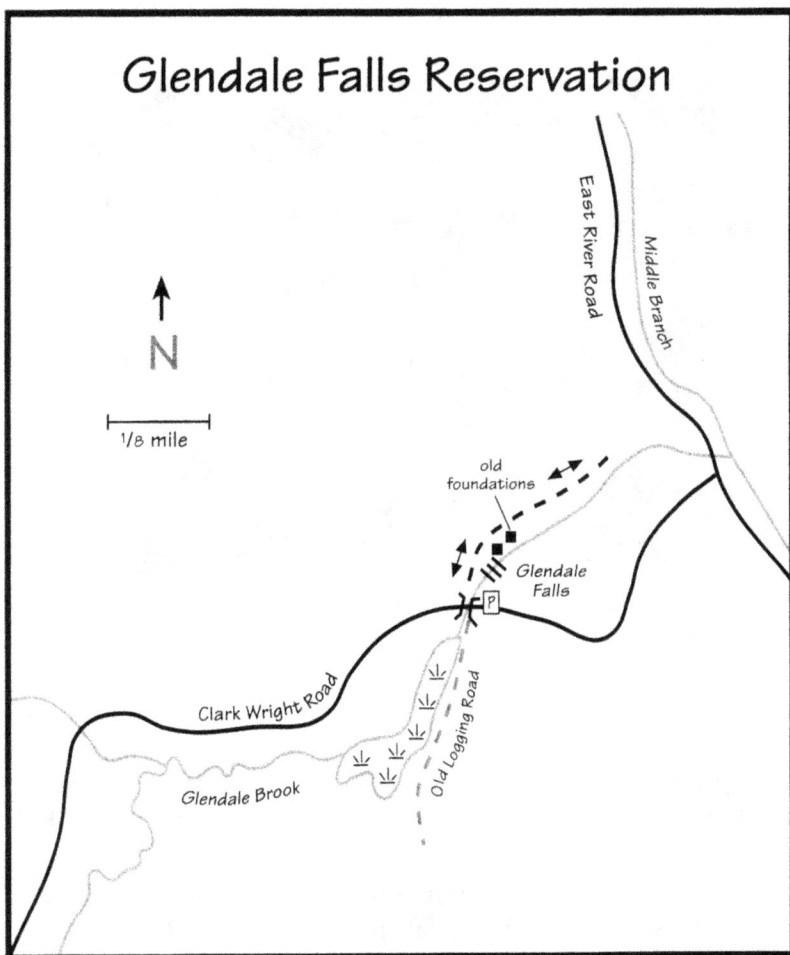

Glendale Falls Reservation

From vantage points along the way, you'll be able to get intimate looks at the gushing water and the dark, tannin-stained pools between the numerous cascades. Small pools host tiny shiners, and numerous water striders skate across the water's elastic surface film. Miniature sand beaches lie where flood waters deposited their loads, and here moisture-loving plants like gray willow and spotted touch-me-not have gained a foothold. Delicate in appearance, clematis, or virgin's bower, vines out over rocks, while sedges grow grasslike in the crevices between them. An uncommon species of fern, **fragile fern**, also thrives in the moist crevices between the moss-covered boulders. Long beech fern is a small species that can be identified by the fact that its lowest leaflets point decidedly downward. Look for it as well as Christmas and marginal wood ferns in the rich woodland, while seeking interrupted and sensitive ferns in wet spots.

An abandoned granite millstone rests in the pools along Glendale Brook.

In spring, when the cascades roar with their greatest volume, the forest floor brightens briefly with the white blossoms of Canada mayflower and false Solomon's seal, yellow sessile-leaved bellwort (also known as wild oats), greenish yellow clintonia, red trillium, and white starflower. In summer look for tall meadow rue as it extends its starry white flowers; tall buttercup, which is in bloom; robin plantain, really a composite with purplish-and-yellow daisylike flowers; and wild roses showing off their delicate pink blossoms.

Listening for birdsong over the tumult of flowing water isn't easy. But you may hear the songs of blue-headed and red-eyed vireos, ovenbirds, and black-throated green and Blackburnian warblers (arguably our most beautiful, found usually in the hemlocks), along with the long, loud, bubbling song of our smallest wren—**winter wren**. Hemlock gorges dissected by brooks are the favorite haunts of this bird.

You can walk about a half-mile downstream before returning to work your way back up the rather steep slope. Hiking up will take you about 15 to 20 minutes. Deer come to the stream to drink and browse on the succulent vegetation, but you'll probably find only their tracks unless you happen to be here at dawn or dusk. Raccoons, too, find food along the brook, hunting with their sensitive noses and dexterous paws.

For a very different walk, cross Clark Wright Road and stroll along the old logging road (no markings, but fairly easy to follow) that roughly follows rocky Glendale Brook upstream. The brook's main sources actually number six. The wet meadow clearings are good places to search for keen-eyed dragonflies, butterflies, and other insects. On a June visit, I was happy to find an attractive arctic skipper, a small, uncommon orangish butterfly that lives in wet boreal environments. Other summer butterflies you may well see include tiger swallowtail, red-spotted purple-white admiral (now considered the same species by lepidopterists), spring azure, and little wood satyr. Birds that prefer brushy thickets dwell here and include the gray catbird, a mockingbird relative. This bird's catlike meow is unmistakable. In wetter habitats look for beautiful nesting yellow, black, and blue colors of the Canada warblers, and listen for the sweet trill of rusty-capped swamp sparrows emanating from the marshy growth. You can walk for about one-half mile before the track becomes overgrown, then retrace your steps to your car in the reservation parking lot.

Getting There

From Route 143 in West Chesterfield where you'll cross the Westfield River, travel west for 2.25 miles to the junction with Route 112. Stay left and travel just under 2.0 miles to the intersection of Routes 143 and 112 at Worthington Corners. Turn right and travel north on Route 143 for approximately 2.2 miles to where it bears left. After driving west and then south for just over 1.5 miles, you'll come to River Road. Turn left and follow River Road south. After 3.25 miles, you'll come to Cone Hill (Smith

Hollow) Road on the right, but stay left on River Road. You'll be paralleling the Middle Branch. After traveling just over 5.3 miles since your original turn onto River Road, turn right onto Clark Wright Road and travel uphill for 0.4 mile to the Glendale Falls Reservation gravel parking area on the right—just before you would cross the brook.

Reservation hours are sunrise to sunset. There are no fees, picnic areas, or rest rooms. Camping, fires, motorized vehicles, and firearms are prohibited. There is no map currently available from The Trustees for this property.

—R.L.

40 Arcadia Wildlife Sanctuary

Easthampton/Northampton
550 acres

❖ 1.75 miles

❖ 1 hour

❖ easy

❖ great for children

Situated in the floodplain of the Connecticut River Valley, Arcadia Wildlife Sanctuary is a great birding location with five miles of trails, traversing forest, and marsh. This Massachusetts Audubon Society sanctuary borders the Mill River and an ancient oxbow of the Connecticut River where migrating birds stop to rest. An observation tower, overlooking a marsh, provides great views and is a big hit with children!

To begin, take the trail to the Old Coach Road to the right of the nature center, into woods of maple, oak, hemlock, and white pine. Be sure to pause for a moment near the rear of the building and scan the bird feeder and nearby trees. On my last visit, a number of goldfinches were flashing brilliantly in the sunshine as they flew from the trees to the feeder.

There is also a **vernal pool** just beyond the bird feeder. These freshwater pools usually dry up by mid-summer, but during the spring they are alive with amphibians: listen for the "peep" of the spring peepers or the "quack" of a wood frog. Because vernal pools are temporary, no fish live in them, which means that the eggs laid by frogs and salamanders will not be eaten. Vernal pools are also rich in nutrients for tadpoles and salamander larvae to feed upon. The drying of the pools in the summer helps speed the decomposition rate of organic matter, which in turn supplies nutrients. (Amphibians face increasing peril as development destroys vernal pools and pesticides work their way into the food chain. There is also concern that depletion of the ozone layer and corresponding increase in ultraviolet radiation is harming amphibian eggs.)

Our walk continues past the vernal pool and swampy area on the Old Coach Road Trail. This trail leads in a northwesterly direction along a ridge that parallels the Mill River a few hundred feet to your right. Pass over an abandoned trolley line that connected Northampton to Springfield in the nineteenth century. Mountain laurel emerges in the understory, making this particular path a great place to walk in the spring. A number of trails intersect the Old Coach Trail, but you should continue on this trail, traveling straight until you reach Hitchcock Brook.

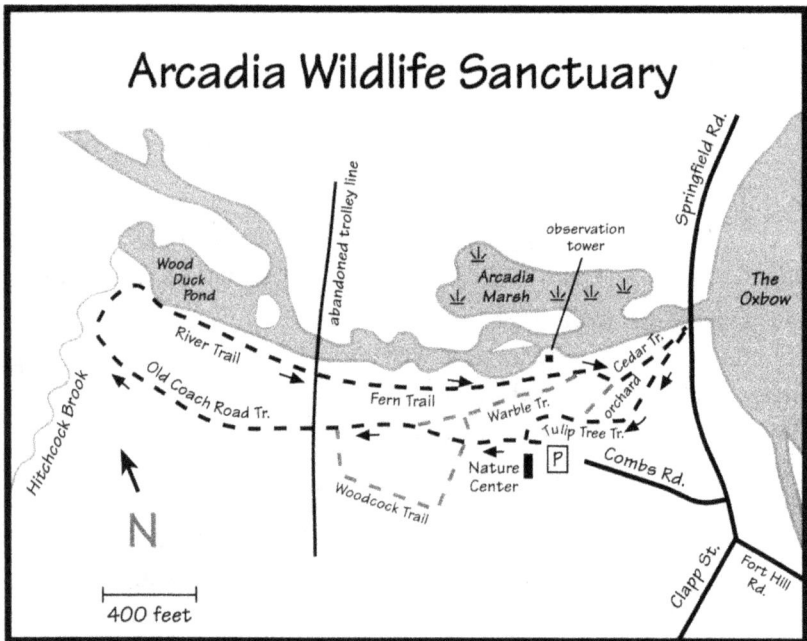

The trail descends a hill at Hitchcock Brook. Bear right rather than cross the brook. In a hundred feet, you reach the River Trail at a backwater of the Mill River called Wood Duck Pond, which, as the name implies, is good habitat for the brilliantly colored **wood duck**. Males have patterns of purple, green, yellow, red, and blue. The female is less colorful but can be identified by its white eye ring. Look for them soaking up the sun on a dead tree branch above the water or feeding on the pond. They are tremendous fliers, capable of dodging trees at great speed.

The nesting boxes you see at the pond are constructed to duplicate the hollow trees wood ducks prefer, using an entrance hole small enough to keep out raccoons. Females line the nest boxes with down plucked from their breasts and incubate the eggs with body heat. When the ducklings hatch, they respond to their mothers' calls and jump from the nests, following the mothers to the safety of the water.

Follow the River Trail to the east where it becomes Fern Trail. Footprints in the mud along the banks of the Mill River may reveal the tracks of raccoon, mink, and the large hand-size prints of great blue heron. If great blue heron find a hunting site to their liking, they will often visit the same place day after day to catch fish. I once saw a heron in the exact same spot for more than 30 days!

Arcadia's observation tower overlooks marsh and forest.

The trail passes by a diversity of ferns, including ostrich ferns with three- to five-foot fronds, and towering shagbark hickory as it follows the Mill River to an **observation tower**. Rising roughly 60 feet, the tower is a great place to rest and scan Arcadia Marsh. Below the tower on a post, two signs mark the high-water level of the floods of 1936 and 1984.

From the observation tower, continue following Fern Trail to an old orchard. On my trip I had the good fortune to see a pileated woodpecker here: a large, rather uncommon woodpecker, roughly the size of a crow with an identifying red crest. You might also see a cardinal. During spring, listen for the bird's series of loud, clear whistles it uses to announce its territory prior to mating. Also be on the lookout for bluebirds, bobolinks, and red-winged blackbirds that frequent the orchard.

   ·   Bear to the left at the orchard onto Cedar Trail and continue to follow the Mill River downstream. A five-minute walk will bring you to the mouth of Mill River where it meets the **Connecticut River Oxbow**, subject of a wonderful painting by Thomas Cole. Prior to 1841, the Connecticut River flowed through this loop. During high water, however, the river abandoned a bend to create a more direct downstream course, leaving the oxbow as a lake.

To return to the parking lot, simply retrace your steps back to the orchard and follow the Horseshoe Trail a short distance southwestward to the nature center. The orchard you pass through has old apple trees and cherry trees, a favorite source of food for cedar waxwings and other birds.

Getting There

From I-91, take the Northampton exit (Exit 18). From the exit ramp, turn right onto Route 5 south. Follow this for almost 1.5 miles and make a right turn onto East Street at a road sign for Easthampton center. Follow East Street for a little more than 1.0 mile and turn right onto Fort Hill Road (marked by a Massachusetts Audubon Society sign). Travel 1.0 mile to the sanctuary entrance.

Open year-round, closed Mondays except for major holidays, admission fee (MAS members free), rest rooms, nature center.

—M.T.

Joseph Allen Skinner State Park

Hadley/South Hadley
390 acres

❖ 1.75 miles

❖ 2.5 hours

❖ difficult

For years, I drove from my home in the Berkshires to Northampton and points east along Route 66, enjoying a wonderful view of the Holyoke Range and its gleaming white summit building. I often wondered what the building was and about the view possible from it. One early September day, I finally made up my mind to find out.

Mt. Holyoke, the nominal western end of the **basaltic Mt. Holyoke Range**, rises more than 800 feet above the broad meanders of the Connecticut River. Some 200 million years ago, two lava flows spilled forth through a crack in the earth's crust, solidifying to form the Holyoke Range. This rock, rich in iron, has oxidized to a dark reddish hue. It fractures along hexagonal planes and produces a distinctive metallic *clink* when struck against another piece of basalt.

The mountain's summit is the site of one of America's oldest mountain resorts, a one-room building constructed in 1821. Later additions and renovations gave rise to the current Summit House. Once it had 40 rooms and catered to the nation's growing middle class. The hurricane of 1938 destroyed most of it. Between 1854 and 1942 a funicular railway transported millions of tourists to the summit. J. A. Skinner donated the property to the commonwealth in 1940.

Today you can drive to the top, but it is far more enjoyable to walk. From the largely open summit, assuming the day is clear, you can gaze out upon the flat, fertile fields of the Connecticut River Valley, some of the richest farmland in mostly rocky New England. Millions of years of erosion and sedimentation, together with thousands of years of spring floods, have deposited a thick layer of rich silt in this broad flood plain. Beyond the valley, you can make out all the major promontories within about a 45-mile radius, including Mt. Snow in Vermont, New Hampshire's Mt. Monadnock (where the 117-mile-long Metacomet-Monadnock [M-M] Trail terminates), and Mt. Greylock in the Berkshires.

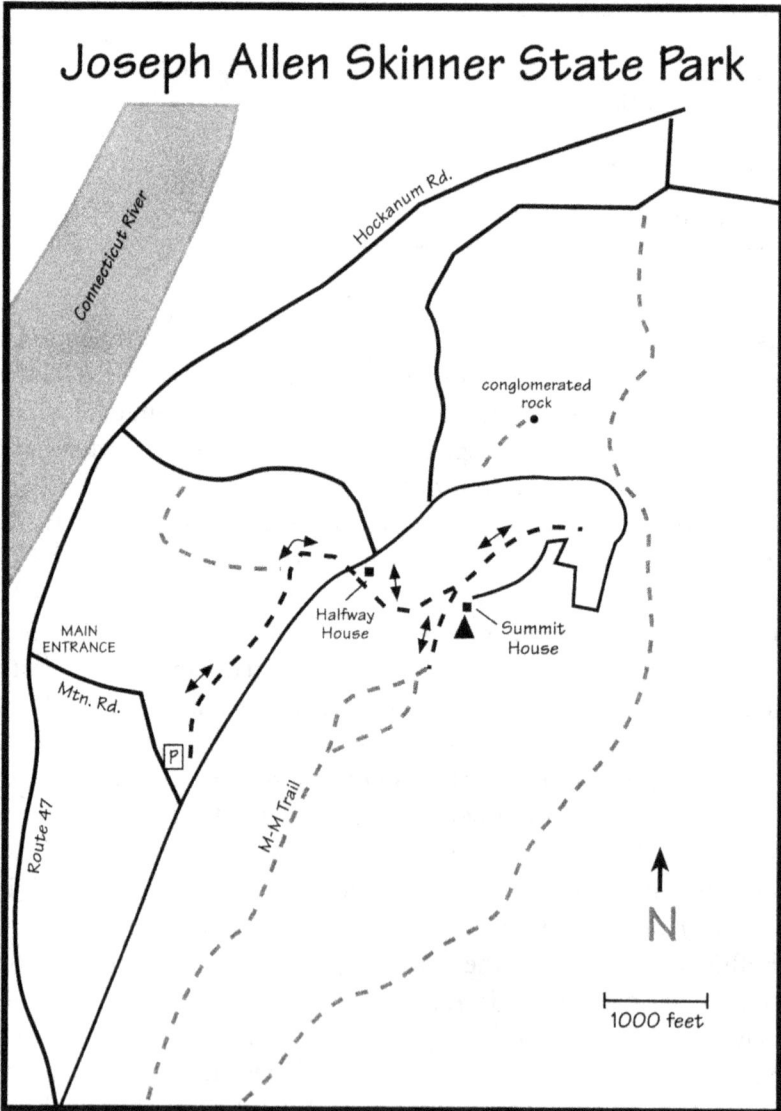

Joseph Allen Skinner State Park

Park in the designated area (with room for eight to 10 vehicles) located left off Mountain Road, just before the road makes a sharp swing to the left to begin the ascent to the top. The road is sometimes gated at this point. The Two Forest Trail begins at the rear of the parking area and proceeds left. It is marked with yellow paint blazes. The starting elevation is about 265 feet above sea level.

Walk over level ground through deciduous forest for a short distance and then climb briefly and steeply to the next plateau along the road. The leaves dropped each fall by the big black birches, gray birches, sugar and red maples, and other trees help to produce a fertile bed for tiny club mosses, ferns (especially evergreen wood fern and hay-scented fern), and spring wildflowers—false Solomon's seal (which has its flowers at the tip, whereas the flowers of Solomon's seal are at the nodes), Solomon's seal, Canada mayflower (also known as wild lily of the valley), and partridgeberry. In late summer, white snakeroot and white aster are abundant. Thousands of ankle-high red oak seedlings will indicate that a bountiful crop of acorns was produced the previous season. Hemlocks become prominent on the slopes, especially to your left. Black-capped chickadees (the Massachusetts state bird) dangle acrobatically from the branches, and bigger, noisy, crested blue jays fill the air with their piercing calls. The trail proceeds east-northeast, and if you peer through the hemlocks you'll see cornfields in the valley to the north. Flocks of Canada geese, with their ever vigilant sentinels keeping a watchful eye; American crows; wild turkeys; and other wildlife eagerly glean the waste grain after fall harvest.

Continue straight on Two Forest Trail. Soon your eyes fall upon a huge cabin-sized basalt boulder known as the **Devil's Football**, because of its odd shape. How did it come to rest here? The rough, hexagonally fissured surface and color add considerably to the comparison. Unfortunately, human-made graffiti mar its surface. Several trails merge at this point. Follow the Devil's Football Trail (blazed blue and yellow) straight to Mountain Road and the Halfway House. A short trail also goes sharply right up to Mountain Road. You should continue straight. At 0.6 mile cross the paved road just below the Halfway House—park headquarters—where you'll be able to see a big gear wheel once part of the old railway system to the summit.

After crossing Mountain Road and walking a short distance to the left, pick up the blue-blazed trail, which becomes noticeably steeper, utilizing a switchback to the left to ascend the dark hemlock slope. Retaining walls have been built to help counteract the force of gravity. The trail is in good condition but stopping often to catch your breath may be a necessity, as it was for me. From the retaining wall it's 0.3 mile to the top. Eastern chipmunks are the most visible mammals in late summer. While you rest you can't help but notice these attractively striped ground squirrels running about, often with cheek pouches crammed full of acorns for the winter larder. They emit shrill chirps and birdlike clucks.

Near the summit the trail forks; stay to the left. When the trail splits again, take the right fork and walk up to the **Summit House** at an elevation of 940 feet. From here parts of four states are visible on a clear day, and interpretive panels on the deck of the building identify major features of the landscape. Other panels relate the interesting history of the Summit House. Gravel walks lead through a manicured picnic area with wonderful views of the Connecticut Valley where you may want to stop for a snack.

Mountain ash, with its rich red berries, dots the landscape at J. A. Skinner State Park.

Following a brief but energetic rain shower that September morning, I noticed a wispy cloud of what turned out to be one-quarter-inch-long winged ants just above the picnic area. The smokelike column of insects was made up of many thousands of ants which, having left the nest, represented an expeditionary force seeking to colonize new ground. The ants were mating and the young queens moved off to found new colonies. During the dramatic clearing following the storm, the bushes and trees attracted my attention as fall migrant songbirds flitted about in search of sustenance. In a few minutes I was able to spot black-throated green warblers, an American redstart, a magnolia warbler, and three red-eyed vireos.

When you're ready to move on, retrace your steps, but take the left (westerly) fork below the Summit House this time. Follow the white-blazed M-M Trail past old rock walls. Enter an oak/hickory woodland of rather low stature. The forest floor is sun flecked, and basaltic outcrops up to 10 feet high punctuate the open ridge-top woodlands. Little bluestem grass, which fades to a rose-wine color in late summer, grows in clumps among the rocks. Mountain ash, sporting clusters of bright red berries, and oaks do well on the thin soils of the Holyoke Range. In spring and fall keep one eye on the sky as hawks set sail on the warm updrafts created by the ridge. Broad-winged (about the size of a crow, with a fan-shaped black-and-white-banded tail), small, long-tailed sharp-shinned, and big resident red-tailed hawks all ride the rising thermals.

Follow the white-blazed M-M Trail as it descends rather steeply for a brief period, then skirts the escarpment edge, affording you a nice view of the valley to the northwest. Descend slightly again and cross a basalt outcrop of the ridge where the **columnar cleavage** of the former lava is readily evident. In places, freezing and thawing have created convenient natural staircases, and the rough texture of this rock makes for sure footing even on flat, glacier-scoured sections. Northern red oak, pignut hickory, fuzzy-stemmed staghorn sumac, wild rose, and raspberry represent the predominant woody growth of the ridge here. After about 25 minutes of walking from the Summit House, come to an open spot where the hill drops away gradually and a truly wonderful view of the largest Massachusetts city in the valley—Springfield—is visible to the south, as is the Connecticut River.

While scanning the horizon with my binoculars, I chanced upon a huge dark bird soaring northwesterly near the river. The brilliant white head and tail told me without a doubt that I was admiring an adult bald eagle! Perhaps this was one of the birds now nesting along the river in West Springfield. A very successful hacking program has returned nesting bald eagles to Massachusetts. Young birds from Canada were brought to Quabbin Reservoir in the 1980s in hopes that they would eventually come to see the place as home and choose to nest there when mature at age five.

The overlook is a convenient spot to turn around and retrace your steps back to below the Summit House to follow the Halfway House Trail (blue blazes), left, back the way you came—eventually to your car along Mountain Road. A reasonably fast walk will get you back to your vehicle in less than one hour if you're in a hurry.

Getting There

From the junction of Routes 116 and 47 in South Hadley, take Route 47 north for 3.5 miles to Mountain Road (Barrus Road on some maps) on the right. Follow Mountain Road for 0.4 mile to the small roadside parking area on the left just before Mountain Road turns sharply left.

Alternately, from the Route 9 exit ramp off the I-91 ramp in Northampton, follow Route 9 east across the Connecticut River on the Calvin Coolidge Bridge. Follow Route 9 for 1.9 miles to Route 47 (Middle Street) on the right. Route 47 makes a 90-degree turn to the left (east) after 0.6 mile. Continue on Route 47 for 3.8 more miles to Mountain Road on the left. Drive up Mountain Road for 0.4 mile to the parking area on your left.

The park is open from sunrise to half an hour after sunset. The Summit House is open 11:00 A.M. to 5:00 P.M., Saturday, Sunday, and holidays, Memorial Day through Columbus Day, weather permitting. There is no fee to park at the lower parking area abutting Mountain Road, but no parking is allowed there between 8:00 P.M. and 8:00 A.M. Rest rooms are located under the porch on the north side of the Summit House. Dogs must be leashed and trash must be packed out.

—R.L.

42 Holyoke Range State Park

Amherst/Granby
2,252 acres

❖ 2.75 miles

❖ 3 hours

❖ moderate

Somewhat surprisingly, it is not the better known Mt. Holyoke but Mt. Norwottock (1,106 feet) that is the highest point of the six-mile-long Holyoke Range. Formed by two major lava flows some 200 million years ago, the basaltic spine of the Holyoke Range is unusual in that it is one of only a relatively few east-west ranges in America and the largest in Massachusetts. The Connecticut River flows through a water gap in the erosion-resistant rock here—a gap that separates this range from the similar Mt. Tom Range on the west side of the river.

Holyoke Range State Park offers an extensive trail system through attractive birch/oak/maple woodlands leading to several promontories with beautiful views. The 117-mile Metacomet-Monadnock Trail (M-M Trail) follows the ridge line and connects the park with adjacent Skinner State Park and Mt. Holyoke (see p. 197) about three miles to the west. Picturesque rock overhangs known as Horse Caves are said to have sheltered the Revolutionary-era tax protester Daniel Shays and his men and horses. Route 116, running through a gap in the range called the Notch, was originally a trail used by Native Americans; now Notch Visitor Center, on the east side of the road, is the gateway to this popular park and its trails.

The route described below will take you eastward from the visitor center to the somewhat open summit of Mt. Norwottock by way of the M-M Trail (some distant views are possible before you reach the summit of Mt. Norwottock); down and up slightly to and through a large split boulder and the Horse Caves; down and up again to the summit of Rattlesnake Knob (813 feet elevation), where you'll appreciate the splendid panoramic view; and then back to the visitor center by way of Southside Trail. The trails are well marked and quite well maintained, thanks in large measure to the Friends of the Holyoke Range. Some trails traverse private property.

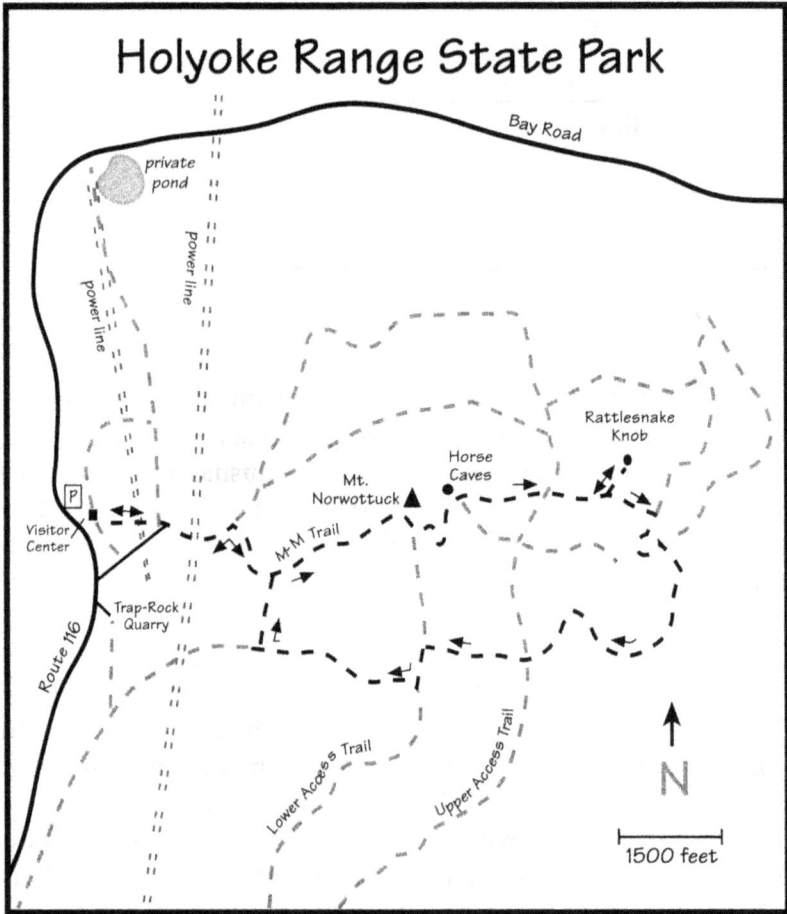

After parking in the large paved lot, you may wish to enter the visitor center to view exhibits and obtain a map and additional information about current trail conditions. Restrooms are available. Follow the orange, white, and blue paint blazes from behind the center (called Laurel Loop) and cross the gravel road (once an old trolley bed). Follow the Metacomet-Monadnock and Robert Frost Trails (follow orange and white blazes) when they jog left, then right over the road. Cross a cleared utility line right of way where birds that prefer edge habitats, such as eastern towhee (listen for its well-known *drink-your-tea* song), gray catbird, and, in the wetter spots, common yellowthroat, reside.

The Metacomet-Monadnock Trail passes through a narrow crevice in a split boulder just above the ledge overhang known as Horse Caves.

Pass near a rock quarry on the right where basalt is mined (notice that the trails here are littered with iron-rich basalt fragments, which produce a characteristic metallic clinking sound as you knock them about while walking). Follow the white blazes as the M-M Trail bears right (Robert Frost Trail continues straight). A private shooting range is located just north of the visitor center, and the firing may be an unwanted distraction as you wend your way up the slopes toward Mt. Norwottock. Fortunately, the sounds will eventually diminish and then disappear altogether as you continue eastward. Mt. Greylock, the state's highest peak, is already visible (38 miles to the northwest) from a point left of the trail well before the summit. In the foreground is the rounded mass of Bare Mountain, just west of Route 116.

Northern red oaks and blue jays, which feast upon the bitter acorns, predominate on these lower slopes. Wildflowers such as heart-leafed aster, which blooms white in late summer; false Solomon's seal; and Canada mayflower are very common on the forest floor. The trail ascends rather steeply at times and enters a moister zone where sugar maple is the most common tree. Christmas fern, an indicator of rich, organic soils, provides color here even in winter. The trail then drops before rising to the summit, where the views from the solid bedrock are stunning.

The view of Amherst, less than five miles to the north, is nice but there's an even better one to the east from the outcrop, to the right of the trail. The observation tower at Quabbin Reservoir is also visible 17 miles away to the east. On a sunny day, bask in the sun on the warm basalt, as we did. Stunted oaks, lowbush blueberry, hair grass (with very thin leaves), and little bluestem grass have taken hold on the sunny, rocky summit. From here you may also see **broad-winged hawks** and **turkey vultures** riding the warm thermals that are deflected up the mountainside.

The trail now descends past basalt outcrops, through a narrow cleft formed by a house-sized boulder that has broken in two, and on to the formation known as the **Horse Caves**, 0.2 mile from the Mt. Norwottock summit. The caves actually were created when sandstone and conglomerate, a sedimentary rock made of rock fragments cemented together, then broke away, leaving a protective overhang. A pair of eastern phoebes (a member of the flycatcher family) apparently have found the stone ceiling suitable for attaching their mud nest. Phoebe nests always have an exterior layer of green moss decorating them—perhaps for camouflage?

Follow the trail downhill to the right where it skirts the bottom of a rock slide (talus slope). The basalt making up this ridge is 600 feet thick. Ages of freezing and thawing have worked loose the chunks of rust-stained basalt along their characteristic hexagonal cleavage planes—with gravity doing the rest. The trail passes through dry, sunny, semiopen deciduous woodland of oak, laurel, blueberry, azalea, and witch hazel in the level area between summits.

Your next destination is Rattlesnake Knob. Bear right at the intersection, then bear left a few hundred feet farther along where the blue-blazed Southside Trail goes right. Bear right where Robert Frost Trail intersects the combined M-M and Robert Frost Trails (marked with white, yellow, and orange blazes). The trail ascends moderately to the right; go right at the next split in the trail. Pass a red metal town boundary marker with A on one side for Amherst and G on the other for Granby.

Pignut hickory, northern red oak, and red maple are the dominant woody vegetation on these slopes. Stay left at the trail junction and walk a short distance uphill to the viewpoint on Rattlesnake Knob (elevation 813 feet). The chances of seeing a rattlesnake here are slim to none; more likely you might encounter the ubiquitous common garter snake sunning itself at the edge of the trail. All snakes play a vital role in keeping prey populations in check, but they are often unfairly maligned. A beautiful panorama of green rolling hills, including the diagonal ridge of Long Mountain, is laid out before you. Small red cedar trees (actually juniper) and shrub-sized **dwarf oak** with shiny, dark-green leaves grow on this southeast-facing rocky outcrop. Listen for the guttural croaks of soaring ravens, or watch the comings and goings of insects on the rocks at your feet. On a visit in September we witnessed a small drama unfold as a tiny ant single-mindedly struggled to drag away a much larger and heavier bronze-colored beetle.

To begin your return hike, walk back down from the Knob and turn left at the combined M-M and Robert Frost Trails (orange and white blazes). Walk down a rather steep, rocky slope where Christmas fern grows abundantly. Three-tenths of one mile below the summit you'll come to a junction with Cliffside Trail, also a bridle trail, blazed with red paint. Turn right onto this wide track and pass through a shady hemlock grove. Soon smooth, light-gray-trunked American beech trees outnumber all others. Many species of birds and mammals feed on the beech's nutritious three-sided seeds, which are enclosed in prickly capsules. Continue on through a small area of dead timber just before the next trail intersection.

A vernal pool is situated on the right at the intersection with the blue-blazed Southside Trail. Dry when we visited, this pool holds water in spring and early summer. Wood frogs and spotted and Jefferson salamanders make overland migrations to court and breed here. They must complete their breeding cycles before the pool dries up in late summer. Follow the Southside Trail straight ahead for about 2,000 feet and cross one of the few streams that carries water year-round on the southern flank of the range. It is an oasis for amphibians like the small green-and-brown pickerel frog. Do not drink the water, however, as most streams in Massachusetts are contaminated by the parasite *Giardia lamblia*.

Almost immediately after crossing the brook, turn right briefly onto the red- and blue-blazed Swamp/Southside Trail. The trail splits and you want to take the blue-blazed Southside Trail left to where it meets Lower Access Trail. Stay right at the next intersection (if you turn left, you'll cross a stream) and continue west on the Southside Trail. Later, cross a dry brook bed in the oak/maple woods and walk gradually uphill. Odd-looking **squawroot** pokes up through the leaf litter under the oaks here. It looks something like an inverted pine cone, with brownish scales and yellowish flowers that bloom in spring. Squawroot is a parasite lacking chlorophyll and must draw nourishment from the oak roots.

The trail then enters drier white pine/oak forest with a shrub layer of highbush blueberry (an indicator of acidic soil) and mountain laurel. At the next intersection, stay right on the blue-blazed Southside Trail (a sign at the intersection indicates the direction of the visitor center). Walk uphill to the junction with the M-M Trail; turn left, then right after about 50 feet. Follow the M-M Trail back to the junction with the Robert Frost Trail and turn left on it. Cross the road and follow the Laurel Loop back to the Notch Visitor Center.

Getting There

Take Route 116 north from the center of South Hadley for 4.5 miles to the Notch Visitor Center parking area on the right. There is a sign for the center on Route 116.

From Route 9 in Amherst, travel south on Route 116 for 5.1 miles to the visitor center on the left. After leaving your locked vehicle, walk left and then left again up the stairs to the big, modern brick-and-stone building that has wildlife exhibits, maps, and restrooms.

Trail hours are dawn to dusk. Visitor center hours are 9:00 A.M. to 5:00 P.M. daily May through September, and Thursday through Monday, 8:00 A.M. to 4:00 P.M., October through April. Signs tell visitors not to leave valuables in their cars and not to drink the water in streams. Dogs are allowed but must be kept on leashes. Some trails are open to mountain bikers, but bikes are not permitted on the M-M Trail. Motor vehicles are prohibited. Since some trails cross private property, be sure not to stray off the trails.

—R.L.

43 Mt. Tom State Reservation

Holyoke/Easthampton
1,683 acres

- ❖ 4.5 miles
- ❖ 4 hours
- ❖ difficult

A colleague, whose given name coincidentally is Tom, grew up in the shadow of the mountain he always identified with so strongly—becoming a nationally known expert in the field of herpetology (the study of scaly [reptiles] and slimy [amphibians] vertebrates) in the process. Perhaps fittingly, Mt. Tom is one of the last strongholds of the eastern timber rattlesnake and copperhead, both endangered species.

This north-south-trending **volcanic spine**, separated from the east-west Holyoke Range by the broad, meandering Connecticut River, has an extensive trail network, including the Metacomet-Monadnock (M-M) Trail. Ponds and wetlands, including vernal pools; extensive oak/hickory forests; and **breathtaking views** provide hours of wonderful hiking and nature study. You'll want to return again and again to explore the variety of natural communities encompassed by the reservation.

Scorching lava flows, welling to the surface some 200 million years ago, solidified to form the rusty basalt columns we see today in the Mt. Tom and Holyoke Ranges. Thought to have been named for an early-seventeenth-century English explorer, Rowland Thomas, Mt. Tom forms a resistant monolith towering 1,100 feet above the mighty river that served as the "highway" for Rowland and early colonists. Industry, agriculture, and, later, higher education continue to be prominent bulwarks of the valley economy. Mt. Tom State Reservation, one of the state's oldest, was established in 1903.

This round-trip walk begins at a picnic pavilion at the intersection of Smiths Ferry and Christopher Clark roads across from reservation headquarters, where ample parking is available. Walk southeast along paved Smiths Ferry Road for 0.1 mile and cross the road to join the white-blazed M-M Trail on the left. A map of the entire 117-mile trail is located here. Pass a building on the left and walk through a stand of big, tall red oaks and eastern hemlocks. Tiny, energetic golden-crowned kinglets search the conifer boughs for insects and other invertebrates. They are usually first located, in spring and fall, by their high-pitched, sibilant calls. The trail is fairly flat and wide as it passes through red maples, hemlocks, and American chestnut sprouts. Tufted titmice, attractive, gray-crested birds with peachy flanks, are year-round residents that whistle *peter, peter, peter.*

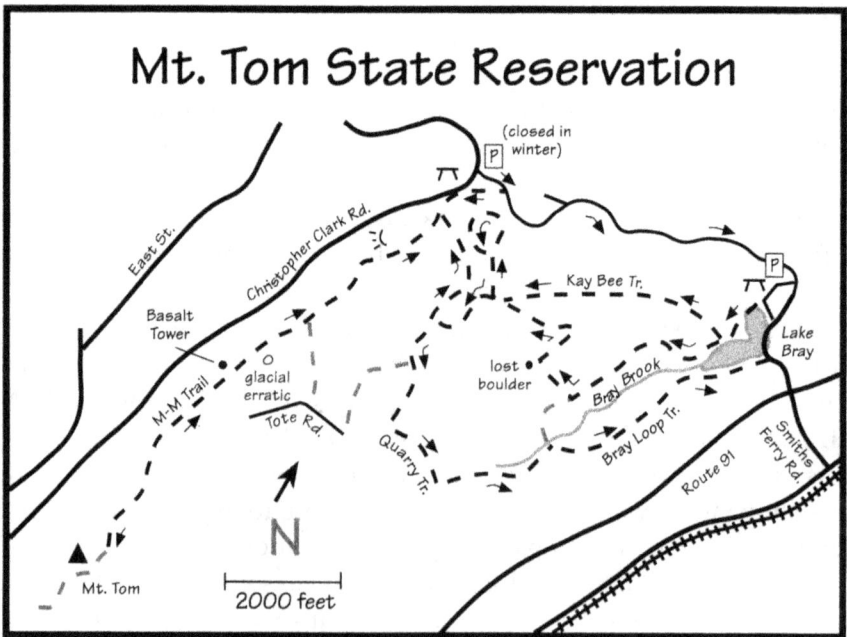

Mt. Tom State Reservation

After about 10 minutes you'll arrive at Quarry Trail junction; a Department of Environmental Management (DEM) maintenance/storage area is on the right. From here it's two miles on the M-M Trail to the Mt. Tom summit. This is where the real walking begins, as you head up rather steeply via a switchback to a partially screened vantage point. The Connecticut River Oxbow (cut off by the river circa 1830) and I-91 to the north will be visible to the right. Scaly, pink-trunked red pines grow on this slope.

They have long, paired needles. The next overlook from the ledge is more open. From here the state's highest point—Mt. Greylock—is visible as a bump 33 miles to the northwest. Easthampton lies directly below you.

The basalt rock hints at its high iron content with a rusty exterior and the metallic clinking sound it makes as you knock pieces together. The path winds up through a crevice in an outcrop adorned by **mountain ash**. Not an ash at all, in autumn it produces large clusters of bright red berries. This fruit, along with its yellow foliage, is truly lovely when seen against the azure blue of the sky. Robins, cedar waxwings, and other fruit eaters can make quick work of the offering. Oak woods now become prominent, and evergreen wood fern grows in blue-green clumps among the rocks.

The trail levels out for stretches, skirting the summit of Whiting Peak (1,010 feet) to the left, allowing you to pay more attention to the woodland asters blooming as white stars in fall. Watch for migrant birds; flickers display their bright-yellow underwing linings as they shoot past. After proceeding 0.7 mile from the Quarry Trail junction, reach the two D.O.C. Trail junctions, left, both blazed in red. Climb up and over a low rock outcrop on the left covered with mountain ash. The rock below forms a sort of "pavement," with the hexagonal cleavage planes of the basalt clearly visible.

As I walked this trail on a splendid sunny day in mid-October, a big black raven, perched on the ledge up ahead, launched itself off the cliff. These rocky crags are favorite perches. **Ravens** are much larger than crows and, in fact, weigh about four times more than their smaller relative. I always enjoy seeing these magnificent birds.

Proceeding now over barren rock where rectangular white blazes are painted directly on ledges, you'll catch your first glimpse of one of the many communications antennas situated on the ridge. Little bluestem grass and abundant stiff aster, with heads of violet flowers, grow on the dry, exposed outcrops. It's difficult to imagine that a mile-thick sheet of ice once rode up and over this basalt ridge, yet clear evidence rests just off the trail. Take a sharp turn to the right and look downhill at a six-foot-long glacial erratic; this boulder is clearly composed of a rock other than basalt. The ice carried this hunk of granite southward some 12,000 years ago.

A clump of small but picturesque gray birches greets you with waving long, pointed yellow leaves as you walk down and approach the precipice. The footing is quite good, but be careful. Model railroaders will recognize reindeer moss, a silvery green lichen that is processed and used to create trees and shrubs on a miniature scale. The path then re-enters woods of oak, red maple, chestnut, witch hazel, and blueberry. Turning over logs, as

I often do in a search for salamanders, I found two individuals of the red-backed species in a low, damp spot left of the trail and then carefully

Glacial ice planed off the top of the landmark basalt tower that stands above Easthampton on Mt. Tom's precipitous west face.

replaced them under their protective log shelters.

The way in which this hardened lava fractures is very convenient for the hiker. The rock forms natural staircases, which are a pleasure to walk up or down. The M-M Trail drops below the antennas to the left. Nearby to the right is a landmark **basalt tower**, reminiscent of a huge petrified tree stump. Proceed up over outcrops, but be heartened by the good footing. Among the rocks grow pussytoes and meadowsweet. Bush clover, a member of the pea family, grows about two feet tall on these sunny outcrops, producing seeds eaten by such birds as white-throated sparrows. From here, you'll be able to see Mt. Monadnock (the terminus of the M-M Trail) 50 miles away to the northeast. **Huckleberry thickets** full of burgundy-red leaves enliven the sunny outcrops, and in the low woodlands, patches of maple-leaf viburnum glow with an unusual and beautiful rosé-wine color.

Scrub oak and sweet fern, both indicators of dry, sandy soils, provide shrubby cover here. The crushed foliage and twigs of sweet fern—not a fern at all—are very fragrant. Wild roses along the path produce red, seed-filled "hips" in late summer. Below the second communications tower a windmill was erected in 1994 by the University of Massachusetts. It has supplied 20 percent of the electricity needed to light the trails of the near-by ski area (the equivalent of power for 40 homes). This sight caused me to reflect upon the merits of providing energy from renewable sources versus the desire to keep such scenic summits safe from development.

Continue straight at a major rock crevice on the left. This is an area of short-stature oak woods providing the first clear view of the Mt. Tom summit antenna farm. Alternating ups and downs lead you between outcrops that provide stunning views to the west and of the Mt. Tom massif itself. The summit is marred by development. A metal fence with Danger High Level Radiation and No Trespassing signs surrounds the antennas—not a pretty sight. The M-M Trail continues down to the ski area and beyond, but this is the turnaround point for this walk—one and a half hours out from the Quarry Trail junction and 1,200 feet above sea level.

If you're like me, you'll want to get away from this "developed" area as quickly as possible. Return back down the trail, as I did, and find a great spot to have lunch and survey the countryside. As I relaxed a raven flew by doing flips, legs down and generally cavorting. Bearberry, I've found, grows on some of the exposed outcrops. This low-growing evergreen member of the heath family usually is associated more with the dune lands of Cape Cod than with the hills of western Massachusetts—but here it is.

Two adult red-tailed hawks (fully adult birds have red tails but immatures don't) circled overhead near the cliff, riding the warm updrafts. Among the oaks growing here are red, white, black, and a little bit of scrub oak, which never attains tree size. Other species of birds may come into view, including big **turkey vultures** that sail just below and parallel with the top of the cliff. As I walked that day, I was struck by how really gorgeous the fall foliage was. It was one of those days when you think, How great it is to be alive!

Returning, you reach the two D.O.C. Trail junctions on the right. (If you wish to vary your return, take the second D.O.C. Trail 0.9 mile to Quarry Trail and then take Quarry Trail 0.3 mile back to the M-M Trail at the maintenance/storage area.)

If continuing on the M-M Trail, watch for trailing arbutus (a May bloomer) and spotted wintergreen, which has attractive dark green and white leaves. You may also notice a few low azaleas and some white, wax-like Indian pipes—parasitic flowering plants containing no chlorophyll.

After about one and a half hours of leisurely walking from the summit, you reach the Quarry Trail intersection. Continue straight and follow it back through the oaks and hemlocks to Smiths Ferry Road. Turn left, cross the road, and walk back down to the picnic pavilion and parking area.

Getting There

From Springfield, take I-91 north to Exit 17A (Route 141). Reach Route 5 (which is not mentioned on the exit sign) in 0.3 mile. Turn left at the traffic light and drive 3.9 miles on Route 5 to Smiths Ferry Road. The entrance to the reservation is on the left. If traveling south on I-91, take Exit 18, turn right at Route 5, and follow it south for approximately 3.2 miles to Smiths Ferry Road on the right. Pass under I-91 as you drive up Smiths Ferry Road into the reservation and reach a contact station. From here, continue 1.6 miles on Smiths Ferry Road, past Bray Lake on the left, to the pavilion and picnic area at the junction of Christopher Clark and Smiths Ferry roads.

Hours are 8:00 A.M. to sunset; gates are locked until 8:00 A.M. Daily parking fee is two dollars per vehicle. Motorized vehicles and mountain bikes are prohibited from trails; hunting not allowed. The rest room building at Bray Lake picnic area is open Memorial Day to Labor Day. A chemical toilet is also available.

—R.L.

44 Sanderson Brook Falls

Chester/Blandford
2,308 acres

❖ 2 miles

❖ 2 hours

❖ easy

The cold, clear waters of Sanderson Brook, a tributary of the Westfield River, gush over vertically contorted rock strata, creating a single dramatic drop as well as alternating pools and cascades in an idyllic woodland setting. Beautiful Sanderson Brook Falls, perhaps 75 feet high in all, is certainly the most notable feature of Chester-Blandford State Forest. Sculpted by three brook systems, the property in northwest Hampden County borders the nearly pristine West Branch of the Westfield River, a major tributary of the mighty Connecticut. In 1994 the Westfield became the first river in Massachusetts to receive National Wild and Scenic River status.

Streams and pools provide ideal conditions for several species of aquatic and semiaquatic salamanders. The woods are home to red-backed salamanders—according to some, the most abundant vertebrate (by biomass) in the eastern forests—as well as some of the most accomplished avian songsters in the woodlands: winter wren, Louisiana waterthrush, and hermit thrush. The first two have loud songs designed to be heard above the sound of flowing water. Listen also for the robinlike phrases of the brilliant, but easily overlooked, **scarlet tanager** in the deciduous woods. It is one of many woodland species that spends the bulk of its year in the rapidly shrinking tropical forests of northern South America, flying north to mate and raise its young.

From the dirt parking area walk up the gradually climbing dirt road. Walk along the northwest-facing slope of a shaded hemlock gorge cut by the modest yet relentless waters of Sanderson Brook, with a steep hillside on the left. Dusky and two-lined salamanders live in the wet environment along the stream edges. Neither species has lungs; instead, both breathe through their moist, sticky skins. Head upstream, climbing progressively higher above the brook. Beside hemlock and yellow birch—my favorite among the hardwoods (I love the fine, peely quality of its golden metallic bark)—you'll also find red and sugar maple, northern red oak, American beech, basswood, and smooth-trunked (except the oldest) black birch.

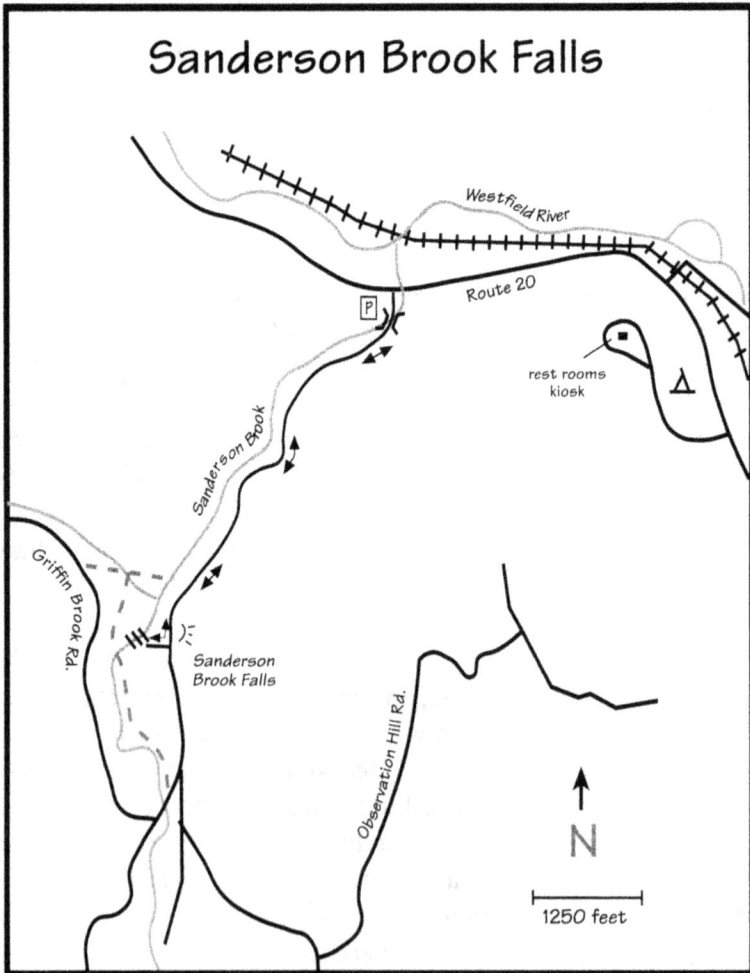

Sanderson Brook Falls

Westfield River

Route 20

P

rest rooms
kiosk

Sanderson Brook

Griffin Brook Rd.

Sanderson
Brook Falls

Observation Hill Rd.

N

1250 feet

The understory includes witch hazel, striped maple (a.k.a. moose-wood or goosefoot maple), and mountain maple—which produces reddish, winged seeds in summer. Here and there are thickets of hobblebush and American yew, which looks a good deal like another of its common names—ground hemlock. In summer, **red-flowering raspberry** is studded with attractive roselike blossoms that will catch your eye. The deep shade below the hemlocks is not conducive to wildflower growth, but in summer you may find the greenish white shinleaf, whorled loosestrife (a yellow-blossomed plant that favors moist ground), and clusters of ghostly white Indian pipes, a flowering plant that lacks chlorophyll. The nodding pipes become more erect with age. In May you'll find blooming clintonia and Canada mayflower (both lilies), wild sarsaparilla, starflower, partridgeberry, and the lovely red-and-white painted trillium.

After about 20 minutes of walking, come to an old auto bridge over Sanderson Brook. Cross the bridge (note the rocky/gravelly bottom of the stream bed—the swift flow washes finer particles downstream), and after a short distance cross the brook again and continue walking up the road toward the falls. After another 15 minutes of walking, look for a well-worn path on the right that goes down the slope toward the base of the falls. It should take you only two minutes to reach it from the road.

In July, the cool breezes from the falls are welcome relief from the heat. A luxuriant growth of mosses and less familiar **liverworts** drape the damp rocks, while the vertically tilted and layered bedrock surrounding the falls is capped by dark-green hemlocks. Odd nonflowering plants, liverworts grow tonguelike on wet rock surfaces among the mosses. Predatory water striders skate across the surface film of the pools. (To take photos of this fairyland scene, given the dimly lit conditions, use ASA 200 or faster film or a tripod.) Even in mid-summer the volume of water is quite considerable. The soothing sound of flowing water is sure to lower your stress level. You'll doubtless want to rock-hop across the brook to clamber up along the left side of the falls for a closer look at the alternating pour-offs and pools, but watch your footing.

The sunny clearing below the falls provides the right conditions for the orange trumpets of spotted touch-me-not, a favorite of ruby-throated hummingbirds. Pink joe-pye weed and white-flowering boneset—once used medicinally—also thrive here. Moisture-loving sensitive and inter-rupted ferns as well as primitive soda-straw-shaped horsetails grow here too. Bush honeysuckle, in contrast, shows off its yellow blossoms in sum-mer from the dry, gravelly slopes above the brook.

After spending time at the falls, you may want to walk to a lookout site along the road above the falls before returning to your vehicle. To reach it, return to Sanderson Brook Road on the same path and turn right. You soon reach a spot where, to the right (west), you can gaze through a gap in the canopy toward the falls. A wooded ridge is visible rising up behind the falls.

To further explore the hemlock stands above and south of the falls, follow the road up another 2,000 feet to a bridge (which is out) over Sanderson Brook. Follow the brook downstream over informal trails and then swing right, downhill, and then uphill back to the road. This area is laced with all-terrain-vehicle tracks but offers some spectacular views from ledges under the hemlocks down into the rocky gorge. After rejoining the road, turn left and head back to your vehicle.

The falls plunge in a single dramatic drop plus alternating cascades and pools for a total distance of about 75 vertical feet.

Getting There

From the intersection of Routes 20 and 112 in the center of Huntington, travel west for 4.3 miles and turn left onto Sanderson Brook Road (there is a brown, wooden Forest and Parks sign on the left for Sanderson Brook Falls at this point). The dirt parking area is located on the right, 0.15 mile from the Route 20 turnoff.

Hours are dawn to dusk. There is no fee for hikers. Motorized vehicles are prohibited. Maps are available from a box at the trailhead. Rest rooms are located at the end of the campground loop road, located on the left off Route 20, approximately 1.0 mile before Sanderson Brook Road.

—R.L.

45 Tolland State Forest

Tolland/Blandford/Otis/Sandisfield
9,000 acres

❖ 3.3 miles

❖ 3 hours

❖ moderate

Because of its elevation atop the undulating Southern Berkshire Plateau, the woodlands of Tolland State Forest are dominated by northern hardwoods. But Otis Reservoir, one of the largest water bodies in western Massachusetts at 1,065 acres, forms the focal point for numerous anglers, hunters, campers, off-road-vehicle users, and others who visit. The trail system is little used by hikers—quite a contrast to the heavily utilized recreation areas—making a sojourn to this property, which imparts a wilderness feeling, rewarding and enjoyable.

After parking in a large paved lot just before the contact station, walk south to the entrance of Gilmore Trail in the direction of the reservoir. Pass the Gilmore Trail exit first (this will be your return point) to reach the outbound trailhead approximately 50 feet farther; turn left onto the trail. Follow it a very short distance and turn right at the first junction. The trail is marked by triangular blue plastic markers (some with a bear-track symbol) and older, painted blue blazes.

Breathe in the wonderful earthy fragrances of this rich, moist forest of American beech; eastern hemlock; and yellow, black, and white birches. The understory contains mountain laurel and tiny club mosses—princess pine (also known as tree club moss), ground cedar, and shining. These attractive evergreen plants spread by underground runners and by minute, dustlike spores borne by candlelike structures. Goldthread, a wetland indicator that is common here under the hemlocks, has shiny green three-part leaves and starry white flowers in May. Hermit thrushes skulk in the shade, uttering their beautiful flutelike songs at dusk. The trail climbs modestly and then enters a white pine stand of medium age. Eastern white pine (also known as old field white pine) is a colonizer of abandoned farmland, forming thick stands of fairly uniform age. Stone walls tell of a time when this ground provided forage for pasturing livestock.

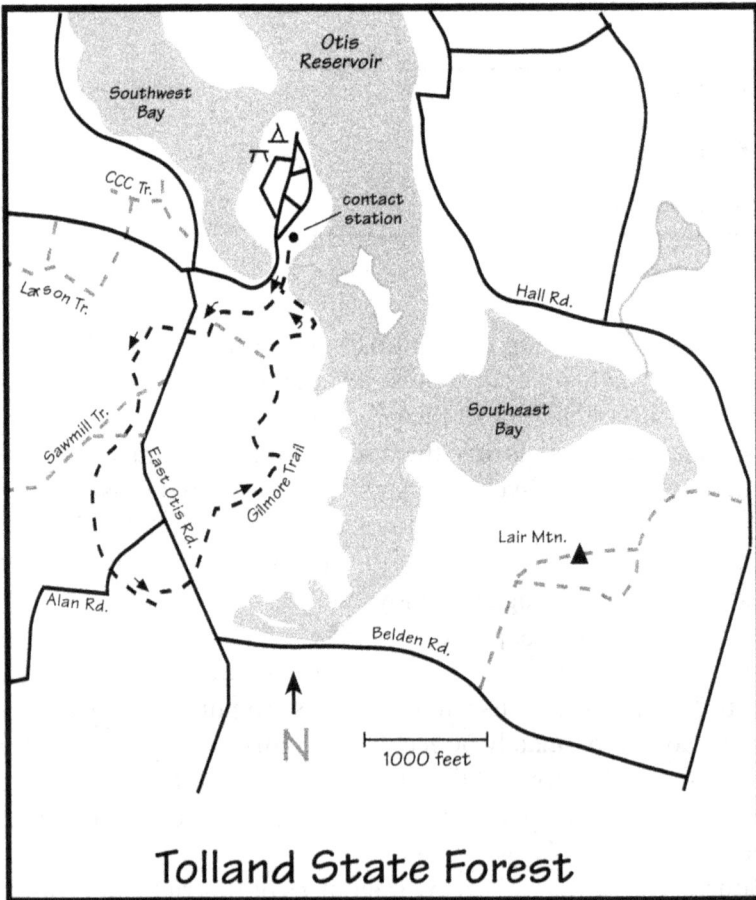

Tolland State Forest

After passing through a sugar maple stand, cross the dirt East Otis Road and find the first sign for Gilmore Trail. Descend through woodland ever so slightly and come to the border of a mowed field—perhaps 1.5 acres—on your right. Walk out into the field and examine the plants and insects, including butterflies, crickets, and grasshoppers. Common flickers frequent open habitats and search for ants by probing their long, stout bills into ant nests in the ground. Openings like these in otherwise closed forest have a special appeal for me. The blue sky is unobstructed, and the warm sunshine on my face always seems to improve my disposition. In early fall watch for hawks, migrating monarch butterflies, and other air-borne creatures.

Smooth, silvery beech, red maple, and white pine define the woods as you return to the trail, which soon makes a sharp left. A large gray boulder on the right has a white quartz vein vertically bisecting it. Quartz is a very hard mineral from which sand grains are made. Even after the bulk of the boulder has worn away, the quartz will probably remain. Shade-tolerant hemlocks—from whose reddish inner bark tannin (used in the leather-tan-ning process) originates—become numerous on the slope that drops off to the right (west).

Soon you reach a spring. Water flows through a red clay pipe that has been sealed in by cemented stones to protect the spring from contamina-tion, but it is recommended that you not drink untreated water such as this. Large yellow birches—the trees with peely, metallic bark—provide blue-headed vireos with nest sites and nesting material. Vireos build cup-shaped nests in the fork of a branch, weaving thin birch-bark strips (usu-ally paper or white birch) into the nest. The trail skirts the top of a fairly old beech/hemlock stand with little understory or ground cover and ascends gradually to some rather large black birches. The sap contains oil of wintergreen. The familiar aroma of this fragrant oil will delight your nose if you break a twig and sniff it.

Just before you reach Sawmill Trail (a woods road used by ORVs), you encounter a small fern glade and the remnants of an old stone wall. Hay-scented fern is partial to sun-dappled rocky pastures, which this once was. In mid-September its fronds were already turning yellow. Hidden beneath your feet, hairy-tailed moles "swim" through the soil seeking—by touch and smell—worms, grubs, and other soil invertebrates. Coming only rarely to the surface, these creatures have dark-gray, plush, reversible fur that facilitates their movement—forward or backward. Aboveground all that betrays their presence is a raised ribbon of soil and an occasional mound of earth.

Pick up Gilmore Trail again after crossing Sawmill Trail. Cross an intermittent stream bed. After crossing another woods road—this one obvi-ously heavily used by off-road vehicles—enter an attractive forest of mostly gray and black birch with some hemlock and beech. An increasing number of blowdowns on this portion of the trail makes it a bit more difficult to nav-igate. Middle-aged and moderately large red oaks now become much more common. Oaks are among the last trees to change color in fall—generally turning to yellowish and then coppery hues. Boulders of gneiss and schist protrude from the forest floor. The wavy lines of the schist show distortions caused by incredible heat and pressure.

Striped maples increase in abundance below the canopy formed by the beech trees. Most of the beeches show signs of fungal disease that causes rough, bumpy lesions in the bark. Beeches reproduce by vigorous sprouting, and large trees often are surrounded by a thicket of small-diameter offspring. The delicious nuts are eaten by many mammals and birds. Black cherry trees also increase in number. Unlike beeches, cherries are very intolerant of shading and, in fact, are among the first trees to colonize abandoned fields, along with pines and gray birches. The brown, hulking skeletons of ancient sugar maples stand erect just before the trail crosses hard-surfaced Alan Road and continues in a southeasterly direction (Gilmore Trail is indicated by signs in both directions).

The trail leads through damp ground populated by sensitive fern (sensitive to frost) and horsetails. The tracks of white-tailed deer show clearly in the damp, dark earth. After passing through an open, wet area thick with ferns, the trail passes through a stand of tall white pines. Woodpeckers flake off the bark of dead trees to expose fat, juicy beetle grubs, and red-breasted nuthatches creep along, surveying bark crevices for spiders and insects. This area is somewhat overgrown and brushy with a thick growth of sapling black birches; young trees possess a dark, shiny, tight-fitting bark marked by small horizontal, corky growths called lenticels that admit air. You'll find white ashes and white pines growing in the next damp open area. White ashes do well in moist ground and produce winged seeds that resemble canoe paddles. Their trunks tend to be tall and straight.

After crossing a stone wall the trail passes through low forest and then through a planted Norway spruce stand to reach East Otis Road. Beneath the dark, towering alien spruces the ground is littered with the large "cores" of spruce cones that have been stripped of their scales by **red squirrels** in order to reach the luscious seeds beneath. These small, seemingly hyperactive squirrels eagerly take advantage of these nonnatives within their midst. On the east side of the road the trail descends gradually and heads northerly through woodland of beech, birch, and maple. Their usual associate— eastern hemlock—occupies the shaded and damp spots like the one ahead.

A small stream flows through the stand and feeds the wetland to the right, an extension of Dismal Bay at the extreme southern end of the reservoir. A bit of searching beneath the flat stones of the two brooks here may produce a three-inch-long two-lined salamander. After gently examining the bronzy yellow stripe down its back, return it to the stream. On warm, damp evenings these amphibians are sometimes found foraging well away from water.

Winterberry, a native holly that grows in wet places and loses its leaves in fall, provides birds with a feast of bright red berries during winter.

There was already some color in the swamp—the red maples—during my mid-September visit. A native holly, **winterberry**, grows along this wetland edge. A low, conifer-studded ridge that borders the far perimeter of the wetland beckons, but it is out of reach. Gingerly working my way around the standing water and through the thick vegetation, I was able to locate beaver-cut red maples quite close to the trail. A pickerel frog leaped to safety as I clambered about.

Gilmore Trail then climbs gradually away from the wetland through hemlock and beech, then sugar maples, and again more hemlock. Here the trail makes a sharp left turn—the one spot where losing the route is a distinct possibility, as a few downed trees obscure the trail. Follow the trail slightly up over rocks through a forest of young beech, sugar maple, and hemlock. The crest of a ridge drops off to the right. These rocky beech woods contain thick growths of beechdrops. These six-inch plants lack chlorophyll and are parasitic on beech roots; in autumn they produce small whitish flowers flecked with purple.

Pass a large rotting sugar maple, right, as the trail climbs gradually. The peace and quiet were palpable here—no human-made sounds were audible as I walked along enjoying the day. I heard the *peeps* of six **spring peepers** calling that mid-September day. Where the trail splits, follow the right fork downhill toward the lake. The old red paint trail blazes are difficult to see here. The trail leads under hemlock trees and over fern-covered rocks.

Continue downhill. The blue plastic blazes resume, and soon the blue waters of Otis Reservoir come into view on your right. The path takes you to the shore and then parallels it. The reservoir was created in 1866 when the Fall River, a tributary of the Farmington, was dammed; the dam was reinforced with granite blocks in 1888. The state forest was established in 1924. During the 1930s the Civilian Conservation Corps (CCC) constructed many of the facilities. Hobblebush grows thickly near the shore, and a few small native red spruces are also found here. I was fortunate to spy a **pied-billed grebe** riding low in the water; it soon disappeared—only to reappear 50 feet farther away 30 seconds later. No doubt it was a migrant. These small grebes are rare and declining freshwater marsh breeders in Massachusetts. Among the most primitive of birds, grebes are nearly helpless on shore since their aft-mounted legs make walking extremely difficult; in the water they are superb divers.

Across Southeast Bay is Lair Mountain (1,674 feet), its fire tower clearly visible. After swinging briefly away from the shore, the trail returns to it amid a forest of beech and hemlock, with hobblebush beneath. It produces bouquets of small white flowers in May. The trail soon emerges from the woods at the parking area where the walk originated.

Getting There

From the intersection of Routes 5 and 20 in West Springfield, take Route 20 west through Westfield for 17.5 miles to Route 23 in Woronoco and turn left onto Route 23. Drive west on Route 23 for 12.0 miles through Blandford to Reservoir Road in Otis on the left. Turn left onto Reservoir Road and drive west to Tolland Road (the third road on the left). Turn onto Tolland Road and drive south along the shore; stay right where Kibbe Road goes left. Continue south to the road leading to the contact station and campground, and turn left at this intersection.

Hours are dawn to dusk. No fees to walk. There are no toilets at the contact station/public boat ramp. Camping is available; reservations can be made. Hunting is permitted.

—R.L.

46 Granville State Forest

Granville/Tolland
2,397 acres

❖ 2 miles

❖ 3 hours

❖ moderate

Though far from being wilderness, this property is sufficiently isolated to give a sense of tranquil remoteness. My wife, Chris, and I felt it during one visit in early September. Perhaps the warm rays of the late-summer sun imparted a feeling of peace and utter relaxation as we lingered along the shores of Bahre Pond, its bordering meadows thick with blooming goldenrod.

Granville State Forest lies in Hampden County; its southern boundary abuts the state of Connecticut. Like much of New England, this land was once the domain of sheep and dairy cows. It is slowly reverting back to northern hardwood forest. This regeneration has created a rich mix of natural and seminatural communities where wildlife viewing can be excellent. Hints of former human occupation remain, such as an old apple orchard and horticultural plantings at an abandoned home site along West Hartland Road.

This loop walk will take you along gurgling brooks, through woodlands rich in wildflowers to an artificial pond, past the old home site, alongside a wild beaver flowage under towering pines, and back to your car. Endowed with a fine reptile and amphibian population, Granville is also a wonderful place to look for mammals and their signs. Coyote, red fox, raccoon, beaver, and numerous smaller creatures abound. Woodland and wetland birds are abundant also. Old fields and meadows of flowering plants host bees, butterflies, beetles, and other winged insects.

The trail begins on the east side of West Hartland Road adjacent to an old millpond flanked by eastern hemlock, white pine, and red maple. During migration, these trees may be full of colorful warblers, vireos, and other birds. Just north of the pond is a camping area. After parking in a turnout along the opposite side of the road, cross the road diagonally to the right and follow the trail around the right of the pond. A wooden bridge over the spillway connects the trail to the camping area; do not cross the bridge. The faded blue triangular blazes are difficult to see but the trail is fairly easy to locate. Walk through dimly lit hemlock woods on a soft, needle-cushioned path.

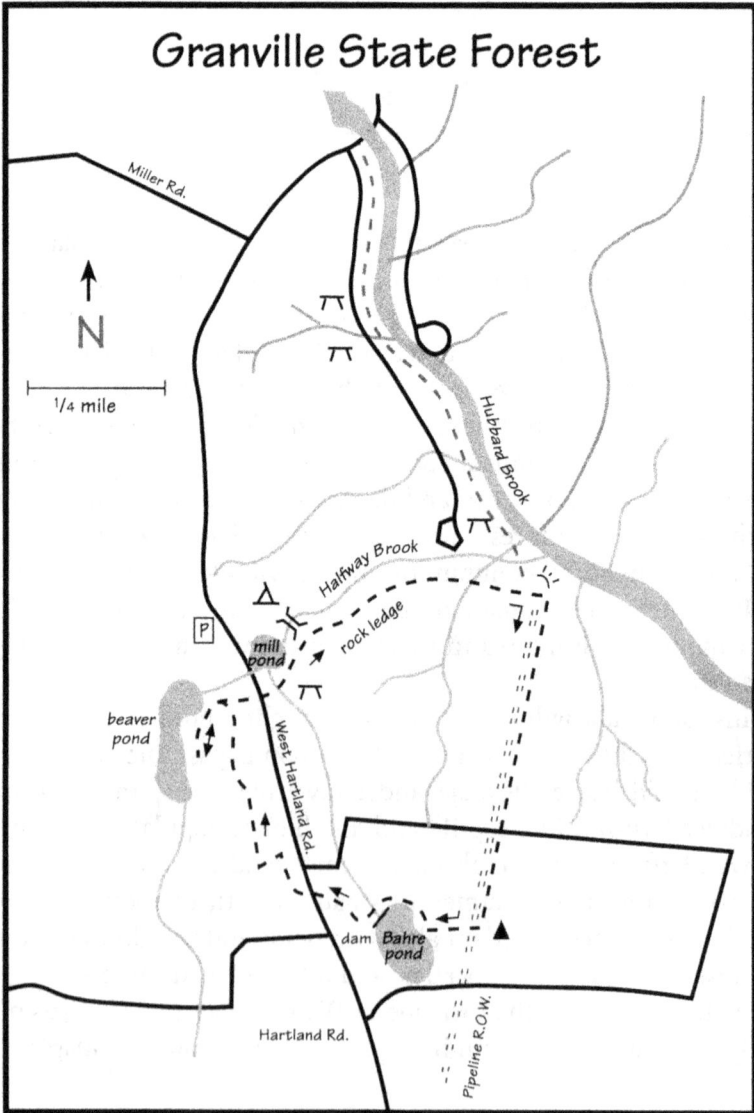

Granville State Forest

At times, the trail climbs slightly above Halfway Brook in a small hemlock gorge. Note a 10-foot rock ledge on the left near the stream. Less than one-half mile from the start, arrive at a **lovely little falls**. Dusky and two-lined salamanders live in the moist environment along the shoreline and under flat stones. Both lack lungs, absorbing oxygen directly through mucus-covered skin into their bloodstreams. A common ground cover here is the fragrant (if you crush a leaf or red berry) wintergreen, whose shiny oval leaves stay green year-round, as the name implies. (Fast film or a tripod is required to photograph in the dim light.)

Just before you reach Hubbard Brook you'll come to a small wet clearing. The trail continues as a narrow grassy path on the right, climbing up the moderately steep hillside along a Tenneco natural-gas pipeline right of way. Take a look at attractive Hubbard Brook (which can be crossed on steppingstones at low flow) before proceeding up the right of way, bordered by hemlock forest. Climb almost 250 feet to an elevation of 1,240 feet. From here look back toward Hubbard Brook for a rather nice view of the forested ridge on the north side of the stream.

After the path peaks, it dips slightly and becomes wet. Brown-blotched pickerel frogs jump suddenly at your approach as you step through the drainage swale. Climbing again, reaching a stand of large white pines on the true crest, look for the wide Bahre Pond Trail marked with blue blazes on the right. The air is filled with the aroma of pine pitch at this sunny spot. This is a good place to pause for a snack or just to listen to the whooshing sound of the wind through the pine boughs. You may also hear the comical trumpeting of tiny red-breasted nuthatches as they creep headfirst down the corrugated conifer trunks.

Leave the gas line and follow Bahre Pond Trail right through woods with tall mountain laurel to a **T** junction. Turning either direction will lead you in only a few moments to the shores of picturesque Bahre Pond, bordered by blooming goldenrods and asters in late summer. The goldenrods literally buzz with honeybees gathering nectar and pollen. On our September visit a big, powerful **northern goshawk** streaked across the blue sky, alternating wing flaps and glides. We also saw a sharp-shinned hawk, the smallest of the goshawk's bird-eating relatives.

An informal path skirts the shoreline. At the marshy southern end of the pond is an old beaver lodge. Ruby-throated hummingbirds dart about, keying in on orange and red tubular flowers such as spotted touch-me-not where nectar, rich in carbohydrates, and minute insects, rich in protein, lurk. They must fatten up prior to their fall migration flight to Mexico and Central America. It is truly amazing that these creatures, weighing only three grams, are capable of flying nonstop across the Gulf of Mexico's 500 miles of open water! **Monarch butterflies** are also on the move, and goldenrod flowers provide them with the fatty nectar that fuels them on their 2,500-mile migratory flight to the volcanic mountains of central Mexico.

The flowage below the earthen dam of Bahre Pond has been dammed by beavers, creating excellent habitat for red-spotted newts and other wildlife.

In late summer **bottle (closed) gentians** and slender gerardia flower in the damp soil near the north end of the pond. The aptly named gentians, whose clustered blossoms never truly open, are a beautiful blue violet. The gerardia flowers are purplish pink and delicate.

At the far right, or north, end of Bahre Pond where the earthen dam is situated, check out the flowage emerging below the dam, right, for pleasing views of beaver habitat and abundant aquatic life. Beaver have constructed a lodge here, and it makes a handy platform from which to scan the dark water. There is a great concentration of **red-spotted newts** here. Within a circular area, perhaps eight feet in diameter, I counted fully 40 of the three-inch-long aquatic salamanders! Red-spotted newts are yellowish green and have six red spots on each flank. Their tails are flattened vertically and provide the propulsion that powers them through the water. Their food consists of aquatic insects, worms, and similar fare, but they are prey to few creatures owing to their toxic skins.

Back on the trail, walk along the top of the dam and soon reach a **T** intersection. Turn right. This car track will take you to a gate and paved West Hartland Road in about 150 yards. Cross the road and walk to the right about 250 feet to reach the former home site. Ancient, gnarled apple trees no longer produce a crop for humans, but deer, raccoons, opossums, squirrels, and other creatures still relish the fallen fruit. At the center of the open area, turn right and follow the car track entering the woods about 100 feet in front of you. The trail proceeds through a pine grove and roughly parallels West Hartland Road. Follow the path to where another trail enters from the left, also marked with blue triangular blazes. Turn left onto this trail for a short detour to two small, picturesque beaver ponds situated along Halfway Brook. Two beaver dams are easily seen here. In summer Canada warblers nest in the bordering shrubbery.

To return to your car, double back to the last trail junction where you turned left and stay left, which will take you through towering white pine with an understory of hemlock and beech. Just after reaching an old stone wall, the trail swings right and follows Halfway Brook downstream back to your vehicle along West Hartland Road. Alternatively, you can walk directly back to your car along Hartland Road from the gated car track (turn right) beyond Bahre Pond, a distance of just a bit more than 0.3 mile.

Getting There

From the junction of Routes 57 and 189 in Granville, travel west on Route 57 for almost 7.0 miles to West Hartland Road on the left. Pass Hartland Hollow Road on the left at about 6.0 miles—do not turn here. Instead, turn left onto gravel West Hartland Road and follow it for 2.1 miles south to the dirt turnout area on the right, opposite the camping area and millpond. Drinking water and restrooms are available here. The trail begins at the far end of the pond, diagonally across the road.

Hours are dawn to dusk, except for campers. There is no entrance fee; there is a two dollar fee to park in the picnic area; camping is six dollars per night (due to increase in 2000); reservations accepted.

—R.L.

47 The Meadows

(Stebbins Wildlife Refuge and Longmeadow Conservation Land) Longmeadow
800 acres

❖ 3 miles

❖ 2.5 hours

❖ medium

The low-lying land along the **Connecticut River** in Longmeadow is where my love of the outdoors first blossomed. It has everything a young person (or an adult) needs for outdoor adventure: meadows, streams, ponds, woods, and New England's longest river, the Connecticut. This large **floodplain** is considered among the **best birding** spots in the Pioneer Valley. Waterfowl migrating along the Atlantic flyway (a primary migration route along the eastern seaboard) use the area as a resting and feeding spot.

A combination of Longmeadow Conservation Land and property owned by the Fanny Stebbins Wildlife Refuge comprise the Meadows. The Allen Bird Club and the town of Longmeadow have been instrumental in protecting the area. Some of the acreage is used for agriculture, just as it has been since the town was first settled in 1644. The rich flats of the river's floodplain are among the most fertile fields in all of New England.

Begin by following the trail westward into the woods of oak and maple, directly opposite the end of Bark Haul Road. (All of the trails at the meadow are flat, making walking very easy.) You will soon pass a small pond on the right. My brother, Bob, has walked the Meadows almost daily for the last seven years. He frequently observes great blue herons, green-backed herons, and kingfishers here. He also tells me that coyotes are sometimes seen crossing the trail ahead.

230

In about five minutes you will cross railroad tracks (which are active) and soon arrive at a four-way intersection near an area of the Meadows called the Sherwood Section. If you follow the path straight ahead you will come to a plantation of spruce and pine. Be on the lookout for cottontails, ruffed grouse, and red fox. The evergreens here give one the feeling of being in a magical, mysterious place where titmice, chickadees, and blue jays stay protected from the winter's wind.

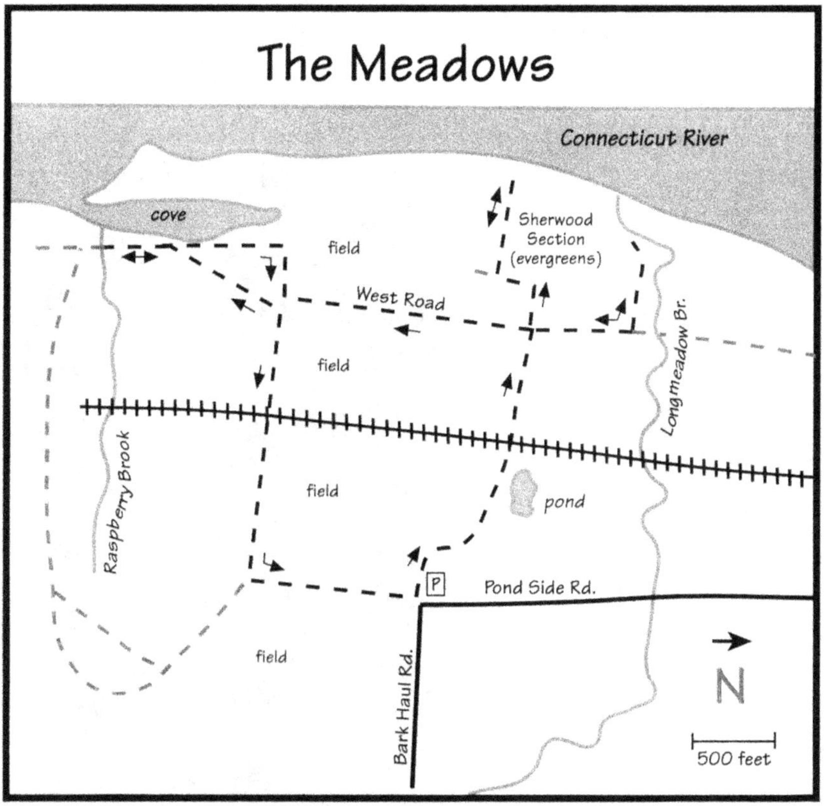

The Meadows

Connecticut River

cove

field

Sherwood
Section
(evergreens)

West Road

field

Longmeadow Br.

Raspberry Brook

field

pond

field

Pond Side Rd.

P

Bark Haul Rd.

field

N

500 feet

From the plantation, it is possible to leave the trail and make your way west to reach the Connecticut River. Enormous trees grow in the dark soil (which is constantly enriched by the flooding river), and there is little undergrowth as you make your way to the mighty Connecticut. The river starts its 409-mile journey in northern New Hampshire at the Canadian border and flows south to Long Island Sound. In all those miles, this section in Longmeadow is the river's widest at 2,100 feet.

Another way to gain access to the river is by returning to the four-way intersection and going north on the trail called West Road. In a short walk you will reach **Longmeadow Brook.** Just before the brook, a trail on the left will take you toward the river. Longmeadow Brook is an interesting stream, with a few trout, lots of bullhead, and, occasionally in the spring, **lamprey eels** that make their way from the river into the brook to spawn. As a boy, I remember catching the eels. Up to three feet long, they have a distinctive round mouth that acts as a sucking organ. They use their mouth and rows of tiny teeth to latch onto other fish and literally suck the life from them. Long ago lampreys were used as food in New England, and smoked eels were considered a delicacy!

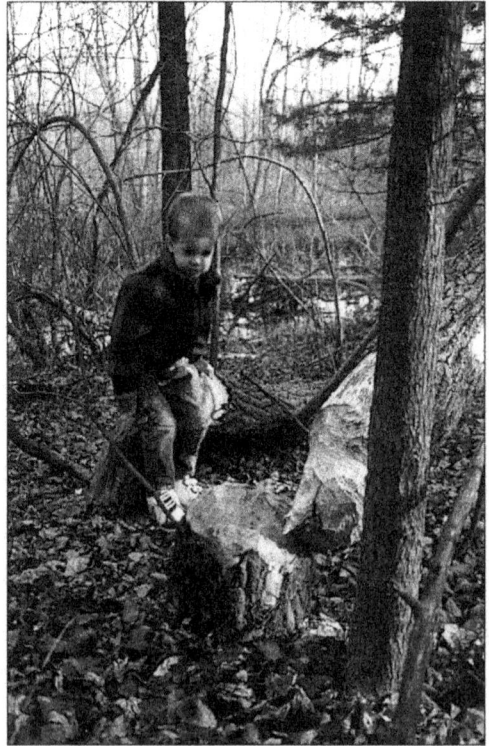

A well-gnawed stump shows the work of beaver to a young explorer.

Continue by following the West Road Trail to the south. You will first pass through woods and wetlands, then through fields frequented by white-tailed deer. Owls, such as the barred owl and great horned owl, hunt the woods and fields at night.

When you reach the end of the fields (about 15 minutes from Longmeadow Brook), you will see a sign for the Eliot Section. Follow the path near the sign in a southwest direction through the woods (to the rear of the sign). When you reach wetlands on your left, look closely through the undergrowth and you will see where **beaver** have gnawed down some trees. It's just a short walk from here to "**the cove.**" Bear left when the trail you are on intersects another, and this will bring you to where Raspberry Brook flows into the cove.

All sorts of birds can be found by the backwater during the warm-weather months: herons, blue-winged teal, cormorant, sanderlings, great egrets, even osprey. **Carp**, a fish introduced to America from Asia, are also found in the cove. The carp is a relative of the goldfish but often grows to 20 pounds. I recall many times seeing (and catching) some of these monsters when the fish would get stranded in small pools in the Meadows after the spring floodwaters receded. Sportsmen consider the carp a trash fish, but battling a 20-pound fish on light tackle—no matter what the species—is a lot of fun!

During low-water periods, it is possible to cross Raspberry Brook and head east along a ridge on a path called the Knoll Trail. This trail crosses the railroad tracks, angles to the north, and then angles west before connecting with Pondside Road. This walk does not cross Raspberry Brook but instead follows the cove back to the original trail. When you reach the split in the trail, stay left along the cove. You will soon reach an open area by a field. Turn right and you will be back by the Eliot Section sign.

Follow the trail east, keeping the fields on your left and woods to your right, and you will soon recross the train tracks, pass more wetlands, and pass another field. In 10 minutes the trail will intersect with another Turn left to reach your car in another 10-minute walk. You should be able to see the highway far to the right. The **meadow**, also to your right, is a fine birding spot.

Each season is special at the Meadows. Wildlife is active in the summer. Autumn's crisp days mean few mosquitoes and good walking conditions. The flat trails are excellent for cross-country skiing in the winter, and birding is super in the spring. My favorite time is early spring—when migrating waterfowl and wading birds return and mosquitoes are few. (Remember to wear boots after heavy rains as the trails get quite muddy.)

Getting There

From I-91 take Exit 1 (Longmeadow) and follow Route 5 south through town for about 3.0 miles (passing the beautiful town green) and look for Bark Haul Road on your right. Follow Bark Haul Road to where it ends at Pondside Road (about half a mile), and park by the welcome sign.

Open year-round, seven days a week, no admission fee, no rest rooms.

—M.T.

Laughing Brook Education Center and Wildlife Sanctuary

Hampden
354 acres

❖ 2.2 miles (approximately 4.0 miles of trails total)

❖ 2.5 hours

❖ easy

Pleasant upland woods of oak and pine, babbling brooks, well-marked trails, and fine interpretive facilities characterize this attractive Massachusetts Audubon Society property located just two miles north of the Connecticut border. Numerous old stone walls tell of a time long ago when this land was predominantly open pasture. One path now leads through maturing forest to a big glacial erratic called Split Boulder, which is a favorite with children. The hills are mostly moderate and you'll find the walking fairly easy.

The flood-plain environment along the sanctuary's three watercourses provides the right conditions for the wood turtle listed as a "species of special concern," as well as mink and belted kingfisher. Complementing the interesting natural communities are several wooden viewing platforms, some roofed. This property was owned previously by naturalist and childrens' storyteller Thornton W. Burgess, who lived here from 1928 until his death in 1965. The Burgess home, dubbed the Storyteller's House, is now open by appointment. It is located along Main Street just west of the education center. Many of the sanctuary's natural features and wildlife were immortalized in Burgess's writings. Laughing Brook itself is the storyteller's name for East Brook, which flows northeast to southwest through the southern part of the property. The Massachusetts Audubon Society purchased the original lands to create the sanctuary in 1966.

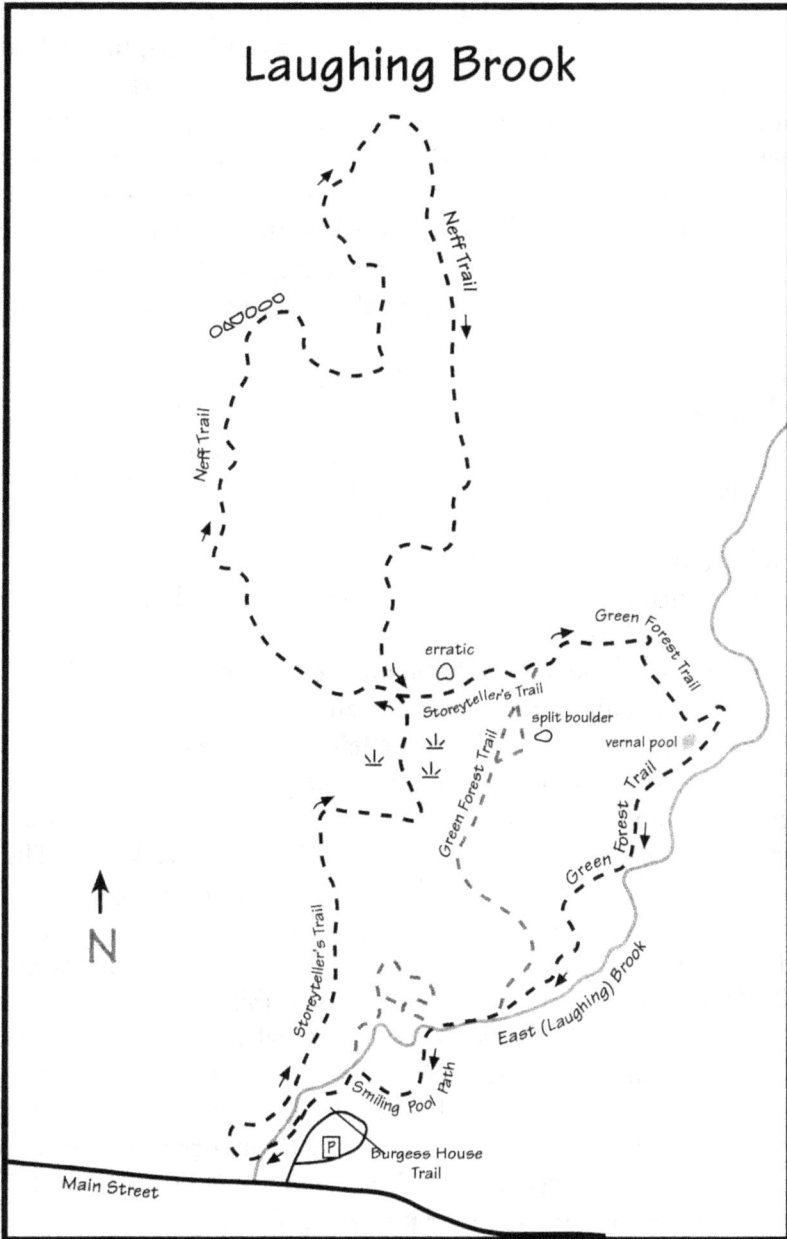

Laughing Brook

Combining several well-maintained trails into a 2.2-mile loop will let you experience the seldom visited "backcountry" of the sanctuary. From the parking lot, enter the education center and register. Interpretive leaflets and a bird checklist are available here, as well as restrooms. After exiting the building to the rear (check the bird feeders out back), turn left at the visitor information board after picking up an interpretive trail map. Follow the Smiling Pool Path along the shrubby margin of an artificial pond. The ornamental shrubs may be full of birds, especially during spring and fall migration seasons. Turn left onto Burgess House Trail, which parallels East Brook. The brook's murmurings are—with a little imagination—reminiscent of giggling laughter—hence the name Laughing Brook. Soon cross the brook on a bridge and walk up a slight slope to a cluster of buildings. The largest of these is the former Burgess home.

Storyteller's Trail begins here. Climb steps to a point 20 feet or more above East Brook. Walk through dry oak woodland and turn left at a Trail Closed sign. Below the oaks—both white and red—small white pine, low-bush blueberry, and black cherry make up the shrub layer. Bracken fern is common, and beneath it soft haircap moss and two club mosses—princess pine and ground cedar—thrive. The powdery mass of spores from club mosses were once used to create the explosive flash used in early flash photography! Blue jays, bold and noisy except during nesting season, are ubiquitous in the oak woodlands. Abundant acorn crops feed a wide array of wildlife including chipmunks, squirrels, and deer.

Some of the oaks, especially those left standing along stone walls, are quite large. **White oak** can be distinguished from red oak by its flakier, light-gray bark and its round-lobed leaves. Its acorns are also sweeter—containing less bitter tannic acid than those of red and black oaks. The trail swings right and then left, passing by a moist area on the right. Cross the wettest section on a short boardwalk, where water-loving ferns—interrupted, sensitive, and royal—as well as marsh marigold thrive, and pass by a stand of young eastern hemlocks. It was near this wet area that my wife, Chris, and I were surprised to see a big brown bat winging through the oak woods late one morning in early October. In addition to choosing attics and barns for its daytime roosts, this bat also uses large hollow trees. Soon this chocolate-brown mammal with a 10-inch wingspan will retire to its hibernation site for a six-month sleep—not to re-emerge until flying insects once again provide food for it next April.

Where the trail splits, stay (straight) left on Neff Trail. You'll pass a cluster of glacial boulders, dropped by the retreating ice, on your right. This forest is different—the soil is wetter and richer in organic matter and it supports different tree species. Sugar maple is more abundant here; in autumn its leaves turn bright yellow. Safely out of sight by day—usually under decaying logs and occasionally under rocks—are three-inch-long

red-backed salamanders (though often gray). I found 13 on our early-October walk.

Rimmed by fall foliage, a small pond near the education center is a good place to observe birds and other wildlife year-round.

Soon the trail splits again; turn left to remain on Neff Trail. The trail descends slightly here and passes rock walls and big, spreading white pines that indicate this was once pastureland. Pines that grow to maturity in woodlands usually exhibit long, straight, single trunks, but those growing in a sunny, recently abandoned pasture have the liberty of growing outward as well as upward. The trail then proceeds through a dry young forest of white pine, birch, and red oak. Hop hornbeam is a major understory tree of these woodlands; the seedpods bear a resemblance to hops. Its small size and thin, brown, flaky bark make it quite easy to identify. The tufted titmouse, which has expanded its range northward over the past 50 years, and white-breasted nuthatch are year-round residents. Listen for the nuthatch's nasal *yank-yank* and *wer-wer-wer-wer* calls.

Descend to a rock wall and, turning right, follow along the rock wall on the left through rich woods of oak and maple with a luxuriant growth of Christmas fern (with a bit of imagination, each leaflet looks something like a tiny Christmas stocking). Follow the path slightly up into a dimly lit hemlock stand; look to your left at the massive trunks of two skeletal oak giants known as the **Twin Oaks**. Although long dead, these monoliths provide refuge and den sites to raccoons, bats, flying squirrels, screech owls, and other wildlife.

The trail now swings right and heads uphill through hemlocks, red maples, and red oaks. Little grows in the deep shade. Cross a low rock wall and descend gradually. Enter a hemlock stand of tall, straight trees growing on a shaded slope that drops away to Big Brook at a distance to the left. Ahead you cross stone walls twice more. Brown creepers hitch up tree trunks, pausing to remove tiny insects and spiders from bark crevices with their thin, down-curved bills, while downy and hairy woodpeckers probe and chisel for insects beneath the bark surface.

At a very large red oak, cross a stone wall and walk through oak/hickory (pignut and shagbark) woods, which soon become oak/maple woods. Some sizable black birch grow here as you pass by a rock outcrop on the left. The ledges are adorned with quite a growth of leafy brown lichens called rock tripe that become green and pliable after absorbing moisture from rain, fog, and dew. This is the highest elevation along the trail. Watch for a red oak with seven trunks, two of which are dead, on your left. Cutting and resprouting produced this multitrunked form.

The path swings right and then left and descends gradually. Soon you'll reach the intersection you passed before; continue straight to the next intersection, where you'll turn left onto Storyteller's Trail. The trail will take you through an area of gray boulders and past a 10-foot rock ledge, left, that contains horizontal crevices. A bit farther along, left, through pine/oak/maple woods is an isolated erratic some 20 feet long. The small, leathery fronds of rock-loving common polypody fern grow in the thin soil that has collected atop the boulders. Turn left onto Green Forest Trail, once an old woods road.

If you wish to see the **Split Boulder**, turn right instead and walk a short distance to a side trail, left, that takes you up a slight rise to the 10-by-25-foot, wedge-shaped granite glacial erratic. It sits amid a forest of white pine, red oak, hemlock, and a few maple. You might decide to stop and have lunch here as we did. Children find the boulder irresistible.

When ready, backtrack to the junction of Storyteller's and Green Forest trails and continue straight ahead. Pass the end of a stone wall and the sanctuary boundary, left, and enter a grove of young, straight-boled white pine; thick green patches of pine seedlings cover the forest floor. White pine seeds are winged and are disseminated by the wind. White pine, which requires bright sunlight, is one of the first tree species to colonize open ground.

A stone wall parallels the path to a big white oak. Turn left and then pass a big white pine on the right. White oak acorns mature in the fall of their first year, whereas red and black oak require two years to mature. If you're here in the fall of a good "mast" year, your walk will be punctuated by the nearly constant sound of acorns dropping upon the recently fallen leaves; the ground may be littered with them. Proceed gradually downhill through hemlocks and watch for a small, wet depression on the right where spongy, silvery green sphagnum moss grows. This is the site of a vernal pool which hosts congregations of breeding salamanders and wood frogs in early spring.

The trail then turns right and brings you to East Brook. The shallow depth and the gravel and rock bottom give rise to the gurgling soliloquy that Burgess so loved. You can also hear noise from Glendale Road. A more natural but rhythmically monotonous sound is made by **true katydids** up in the trees. Their characteristic, loud *Katy-did, Katy-didn't* calls can't be missed. The insects rub their wings together to "sing"; the song has territorial and courtship implications.

You'll soon pass a large white pine on the left and cross a small seepage area where hemlocks, maples, and oaks line the brook banks. White pines often attract carpenter ants, and pileated woodpeckers are carpenter ant specialists—finding and chiseling out huge rectangular cavities to get at the ants. Far from damaging the tree, the big, red-crested woodpecker simply practices the fine art of the tree surgeon by removing the injurious ants and the dead tissue.

Stop along the sandy banks of the brook to look for signs of nocturnal forest life. Tracks of white-tailed deer that have come to the brook to drink are usually visible in the soft, wet sand. Watch, too, for small dark-brown scats of semiaquatic predators such as mink. When bounding, **mink** leave paired tracks about 12 to 18 inches apart. Continue past the junction of the very short Lone Little Path on the right. The trail then swings right for a very nice view of East Brook and a big boulder (another glacial erratic) on the opposite bank.

Soon you'll join the other end of Green Forest Trail—continue straight along the brook. The trail then moves away from the brook temporarily and returns to cross it later. Cross the brook over the wide wooden bridge. From the bridge, you can get a good look down into the clear water. Head back toward the pond and the education center; notice lots of planted autumn olive. The juicy red berries are eaten by birds. Check out the shrubs for northern cardinal, American robin, gray catbird, and house finch. The pond itself contains tiny fish, tadpoles, and aquatic insects. Check the skies for big, black, teetering turkey vultures.

Several other short paths are located on the opposite side of Main Street—on both sides of the Scantic River—from the parking area.

Getting There

From I-91 in Springfield take Exit 2 (northbound) or Exit 4 (southbound) onto Route 83 (Route 83 becomes Sumner Avenue). Follow Sumner Avenue east for 3.6 miles and bear right on Allen Street. Continue on Allen Street for 4.7 miles into Hampden and make a left turn at the traffic light onto Main Street. Follow Main Street for 2.0 miles to the large gravel parking area and education center on the left.

Hours are 10:00 A.M. to 4:00 P.M., Tuesday through Saturday, and 12:30 to 4:00 P.M. on Sundays and Monday holidays. Trails are open dawn to dusk. Admission fees are three dollars for nonmember adults, two dollars for children three to 12 and persons 65 and over; free for children under three and members of Massachusetts Audubon Society. The facility is wheelchair-accessible and rest rooms are available. There is a regular year-round schedule of public education programs available from the center. Dogs, firearms, alcoholic beverages, and vehicles are prohibited.

—R.L.

49 Norcross Wildlife Sanctuary

Monson/Wales
5,000 acres

❖ 1.5 miles

❖ 1.5 hours

❖ easy

Established in 1939 by Arthur D. Norcross of the Norcross Greeting Card Company, this property is quite different from most. At more than 5,000 acres, it represents one of the largest private land holdings in Massachusetts. The relatively small portion that is open to the public, known as the Pocket Sanctuary, is a biological microcosm of the much larger tract. Incorporated within its few acres are cedar and shrub swamps, meadows, and pine-oak woodland, as well as created gardens of hollies, conifers, herbs, and even an acidic bog reminiscent of the New Jersey Pine Barrens.

The sanctuary's stated purpose is "the conservation of wildlife and the active practice of conservation for the benefit of the public." The collection and propagation of wild plants at Norcross sets it apart from most other protected open spaces. Here you will find species native to the entire eastern seaboard, from the Carolinas to Canada, situated along attractive, well-maintained, and well-marked paths that lead through an amazingly diverse set of natural communities within a small area—a "pocket" sanctuary to be sure.

A ramble along the sanctuary's wood-chip paths is a botanical learning experience, as many plants are labeled, or simply an enjoyable jaunt amid lovely surroundings suitable for the entire family.

After parking in the gravel lot, walk the short distance to the reception building. Visitors must register but admission is free, thanks to the Norcross Foundation. Restrooms are located here. The building houses exhibits on the area's fauna and flora. Color photos of plants currently in bloom and a variety of handout materials will help you identify some of **what** you see after you exit to the right through the double doors.

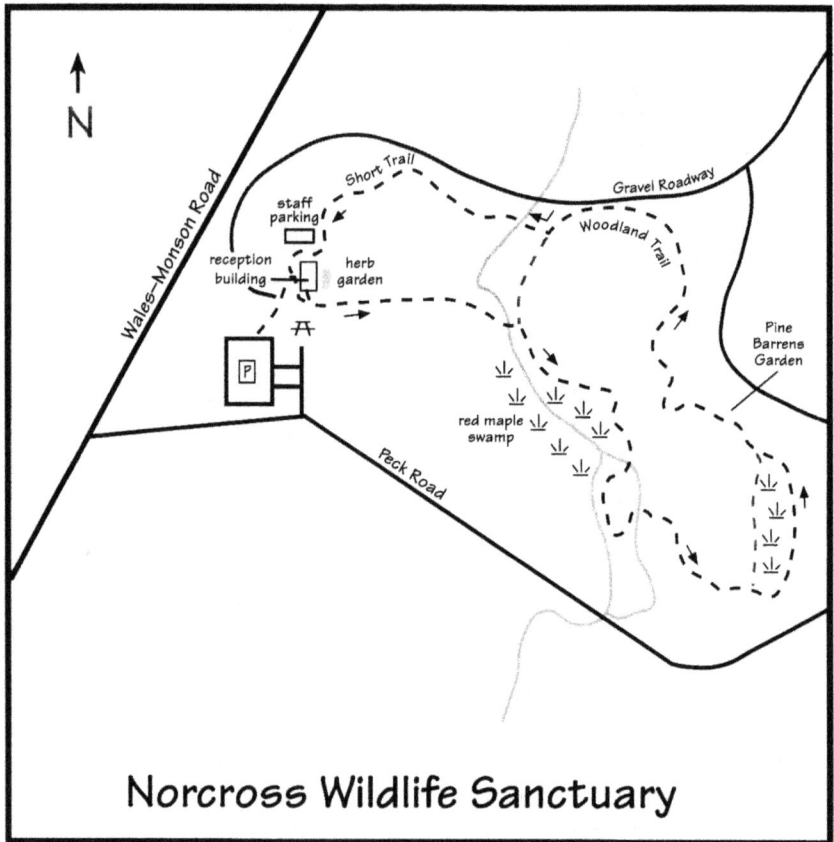

Norcross Wildlife Sanctuary

Walk down a gradual hill into young woodland of red maple, white pine, and black cherry, where during late spring and early summer oven-birds, red-eyed vireos, veerys, and tufted titmice jealously guard their breeding territories from rivals of their own kind. Remnants of stone walls indicate former pasturing. Soon a **red maple swamp** comes into view on the right where the broad arching leaves of **skunk cabbage** form an almost solid layer. Cinnamon fern and winterberry, a native holly that looses its leaves in fall, provide bright red fruits for **ruffed grouse** and other birds. My approach on a hot early-June day caused an annoyed grouse to flush and begin fussing at me from the safety of a maple bough. Here blue-winged warblers sing their *bee-buzz* songs from the shrubs while New York fern (a delicate species whose fronds taper at both ends) border the path on the right. Lowbush blueberry and related taller huckleberry thrive in the acid soils beneath the white pines of the upland. White-blossomed starflower blooms here in late spring. A pleasant gurgle alerts one to the presence of a small brook that you soon cross on an appropriately sized wooden bridge, amid more red maple swamp. Some of the trees and shrubs bear labels, and black birch, with its smooth, dark bark, is common.

At a **T** intersection, where a handsome stand of **cinnamon fern** flourishes in the moist soil, turn right on the yellow-blazed trail toward the Circle Garden. The pleasant sound of flowing water accompanies you through this attractive woodland. Skunk cabbage, one of the first flowers to bloom in late winter, and red maples dominate the wetland. Witch hazel, the small tree from which the astringent originated, displays straggly but welcome flowers in late fall when all else has long since set seed. Split-log benches beckon one to pause and savor the scene. Numerous tree trunks are fitted with wooden boxes for cavity nesters such as chickadees, nuthatches, and wrens. White-footed mice appropriate them as well. Below the pines, Canada mayflower enhances the forest floor in spring, while high in the pine boughs blue-headed vireos sing their inquisitive refrains.

Reach a three-way split and follow the boardwalk to the right. Walk amid red maples; arrowwood shrubs; cinnamon ferns with long, fawn-colored fertile fronds; and leafy skunk cabbage to cross a pebble-bottomed brook. The boardwalk then forks; follow the newer right section to explore briefly a nearby artificial pond where bullfrogs rumble their sonorous bellows in summer. Fragrant sweet fern and blue **lupine** favor the sandy soil along the chipped path. Retrace your steps to the boardwalk split and continue on the boardwalk to cross the brook almost immediately, and then again. House wrens utter their bubbling refrains from the woodland edge. Turn right at a four-trunked red maple, a prolific sprouter when cut. Follow along the brook; here many plants are labeled with both common and scientific names. Tall golden ragwort grows wild on the mossy rocks of the streambed as black-winged damselflies flutter above it.

At another trail split, turn right into the Circle Garden area. Stay right at another **Y** intersection. An eastern garter snake lay basking and butterflies visited robin plantain flowers in a small clearing during a June visit. The screened-in Propagating Garden area is visible on the right. A few feet farther along, the five-toed paw prints of a raccoon caught my eye in the muddy stream bottom. After completing the short loop, turn right and reach a three-way intersection; cross a small bridge with metal railings to the right. The Fern Lime Cobble here contains some rare species that require alkaline (sweet) soils. Turn right at the **Y** and walk up the "boxed gravel" stairs to emerge into a sunny field where the change in temperature from the shaded woodland can be dramatic. In late spring yellow hawk-weed blossoms predominate. Bear right toward the Wood and Rock Museum. Baltimore orioles favor the tall trees along these woodland edges for nest sites. Turn left at the museum to follow a mowed path to the Cedar Swamp Trail as darting blue-green and white tree swallows snatch insects from the air above the meadow.

Enter shaded woods again on a yellow-blazed trail. Pass a cemented stone wellhead and cross a trickling stream. Planted **northern and southern white cedars** do well in the acid soil. The burry phrases of a warbling vireo drifted through the air on my June outing. More familiar perhaps is the *witchity, witchity, witch* of the diminutive common yellowthroat, another wetland species. Follow along the field edge where Asiatic day lilies grace the split-rail fence in summer. Gray catbirds make homes in the shrubby tangles along field edges; catlike *meows* call attention to them. Juxtapositions of distinct habitat types, like those of Cedar Swamp and Wildflower Meadow here, are characteristically wildlife rich. Song sparrows, northern cardinals, and yellow warblers take advantage of the bountiful food supply. Delicate blossoms of **blue-eyed grass and yellow-eyed grass** provide a focus of attention within the pathway itself. Both have grasslike leaves, but only the blue-eyed is a member of the iris family.

You re-enter shade as you bear left, still skirting the cedar swamp. A rock wall and a field beyond lie to the right. At a split in the trail, follow either fork (they form a small loop) just before reaching the gravel road within sight of the two buildings you passed earlier. Follow the sign across the road and down a narrow path to the **Pine Barrens Garden**. Along the way a "tree finder" identifies species that you aim it at. The re-created pine barrens environment is the most unusual on the sanctuary. Arthur Norcross saw to it that large quantities of soil and accompanying plants from New Jersey were relocated to this bulldozed depression. **Pitcher plant, fly poison** (which grows a handsome cone of delicate white flowers), Labrador tea, alder, sphagnum moss, sweet gale, cotton grass, and other bog plants define this unique community.

As you leave the Pine Barrens Garden, the sound of running water alerts you to the gravity-fed irrigation system that provides it with life-giving water; black plastic pipes carry the water. Continue straight (on the left, **east-**

ern bluebirds nest in the box near the bench) and turn right at the Holly Circle/Upper Trail sign. Small holly trees form an understory beneath the native white pine and oak woodland. At the **T** intersection follow the red-blazed trail right, and right again almost immediately. Ubiquitous eastern chipmunks commence their monotonous chipping notes if one intrudes upon their privacy. Walk up a gradual grade on the wood-chip path bordered by dense **huckleberry** and two-foot-tall lowbush blueberry under the pines. Red maples, able to survive in wet and dry soils, are also common. Along with the white pines are large (18-inch diameter) **pitch pines** and white oaks. Pitch pines are unique among our pines in that their needles often sprout directly from the trunk.

To compensate for the lack of large, old trees that could serve as den and nest sites, numerous nest boxes have been installed. Brush piles also have been situated to provide shelter for mammals and other wildlife. Bril-

Edge habitats, such as where Wildflower Meadow meets the White Cedar Swamp, are especially rich in wildlife.

liant, but seldom seen, scarlet tanagers sing their hoarse robinlike phrases from the oak canopy. A gravel roadway is visible on the right but numerous red arrows point the walker in the proper direction. The aroma of warm pine pitch wafts to your nostrils as you descend very gradually through pleasing dry woodland that nonetheless lacks the plant diversity of moist deciduous woods. The gauzy traps of **funnel-web-weaving spiders** constitute a virtual minefield for wandering insects on the forest floor. Reach a skunk cabbage swamp at the base of the low hill on the right and then a **Y** intersection. Continue straight ahead and immediately cross a flowing brook with marsh marigold and **royal fern**. Follow the wood-chip path uphill under red maples and past azalea shrubs to the Fern Area, a small looped garden to the right of the main trail. **Pin oaks** and Juneberry (shad) trees add interest to the woodland scene. At the time of our publication, the Fern Area was scheduled to be removed due to poor growth; some ferns were to be relocated. Retrace your steps to the start of the loop and turn right toward the Conifer Grove, walking through a young stand of white pine, red maple, and quaking aspen. On your left is a small acid-rock garden. Angular chunks of gray granite and gneiss rock decay very slowly to produce acidic soil. A large bench located in a small grassy clearing is a nice place for a rest. Red squirrels frequent the planted firs, harvesting seed-filled cones.

Resume your walk over the needle-covered path. Bear right at the end of the grove and reach a gravel road and trail junction. Cross the road to Short Trail and Hickory Grove. The Short Trail area is surrounded by seven-foot-high black mesh fencing designed to keep white-tailed deer out. Enter through a gate and be sure to close it behind you. Numerous labeled plants bloom in the dappled sunlight of this lovely hillside garden. Turn right to exit the area through another gate along a stone wall remnant. The narrow trail winds through open woods of pignut and shagbark hickories, as well as sugar and Norway maples.

Reach a gravel road and turn right toward the reception building and parking area beyond; just before the parking area is a shaded picnic area. Before doing so, however, you may wish to visit the Herb Garden located in back of the building, down a wood-chip trail. Tree swallows and bluebirds utilize the paired next boxes in the small meadow there.

Getting There

From the east, take I-90 west to Exit 9 (I-84 at Sturbridge) and follow it 1.0 mile south to Exit 4. Follow MA 20 west for approximately 7.0 miles to Brimfield. Turn left onto MA 19 and drive south 4.3 miles to Wales. Turn right onto Monson Road and follow it west for approximately 2.5 miles to

Peck Road on the left. The sanctuary entrance is 0.1 mile down Peck Road on the left.

From the west, take I-90 east to Exit 8 (Palmer). Follow MA 32 south for 6.6 miles through downtown Monson to Wales Road on the left. Turn left onto Wales Road (where the road splits at 0.4 mile, stay right toward Wales). Follow Wales Road for an additional 3.2 miles past the split to Peck Road on the right.

Open May 1 to Thanksgiving, depending on weather conditions; snow closes trails. Call ahead to make sure trails are open: 413-267-9654. Hours are 9:00 A.M. to 4:00 P.M., Tuesday through Saturday; closed Sundays and holidays. Open Mondays beginning in June. No dogs allowed.

—R.L.

Mt. Orient and
50 Amethyst Brook
Conservation Area

Amherst/Pelham

- ❖ 3 miles/2.5 miles

- ❖ 2 hours

- ❖ moderate

- ❖ great for kids

Amethyst Brook Conservation Area is a popular walking spot, with good reason. Much of the trail follows the course of crystal-clear Amethyst Brook through woodlands of pine, oak, hemlock, and maple before beginning the climb to the summit of Mt. Orient. While I would not call the view from the mountain spectacular, there is a nice vista at a rock outcrop where you can stop for a rest or picnic.

Our walk is on the Robert Frost Trail, a six-town pedestrian path that starts at the visitor center at the Holyoke Range State Park and ends 33 miles to the north at Mt. Toby State Forest. Also on the property is the Metacomet-Monadnock Trail.

Our walk begins on the Robert Frost Trail, which leaves the parking lot in a northerly direction and enters an open field—a good place to spot deer, fox, or hawks, especially in the early morning or early evening. The trail forks just two minutes into your walk, and you should bear left following the orange paint dots on trees, which designate the Robert Frost Trail. In two more minutes you will cross a footbridge over Amethyst Brook. Take a moment to look at the rushing waters of this stream and how the light plays on the water's ripples—few things are more inspiring than a mountain brook, and this one has the power to put an extra spring in your step.

I love walking with the stream by my side and the dark hemlocks overhead. Behind every boulder in the stream I imagine there's a small brook trout holding in the pocket water, and on each walk I make a mental note to bring my fishing rod on the next trip, but somehow I always forget. Adding to the sense of peace from the gurgling stream is the chattering of red squirrels, which are nearly always found wherever there are hemlocks.

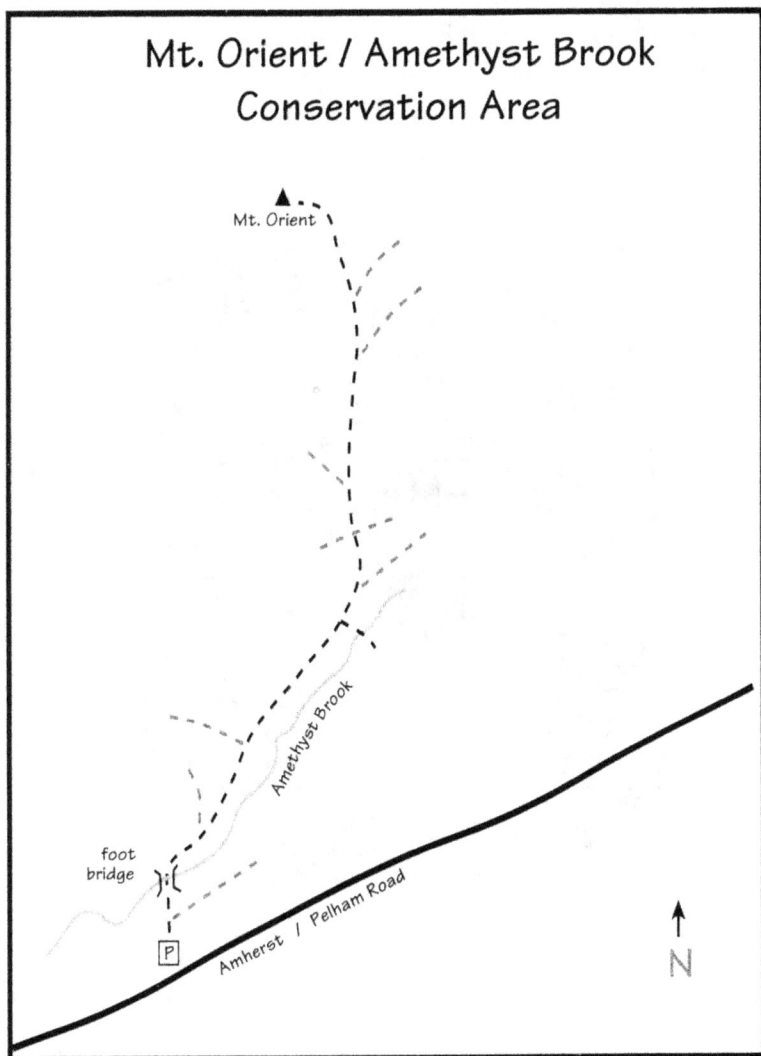

Mt. Orient / Amethyst Brook
Conservation Area

Mt. Orient

Amethyst Brook

foot
bridge

P

Amherst / Pelham Road

N

After about five minutes of walking by the stream the trail forks and you should stay to the right, keeping close to Amethyst Brook on your right. (From here on, the trail we are taking is marked with orange dots. You can ignore any side trails.)

On one of my walks here I saw raven, with its distinctive wedge-shaped tail. Ravens are jet black, looking much like crows but three times as large. While crows often will be seen picking at roadkill, ravens are wilder birds and prefer to feed away from civilization, searching for winter-killed deer and moose. Because of their carnivorous eating, ravens once were killed by farmers in New England, who blamed them for killing lambs and sheep. Now the raven population is coming back, and they are found all over Maine, Vermont, and New Hampshire, and in the forested areas of Massachusetts.

The trail to Mt. Orient crosses a rushing brook.

About 20 minutes from the start of the hike, you arrive at a second footbridge that crosses the stream to the right, but you should stay far to the left, following the orange paint dots. About 100 feet down the trail you arrive at a sign that says Leaving Conservation Land, followed by a path that crosses the Robert Frost Trail. Stay straight, following the orange dots. The trail soon begins the gradual climb up Mt. Orient, then crosses a tiny stream on steppingstones. Mountain laurel, a shade-loving plant, grows in the understory. In the late spring, the delicate pink and white flowers of the mountain laurel grace the forest.

Smaller trails fork off the Robert Frost Trail, so remember to follow the orange dots. Another tiny brook must be crossed where water cascades over a small ledge in the springtime. Exposed rock ledges appear, and if you don't mind doing a little bushwhacking you might find a porcupine den inside one of the small caves in the rock. Often, porcupine scat (about three-quarter-inch, pellet-sized droppings) spills from the cave's opening. Another sure sign of the porcupine can be detected on the hemlock trees. If the outer branches appear to have been cut or the tops of the trees look ragged and stunted, there is a good chance the damage was caused by porcupines feeding.

Roughly 20 minutes from the second footbridge you arrive at the steepest part of the path. From here it's just a five-minute walk to the rock ledge that affords a westward view of the Holyoke Range. After the vigorous climb of the last five minutes, be sure to give yourself a water break here and be warmed by the rays of the sun before retracing your steps back to your car.

Getting There

From Route 202 in Pelham take Amherst Road (westbound) and follow it for 4.7 miles to the parking lot for Amethyst Brook Conservation Area on the right. If you are coming from East Amherst on South East Road, take Pelham Road eastbound and follow it 0.8 mile to parking lot on the left.

—M.T.

Recommended References and Reading

Birding by Ear: Guide to Bird Song Identification and *More Birding by Ear: Eastern and Central*, three CDs or cassettes by Richard K. Walton and Robert W. Lawson. Peterson Field Guides. Published by Houghton Mifflin Company. 1989, 1994. Both teach songs of common species by comparison method.

Changes in the Land: Indians, Colonists, and the Ecology of New England by William Cronon. Published by Hill and Wang. 1983. An interesting melding of human and natural history.

The Changing Face of New England by Betty Flanders Thomson. Published by Houghton Mifflin Company. 1977. An ecological and land-use perspective.

Golden Guides published by Golden Press. Titles include: *Pond Life, Insects, Butterflies and Moths, Mammals, Birds, Nonflowering Plants, Trees, Reptiles and Amphibians,* and *Rocks and Minerals.* Excellent introductory identification guides.

A Guide to New England's Landscape by Neil Jorgensen. Published by Globe Pequot Press. 1977. A geologic perspective.

Newcomb's Wildflower Guide by Lawrence Newcomb. Published by Little, Brown and Company. 1977. Guide utilizes keys to identification; wonderful illustrations.

Peterson Field Guides published by Houghton Mifflin Company. Titles include: *Eastern Birds, Mammals, Animal Tracks, Reptiles and Amphibians (Eastern and Central), Eastern Butterflies, Trees and Shrubs, Wildflowers, Ferns,* and *Eastern Forests.* All are excellent.

A Sierra Club Naturalist's Guide to Southern New England by Neil Jorgensen. Published by Sierra Club Books. 1978. An ecological examination of natural communities and their characteristic plants and animals.

Stokes Nature Guides. Published by Little, Brown and Company. Titles include: *Nature in Winter; Bird Behavior I, II,* and *III; Animal Tracking and Behavior; Observing Insect Lives;* and *Amphibians and Reptiles.* These books are behavior oriented and excellent.

Wild Mammals of New England by Alfred J. Godin. Published by the Johns Hopkins University Press. 1977. The most complete work on the region's mammal life.

About the Authors

Michael J. Tougias *(Pronounced TOH-gis)*

Michael Tougias is a lecturer and *New York Times* bestselling author and co-author of thirty-one books for adults and six for young adults and children.

Fatal Forecast: An Incredible True Tale of Disaster and Survival at Sea was praised by the *Los Angeles Times* as "a breathtaking book—Tougias spins a marvelous and terrifying story." *The Finest Hours,* which Tougias co-authored, tells the true story of the Coast Guard's most daring rescue. A finalist for the Massachusetts Book Award, the book was made into a movie by Disney. *Ten Hours Until Dawn: The True Story of Heroism and Tragedy Aboard the Can Do in the Blizzard of 78,* was selected by the American Library Association as one of the "Top Books of the Year" and described as a "white-knuckle read, the best book of its kind." His latest books are *A Storm Too Soon, Rescue of the Bounty in Superstorm Sandy,* and *Above & Beyond.*

Several of Tougias's books were adapted for middle readers (ages 8-13) and for chapter books with MacMillan Publishers. His series is "The True Rescue Series" and it includes *Into the Blizzard, Attacked At Sea, A Storm Too Soon,* and *The Finest Hours.*

Tougias's most popular books include:

- *Rescue of the Bounty: A True Story of Disaster and Survival in Superstorm Sandy,* Simon & Schuster, co-author Douglas Campbell

- *A Storm Too Soon: A True Story of Disaster, Survival, and an Incredible Rescue,* Simon & Schuster

- *Overboard! A True Blue-Water Odyssey of Disaster and Survival,* Simon & Schuster

- *Fatal Forecast: An Incredible True Story of Disaster and Survival at Sea,* Simon & Schuster

- *Ten Hours Until Dawn: The True Story of Heroism and Tragedy Aboard the Can Do,* St. Martin's Press, American Library Association Best Book of the Year Selection

- *The Finest Hours: The True Story of the US Coast Guard's Most Daring Sea Rescue,* Simon & Schuster, co-author Casey Sherman, finalist for the Massachusetts Book Award

- *The Waters Between Us: A Boy, A Father, Outdoor Misadventures, and the Healing Power of Nature*

- *Until I Have No Country: A Novel of King Philip's Indian War,* Christopher Matthews Publishing

- *King Philip's War: The History and Legacy of America's Forgotten Conflict*, WW Norton, co-author Eric Schultz

- *Above & Beyond: John F. Kennedy and America's Most Dangerous Spy Mission*, PublicAffairs, co-author Casey Sherman

- *There's a Porcupine in My Outhouse: Misadventures of a Mountain Man Wannabe*, On Cape Publications, winner of the Independent Publishers Association Best Nature Book of the Year Award

- *So Close to Home: A True Story of an American Family's Fight for Survival During WWII*, Pegasus Books, co-author Alison O'Leary

- *River Days: Exploring the Connecticut River from Source to Sea*, On Cape Publications

- *AMC's Best Day Hikes Near Boston*, Appalachian Mountain Club

- *Nature Walks in Central and Western MA*

- *Exploring the Hidden Charles*

- *Country Roads of Massachusetts*

- *Quiet Places of Massachusetts*

- *New England Wild Places*

- *The Cringe Chronicles (with Kristin Tougias)*

- Middle reader adaptations: *The Finest Hours, A Storm Too Soon, Attacked At Sea, In Harms Way,* and *Into the Blizzard. All part of the True Rescue Series.*

- *Claws (a middle reader book)*

- *Chapter Books for Children: The Finest Hours, A Storm Too Soon*

- *Quabbin: A History and Explorers Guide,* On Cape Publications

- *The Blizzard of '78*, On Cape Publications

Michael Tougias has been featured on ABC's *20/20*, the Weather Channel, National NPR among other appearances. He offers slide lectures for each of his books and speaks at libraries, lecture series, schools and colleges across the country. He also speaks to business groups and associations on leadership and decision-making including such programs as Leadership Lessons from the Finest Hours; Survival Lessons: Decision Making Under Pressure; and Fourteen Steps to Strategic Decision Making: JFK and the Cuban Missile Crisis. He lives in Florida and Massachusetts. For more information, videos of some of the rescues Tougias writes about, or to contact the author, visit www.michaeltougias.com.

René Laubach has been director of Massachusetts Audubon Society's Berkshire Wildlife Sanctuaries since 1985. Growing up in Michigan, he spent 14 years in museum work before assuming his current position. Since moving to western Massachusetts, René served as president of the Hoffmann Bird Club in 1989 and 1990. He resides in the Berkshire Hills town of Becket, where he sat on its Conservation Commission until 1997. Both René and his wife are avid, licensed bird banders and walkers. Together they completed the Massachusetts portion of the Appalachian Trail in 1991.

Laubach has authored articles for the Massachusetts Audubon Society's *Sanctuary* magazine and several scientific journals dealing with birds. With his wife, Christyna, and John B. Bowles, he wrote *A Guide to the Bats of Iowa*, published by the Iowa Department of Natural Resources, and with his wife, *The Backyard Birdhouse Book: Building Nestboxes and Creating Natural Habitats*, published by Storey Books. He is also author of *A Guide to Natural Places in the Berkshire Hills,* published by Berkshire House, and the AMC's *Nature Walks in Connecticut* (with Charles W. G. Smith). His most recent work is *Audubon Society Guide to the National Wildlife Refuges: New England,* published by St. Martin's Press. When not exploring New England, he enjoys leading natural-history tours to the American Southwest and Latin America.

About the AMC

Since 1876, the Appalachian Mountain Club has helped people experience the majesty and solitude of the Northeast outdoors. We offer outdoor skills workshops, guided trips, and lodging options for all levels of outdoor adventuring. Our conservation programs include trail maintenance, air and water quality research, and advocacy work to preserve the special outdoor places we love and enjoy for future generations.

Join the Adventure!

Take a hike, ride a bike, paddle a canoe. We believe that people who enjoy breathing fresh air, climbing mountains, splashing in streams, and walking on trails have more fun and take better care of the outdoors. Join the fun today. Call 617-523-0636 for membership information.

Outdoor Adventures

From beginner backpacking to advanced backcountry skiing, we teach outdoor skills workshops to suit your interest and experience. If you prefer the company of others and skilled leaders, we also offer guided hiking and paddling trips. Our five outdoor education centers guarantee year-round adventures.

Huts, Lodges, and Visitor Centers

With accommodations throughout the Northeast, you don't have to travel to the ends of the earth to see nature's beauty and experience unique wilderness lodging. Accessible by car or on foot, our lodges and huts are perfect for families, couples, groups, and individuals.

Books and Maps

We can lead you to the best hiking, biking, skiing, and paddling destinations from Maine to North Carolina. With more than 50 books and maps published, we're your definitive resource for discovering wonderful outdoor places. For ordering information call 1-800-262-4455.

Check us out online at www.outdoors.org, where there's lots going on.

Index

Agelid, woolly, 158
Alder, 244
Ants, 200, 207, 220, 239
Apple, 196, 225, 229
Arbutus, trailing. *See* Mayflower, Canada
Arrowwood, 140, 243
Ash, 20, 57, 131
  mountain, 201, 211
  white, 129, 147, 158, 170, 172, 174,
    180, 222
Aspen (popple, poplar), 7, 18
  quaking (trembling), 20, 147, 246
Aster, 23, 56, 227
  blue, 57
  violet, 57, 211
  white, 120, 199, 206, 211
  wood, 120, 145, 163, 174, 211
Azalea, 1, 150, 206, 213, 246

Baneberry, 157
Basswood, 216
Bats, 236, 238
Bearberry, 164, 213
Bears, black, 62, 70, 85, 93, 102, 136, 138,
  148, 151, 172, 174, 181
Beavers, xxiii, 42, 48–49, 58, 63, 71, 73, 84,
  116, 123, 129, 131, 132, 138, 145,
  146, 223, 225, 233
  dams/lodges of, 45, 65, 67, 108, 111,
    113–15, 117, 128, 130, 140, 227–29
  warning "thwack" of, 45, 49
Beech, 6, 9, 18, 31, 57, 85, 99, 121, 128–31,
  137, 138, 140, 141, 145, 147, 152,
  158, 167, 169–74, 181, 183, 185, 188,
  207, 216, 219, 221–24, 229
Beechdrops, 223
Beech fern, 170, 180, 190
Bees, 225, 227
Beetles, 207, 222, 225
Bellwort, 130, 173, 190
Birch, 1, 6, 18, 19, 38, 41, 57, 61, 90, 107,
  108, 115, 123, 128, 152, 167–68,
  171, 183, 185, 188, 203, 237
  black, 104, 120–21, 129, 131, 156, 158,
    159, 162, 164, 169, 173, 199, 216,

    219, 221, 222, 238, 243
  gray, 9, 18, 85, 99, 117, 121, 156–58,
    173, 199, 211, 221, 222
  white (paper, canoe), 3, 19, 41, 48, 65,
    78, 81, 99, 121, 124, 132, 147,
    156–58, 173, 219, 221
  yellow, 129, 130, 145, 147, 157, 158,
    167, 169, 170, 172–74, 180, 216,
    219, 221
Bitterns, xxi
Blackberry, 19
Blackbirds, 54, 196
Blackflies, 41
Bloodroot, 187
Blueberry, 9, 90, 104, 105
  highbush, 42, 85, 115, 208
  lowbush, 42, 99, 121, 124, 147, 150,
    159, 164, 165, 206, 236, 243, 245
Bluebirds, 4, 20, 29, 54–57, 124, 196,
  244–46
Blue-eyed grass, 244
Blue jays, 34, 53, 121, 131, 199, 206, 231,
  236
Bluestem, 100, 201, 206, 211
Bobcats, 42, 62, 76–77, 138, 148
Bobolinks, 54, 56, 196
Boneset, 217
Bracken fern, 146, 156, 236
Bullhead lily, 111
Bullheads, 232
Bunchberry, 138
Bur reed, 141
Buttercup, 185, 190
Butterflies, xxiii, 56, 141, 170, 220, 225, 243
  admiral, 145, 179, 191
  arctic skipper, 191
  black swallowtail, 23
  fritillary, 179
  inornate ringlet, 123–24, 179–80
  monarch, 23, 121, 123–24, 179, 221,
    228
  pearl crescent, 123–24
  spring azure, 123–24, 191
  sulphur, 180
  tiger swallowtail, 123–24, 130, 186, 191

Butterflies *cont.*
  viceroy, 179
  white, 180
  wood nymph, 179
  wood satyr, 191
Buttonbush, 23, 146

Caddis flies, 187
Cardinal flower, 22, 40, 48
Cardinals, 196, 239, 244
Carp, 233
Catbirds, gray, 141, 191, 205, 239, 244
Cedar, 241
  northern white, 244
  red, 165, 207
  southern (Atlantic) white, 34, 36, 244
Cherry, 196
  black, 115, 124, 131, 180, 222, 236, 242
Chestnut, 9, 34–35, 85, 104, 110, 121, 210
Chickadees, 34, 53, 104, 164, 169, 199, 231, 243
Chimney swifts, 164
Chipmunks, 7, 38, 51, 72, 89, 111, 126, 131, 166, 173, 185, 199–200, 236, 245
Christmas fern, 121, 155, 162, 170, 180, 190, 207, 237–38
Cinnamon fern, 35, 39–40, 129, 131, 159, 172, 206, 242–43
Clematis (virgin's bower), 190
Clintonia (blue-bead lily), 139, 169, 172, 190, 217
Clover, bush, 212
Club moss, 9, 104, 152, 185, 199
  cedar, 172, 173
  shining, 169, 172, 180, 219
  tree (princess pine), 104, 108–9, 172, 219, 236
Columbine, 126
Cormorants, 233
Cotton grass, 244
Cowbirds, 142
Coyotes, xxi, xxii, 42, 50, 58, 62, 66, 67, 78–79, 84, 111, 128, 137, 148, 225, 230
Cranberry, 113
Crayfish, 21, 22, 60, 67, 187
Creepers, brown, 104, 111, 141, 163, 169, 238

Crickets, 220
Crows, 78, 90, 105, 110, 199, 211, 250

Damselflies, black, 130, 243
Day lily, 244
Deer, white-tailed, 3–4, 11, 16, 20, 29, 37, 42, 50, 58, 61, 64–67, 70, 72–74, 76, 84, 95, 127, 131, 134, 137, 138, 144, 172, 176, 222, 229, 232, 236, 239, 246, 248, 250
  how to find, xxi, xxii, 7–8, 191
Deerflies, 146
Dogwood, 57
Dragonflies, xxiii, 117, 128, 191
Ducks, xxi
  mergansers, 185–86
  teal, 233
  wood, 20, 57, 58, 67, 194–95

Eagles, 18–19, 66–67, 105, 201
Eels, lamprey, 232
Efts, red, 138, 145, 181
Egrets, 233
Elderberry, 163, 174
Elm, 78

Finches, 239–40
Fir, 78, 246
  balsam, 143
Fishers, 38, 42, 60, 67, 84, 95, 148
Flickers, 20, 211, 220
Flycatchers, 98, 206
  alder, 132
  great crested, 126
Fly poison, 244
Foamflower, 172
Foxes, xxii, 3–4, 11, 16, 50, 58, 95, 248
  red, xxi, 20, 37, 65, 72, 74, 76–77, 84, 127, 146, 225, 231
Foxglove, false, 121, 150
Fragile fern, 190
Frogs, 3, 20–23, 38, 57, 60, 67, 103, 170
  bull-, 243
  green, 116, 130, 159
  leopard, 130
  pickerel, 207, 223, 227
  spring peepers, 116, 172, 193, 223
  tadpoles, 23, 124, 130, 193, 240
  wood, xxiii, 12, 105–6, 124–25, 130, 193, 207, 239

Geese, Canada, 117, 199
Gentian, bottle, 228
Geranium, wild, 159, 185
Gerardia, 228
Ginger, wild, 126, 158
Golden alexander, 185
Goldenrod, 23, 54, 56, 67, 100, 120, 227, 228
Goldfinches, 193
Goldthread, 140, 169, 219
Goshawks, xxiii, 52–53, 61, 96, 227
Grasshoppers, 220
Grebes, pied-billed, 224
Green darners, 117
Grosbeaks, 121, 158, 180, 186
Ground cedar, 219, 236
Ground hemlock. See Yew, American
Groundhogs (woodchucks), xxii, 20
Grouse, ruffed, xxii, xxiii, 9, 16, 20, 34, 37, 58, 61, 65, 73, 74, 85, 96, 130, 136, 152, 231, 243
Grubs, 60, 221, 222
Gum, black (sour), 85
Gypsy moths, 104

Haircap moss, 236
Hair grass, 206
Harebell, 165
Hares, snowshoe, 38
Hawks, xxi, 18–19, 29, 43, 54, 65, 90–91, 110, 121, 221, 248
  broad-winged, 100, 201, 206
  Cooper's, 105
  gos-, xxiii, 52–53, 61, 96, 227
  red-shouldered, 115, 146
  red-tailed, 20, 73, 91, 146, 152, 201, 213
  sharp-shinned, 100, 201, 227
  sparrow (kestrel), 105
Hawkweed, 130, 159, 244
Hay-scented (boulder) fern, 104, 121, 145, 155, 158, 159, 172, 174, 199, 221
Helleborine, 145
Hemlock, 4, 6, 18, 19, 28, 34, 38, 41, 45, 47–50, 53, 57, 59–61, 64, 69, 72, 76, 82, 84, 85, 94, 95, 97, 99, 104, 107, 108, 115–17, 121, 123, 128–32, 134, 137–40, 145, 147, 152, 154–58, 162, 164, 167–70, 172, 173, 175, 178, 183–85, 188, 191, 193, 199, 207, 210, 214–19, 221–27, 229, 236, 238, 239, 248, 249, 251

old-growth, 25–26, 150, 180
Herons, xxii, 29, 58, 233
  blue, xxii, 3, 63, 67, 73, 195, 230
  green, 3, 230
Hickory, 18, 121, 159, 209
  pignut, 104, 201, 207, 238, 246
  shagbark, 195, 238, 246
Hobblebush, 84, 108, 130, 131, 150, 168–70, 172, 174, 185, 188, 216, 224
Holly, 245
Honeysuckle, bush, 159, 217
Hop hornbeam, 173, 189, 237
Horsetails, 183, 217
Huckleberry, 164–65, 212, 243, 245
Hummingbirds, ruby-throated, 217, 227–28

Indian cucumber-root, 84, 129–30, 170, 172, 174
Indian pipes, 213, 217
Indian tobacco, 145
Interrupted fern, 156, 183, 190, 217, 236
Iris, 57, 147
Ironwood (musclewood), 189

Jack-in-the-pulpit, 177
Joe-pye weed, 217
Juncos, 125, 146
Juneberry (shad), 189, 246
Juniper, 207

Katydids, true, 239
Kestrels (sparrow hawks), 105
Kingfishers, 73, 114, 186, 230, 234
Kinglets, 107, 117, 210

Labrador tea, 244
Lady's slipper (moccasin flower), 90, 121, 134, 139, 169
Laurel, 52, 131, 139, 206
  mountain, 6, 19, 42, 50, 53, 76, 84, 88, 90, 95, 104, 105, 108–10, 115, 121, 125, 130, 141, 150, 159, 166, 175, 185, 188, 194, 208, 219, 227, 251
  sheep, 45, 105, 110, 115
Leafhoppers, 12, 95
Leatherleaf, 45, 111, 115–16
Liverwort, 217
Lobelia, 145
Loons, 67, 105
Loosestrife, 217
Lupine, 243

Maidenhair fern, 147, 156, 157
Maple, 1, 3, 11, 20, 38, 48, 49, 52, 54,
    57, 61, 64, 69, 71, 72, 76, 78, 107,
    108, 123, 128, 131, 138, 141, 152,
    158, 162, 182, 185, 188, 193, 203,
    208, 230, 238, 239, 248
  mountain, 168, 216
  Norway, 246
  red (swamp), 32, 50, 53, 80, 85, 99,
    104, 111, 113, 115, 117, 121, 124,
    130, 156, 159, 167, 169, 170, 172,
    173, 199, 207, 210, 212, 216, 221,
    223, 225–26, 242, 243, 245, 246
  striped (moosewood, goosefoot), 88,
    104, 157, 168, 173, 189, 216, 222
  sugar, 18, 129, 143–45, 147, 156, 163,
    172–74, 179, 180, 199, 206, 216,
    220, 222, 223, 236–37, 246
Marsh marigold, 236, 246
Mayflies, 187
Mayflower, Canada (trailing arbutus, wild
lily of the valley), 11, 19, 99, 103, 109,
    121, 126, 139, 150, 159, 166, 172,
    173, 180, 185, 190, 199, 206, 213,
    217, 243
Meadowlarks, 54, 56
Meadow rue, 157, 174, 190
Meadowsweet, 124, 212
Mergansers, 185–86
Mice, xxii, 38, 65, 73, 77, 95, 105, 243
Mink, xxi, 20, 21, 71, 77, 128, 195, 234,
  239
Minnows, 21
Moles, 221
Moose, 43–44, 62, 85, 88–89, 102, 250
Mosquitoes, 41, 146, 186, 233
Mountain lions, 136–37
Muskrat, xxi, 21, 68, 73
Mussels, 22, 67

Newts, red-spotted, xxiii, 103, 116, 128,
  130, 138, 145, 229
New York fern, 104, 145, 155, 169, 180,
  243
Nuthatches, 104, 131, 243
  red-breasted, 99, 155, 169, 180, 227
  white-breasted, 111, 237

Oak, 1–3, 9, 11, 16–18, 20, 23, 28, 29,
    32, 38, 48, 64, 69, 71, 72, 76, 78,

    80, 88, 90, 91, 104, 105, 108, 115,
    123, 158, 159, 162, 163, 183, 193,
    203, 208, 209, 211, 214, 230, 234,
    241, 248
  black, 156, 213, 236, 239
  chestnut, 164
  dwarf, 207
  old-growth, 15
  pin, 246
  red, 15, 85, 107, 121, 131, 147, 150,
    156, 173, 199, 201, 206, 207, 210,
    213, 216, 221, 236–39
  scrub (bear), 164, 213
  white, 119, 121, 150, 159, 213, 236,
    239, 245
Olive, autumn, 239–40
Opossums, 11, 20, 117, 229
Orchid, 123
Orioles, Baltimore, 244
Ospreys, 29, 233
Ostrich fern, 156, 195
Otters, xxii, 67, 148, 176
Ovenbirds, 126, 156, 162, 163, 171, 174,
  191, 242
Owls, xxi, xxii, 10, 54, 60, 71, 90, 96
  barred, 137, 232
  great horned, 20, 130, 232
  screech, 20, 73, 238

Partridge, 29, 77
Partridgeberry, 6, 99, 111, 129–30,
  154–56, 163, 171, 199, 217
Peat moss. *See* Sphagnum moss
Pepperbush, sweet, 35
Pewees, wood, 20, 136, 163, 186
Phoebes, 98, 114, 206
Pine, xxii, 3, 4, 10, 12, 31–32, 38, 41, 45,
    47–51, 60, 62, 69, 111, 157, 166,
    175, 178, 180, 185, 225, 231, 234,
    241, 244, 248
  old-growth, 1, 180
  pitch, 109, 245, 246
  red, 31, 65, 71, 78, 82, 125, 156, 174,
    210–11
  white, 1–3, 9, 11, 18, 28, 29, 48, 50, 57,
    59, 65, 72, 82, 97, 99, 103, 104,
    107, 109, 113, 115–17, 131, 142,
    154–56, 163, 164, 170–72, 180, 183,
    193, 208, 220–22, 225–27, 229,
    236–39, 242, 243, 245, 246

Pitcher plant, 111–12, 244
Poison ivy, xix, 163, 184
Polypody fern, 156, 169, 174, 238
Poplar. See Aspen
Popple. See Aspen
Porcupines, xxii, 38, 42, 44–45, 58, 64,
    65, 72, 84, 95, 106–7, 128, 148, 251
Princess pine (tree club moss), 104,
    108–9, 172, 219, 236
Pussytoes, 212

Quail, 29
Queen Anne's lace, 23

Rabbits, xxii, 50, 77, 95, 130
  cottontail, 3, 37, 72, 73, 231
  snowshoe, 73
Raccoons, xxi, xxii, 3–4, 11, 20–22, 29,
    60, 67, 72, 74, 95, 117, 176, 191,
    194, 195, 225, 229, 238, 244
Ragged robin, 174
Ragwort, 126, 243
Raspberry, 157, 159–60, 163, 170, 174,
    201, 216–17
  black, 124
  red, 124
Rattlesnake weed, 159
Ravens, 105, 110–11, 136, 165, 207, 211,
    213, 250
Redstarts, 156, 163, 171, 174, 180, 200
Reindeer moss, 109–10, 211
Rhododendron, 1, 5, 50
Robin plantain, 185, 190–91, 243
Robins, 115, 140, 211, 239
Rose, wild, 156, 159, 191, 201, 213
Royal fern, 236, 246

Salamanders, 12, 23, 105, 138, 193, 239
  blue-spotted, 13
  dusky, 170, 180, 215–16, 227
  Jefferson, 125, 130, 207
  red-backed, 99, 158, 163, 181, 212,
    215, 237
  spotted, 125, 130, 207
  spring, 63
  two-lined, 108, 170, 187, 215–16, 222,
    227
Salmon, Atlantic, 183
Sanderlings, 233
Sapsuckers, yellow-bellied, 141, 171

Sarsaparilla, wild, 129–30, 156, 174, 185,
    217
Sedge, 172, 183
Sensitive fern, 190, 217, 236
Shadbush, 57
Shiners, 190
Shinleaf, 171, 217
Shrews
  masked, 102
  short-tailed, 128
Skunk cabbage, 22, 35, 40, 242, 243, 246
Skunks, 130
Snakeroot, 120, 157, 171, 199
Snakes, 20, 21, 23, 29
  black racers, 11
  copperheads, 209
  garter, 11, 207, 243
  rattle-, 207, 209
  water, 73
Solomon's seal, 185, 199
Solomon's seal, false, 126, 129–30, 156,
    157, 173, 185, 190, 199, 206
Sparrows
  song, 244
  swamp, 191
  white-throated, 212
Sphagnum (peat) moss, 9, 36, 45, 111,
    113, 239, 244
Spiders, 222, 238, 246
Spiraea, 170
Spittlebugs, 156
Spleenwort, 156
Spruce, 4, 69, 82, 119, 146, 173, 231
  black, 45
  blue, 78
  Norway, 71–72, 222
  red, 71–72, 128, 130, 138, 143, 169,
    170, 172, 224
Squawroot, 208
Squirrels, 10, 38, 73, 95, 131, 181, 229,
    236
  flying, 51–52, 125, 238
  gray, 166
  red, 51, 60, 65, 78, 99, 111, 126, 158,
    166, 180, 185, 222, 246, 249
Starflower, 103, 185, 190, 217, 243
Starlings, 55
Sumac, 18, 19
  staghorn, 8–9, 201
Sundew, 36–37

Swallows, 57, 124, 128, 149, 244, 246
Sweet cicely, 157
Sweet fern, 213, 243
Sweet gale, 111, 244

Tamarack, 45
Tanagers, scarlet, 73, 121, 141, 158, 163, 215, 245
Teal, 233
Thrushes, 96, 158, 173, 180, 186
  hermit, 73, 125, 131, 141, 158, 163, 169, 171, 215, 219–20
  russet-headed, 150
  Swainson's, 138–39, 170
Ticks, xix
Titmice, 34, 53, 162, 210, 237, 242
Toads, 60, 172
Touch-me-not, 190, 217, 227
Towhees, 204–5
Trefoil, tick, 163
Trillium
  painted, 139, 180, 217
  red (wake-robin), 130, 139, 157, 169, 180, 185, 190
  white, 134
Trout, 59, 187, 232
  brook, 134, 167, 170, 176, 183, 249
  brown, 183
  rainbow, 183
Turkeys, wild, 20, 71, 84, 85, 95, 131, 172, 176–78, 181, 199
Turnip, wild, 177
Turtles, 29, 57, 60
  painted, 73, 111, 116, 128
  snapping, xxi–xxii, xxiii
  spotted, 23
  wood, 234

Veeries, 162, 186, 242
Viburnum, maple-leaf, 104, 121, 165–66, 212
Violet, 170, 180, 185
Vireos, 226, 244
  blue-headed, 141, 169, 171, 173, 243
  red-eyed, 141, 147, 150, 156, 158, 162, 169, 173, 180, 191, 200, 242
  solitary, 191, 221
  yellow-throated, 165
Vultures, 105
  turkey, 18–19, 43, 90, 152, 206, 213, 240

Walnut, 78
Warblers, 20, 73, 96, 180, 226
  black-and-white, 131, 157, 163, 169
  Blackburnian, 157, 169, 171, 173, 191
  blue, 104–5, 125, 128, 131, 139, 150, 159, 173, 243
  Canada, 126, 131, 152, 180, 191, 229
  chestnut-sided, 126, 132, 141, 170
  green, 131, 139, 156, 169, 171, 173, 191, 200
  magnolia, 139, 169, 173, 200
  pine, 163
  yellow, 244
Waterlily, 116
Water striders, 190, 217
Waterthrushes
  Louisiana, 215
  northern, 139
Waxwings, 196, 211
Weasels, xxi, 4, 38, 84, 95
Widgeons, 29
Willow, 183, 190
Winterberry, 6, 84, 111, 115, 223, 242–43
Wintergreen, 111, 121, 150, 227
  spotted, 213
  striped, 121
Witch hazel, 6–7, 150, 166, 189, 206, 216, 243
Wolves, 70, 71
Woodchucks (groundhogs), xxii, 20
Wood fern, 121, 152, 156, 162, 168–69, 180, 190, 199
Woodpeckers, 96, 222
  downy, 73, 104, 238
  hairy, 20, 73, 238
  pileated, 7, 11, 17, 42, 131, 137, 166, 196, 239
Wood sorrel, 169, 174
Worms, 221, 229
Wrens, 243
  winter, 130, 158, 170, 191, 215

Yellow-eyed grass, 244
Yellowthroats, 20, 126, 132, 160, 205, 244
Yew, American (ground hemlock), 145, 168, 216